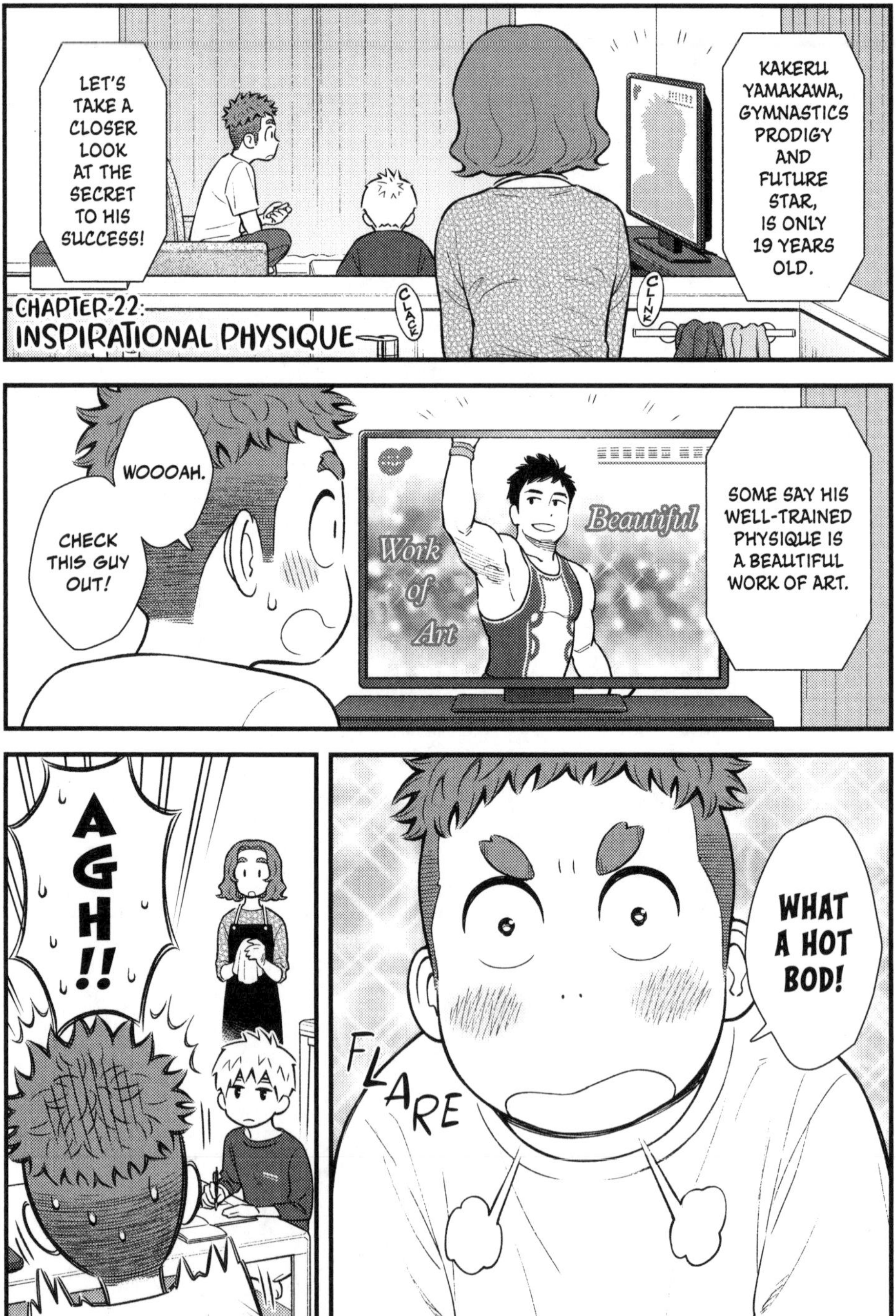
KAKERU YAMAKAWA, GYMNASTICS PRODIGY AND FUTURE STAR, IS ONLY 19 YEARS OLD.
CLINK
CLACK
LET'S TAKE A CLOSER LOOK AT THE SECRET TO HIS SUCCESS!
CHAPTER 22: INSPIRATIONAL PHYSIQUE
SOME SAY HIS WELL-TRAINED PHYSIQUE IS A BEAUTIFUL WORK OF ART.
Beautiful
Work of Art
WOOOAH.
CHECK THIS GUY OUT!
WHAT A HOT BOD!
FLARE
AGH!!

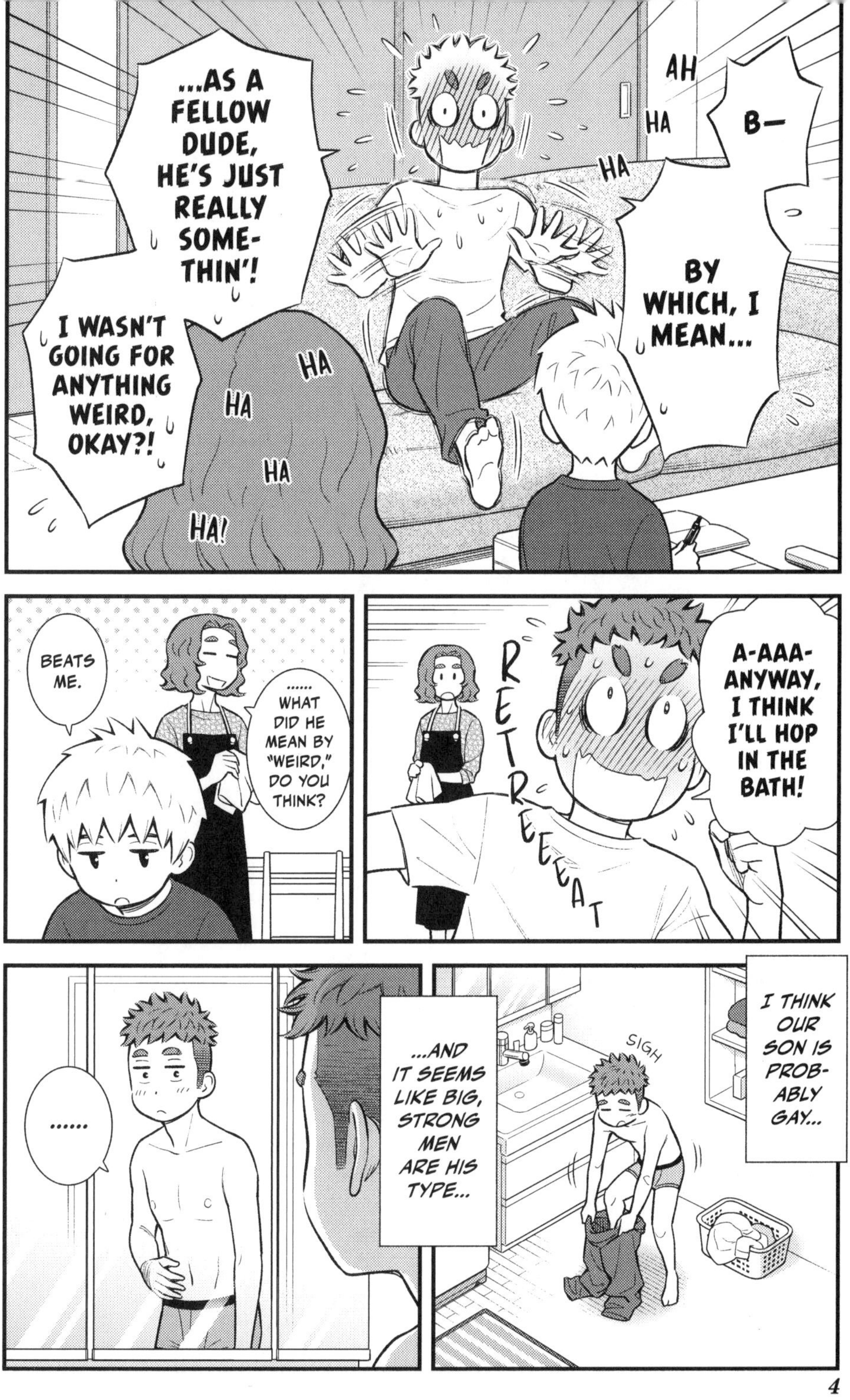
AH HA HA
B—
BY WHICH, I MEAN...
...AS A FELLOW DUDE, HE'S JUST REALLY SOME-THIN'!
HA HA HA HA!
I WASN'T GOING FOR ANYTHING WEIRD, OKAY?!
A-AAA-ANYWAY, I THINK I'LL HOP IN THE BATH!
RETREEEEAT
......WHAT DID HE MEAN BY "WEIRD," DO YOU THINK?
BEATS ME.
I THINK OUR SON IS PROBABLY GAY...
SIGH
...AND IT SEEMS LIKE BIG, STRONG MEN ARE HIS TYPE...
......

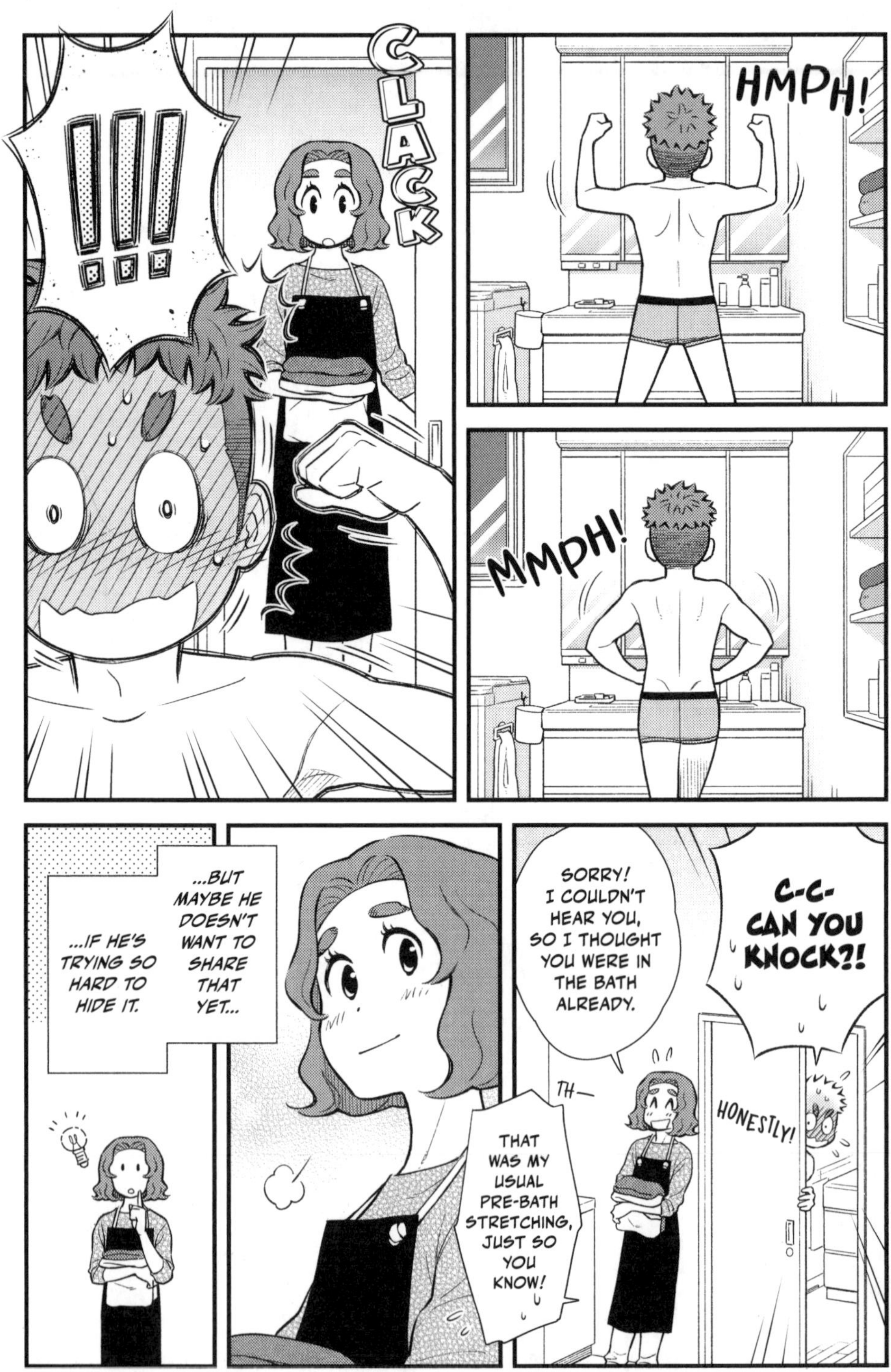
HMPH!
MMPH!
CLACK
!!!!
C-C-CAN YOU KNOCK?!
SORRY! I COULDN'T HEAR YOU, SO I THOUGHT YOU WERE IN THE BATH ALREADY.
HONESTLY!
TH—
THAT WAS MY USUAL PRE-BATH STRETCHING, JUST SO YOU KNOW!
...BUT MAYBE HE DOESN'T WANT TO SHARE THAT YET...
...IF HE'S TRYING SO HARD TO HIDE IT.

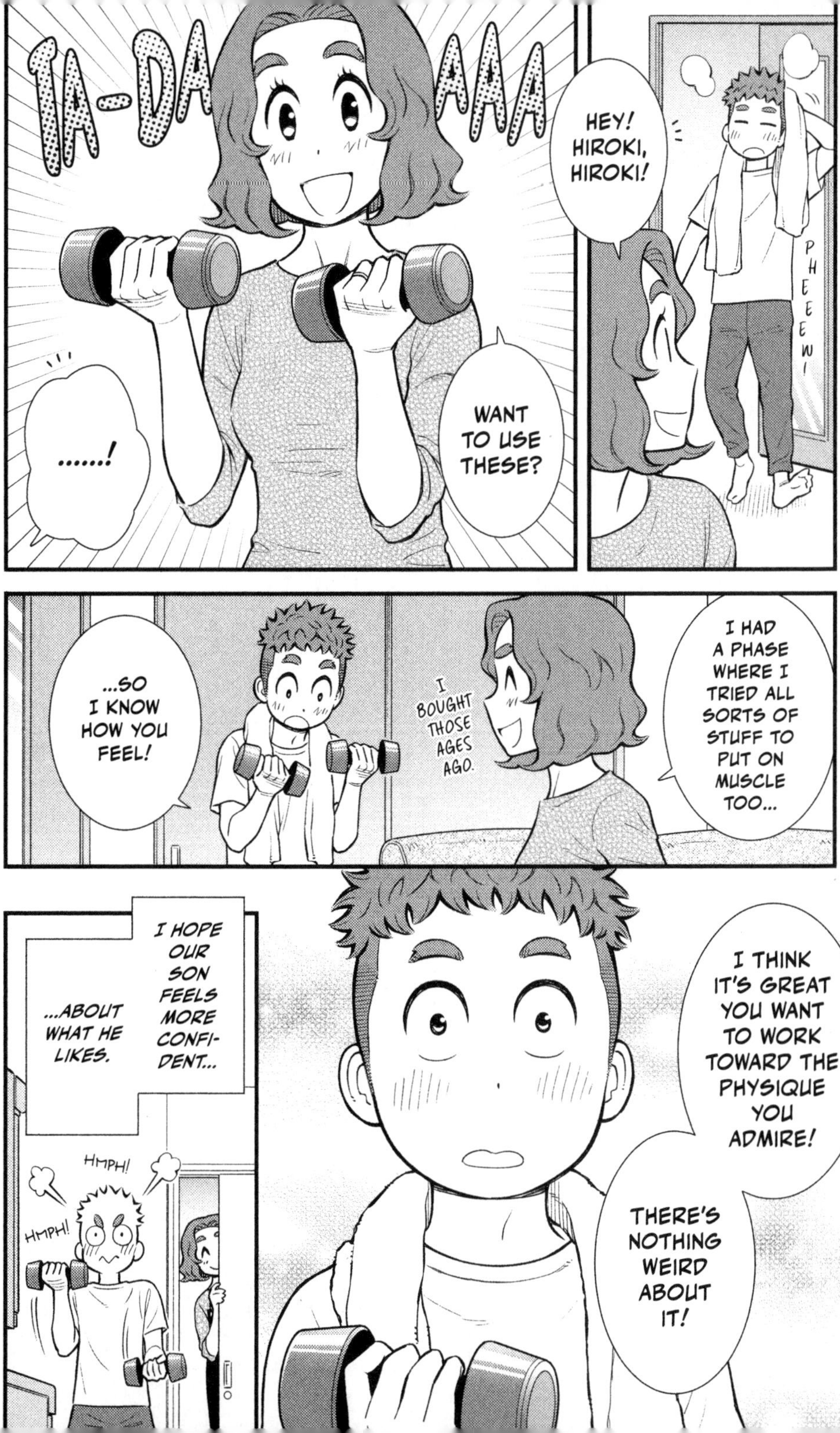
HEY! HIROKI, HIROKI!
PHEEEW!
TA-DAAAA
WANT TO USE THESE?
......!
I HAD A PHASE WHERE I TRIED ALL SORTS OF STUFF TO PUT ON MUSCLE TOO...
I BOUGHT THOSE AGES AGO.
...SO I KNOW HOW YOU FEEL!
I THINK IT'S GREAT YOU WANT TO WORK TOWARD THE PHYSIQUE YOU ADMIRE!
THERE'S NOTHING WEIRD ABOUT IT!
I HOPE OUR SON FEELS MORE CONFI-DENT...
...ABOUT WHAT HE LIKES.
HMPH!
HMPH!

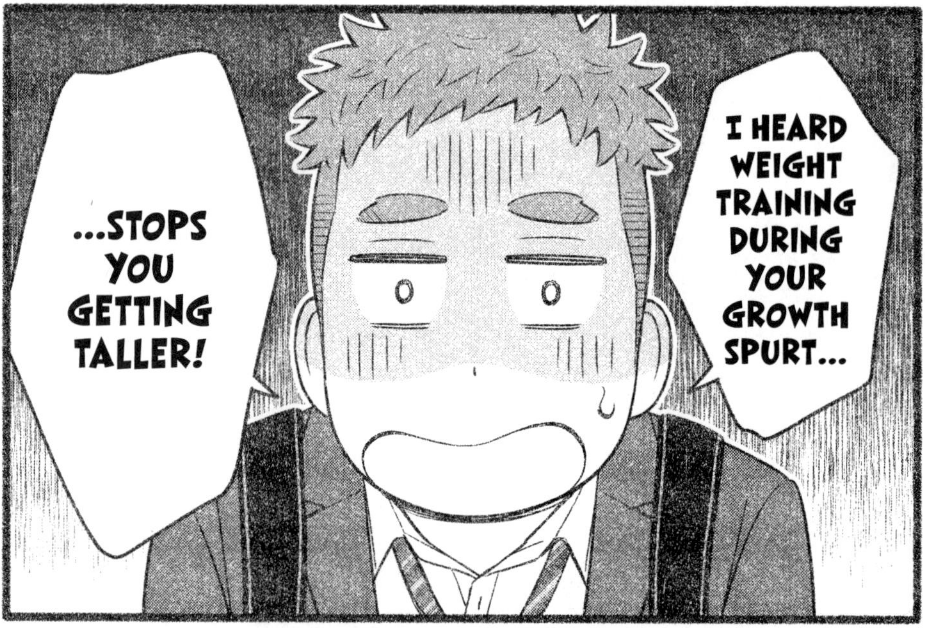
I HEARD WEIGHT TRAINING DURING YOUR GROWTH SPURT...
...STOPS YOU GETTING TALLER!
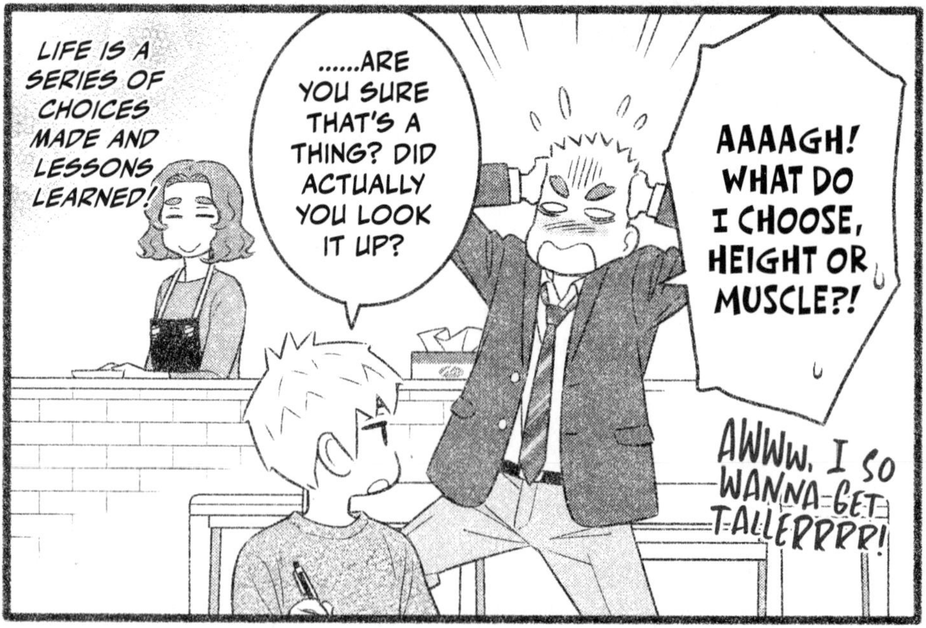
AAAAGH! WHAT DO I CHOOSE, HEIGHT OR MUSCLE?!
AWWW, I SO WANNA GET TALLERRRR!
......ARE YOU SURE THAT'S A THING? DID ACTUALLY YOU LOOK IT UP?
LIFE IS A SERIES OF CHOICES MADE AND LESSONS LEARNED!

I Think
Our Son
Is Gay

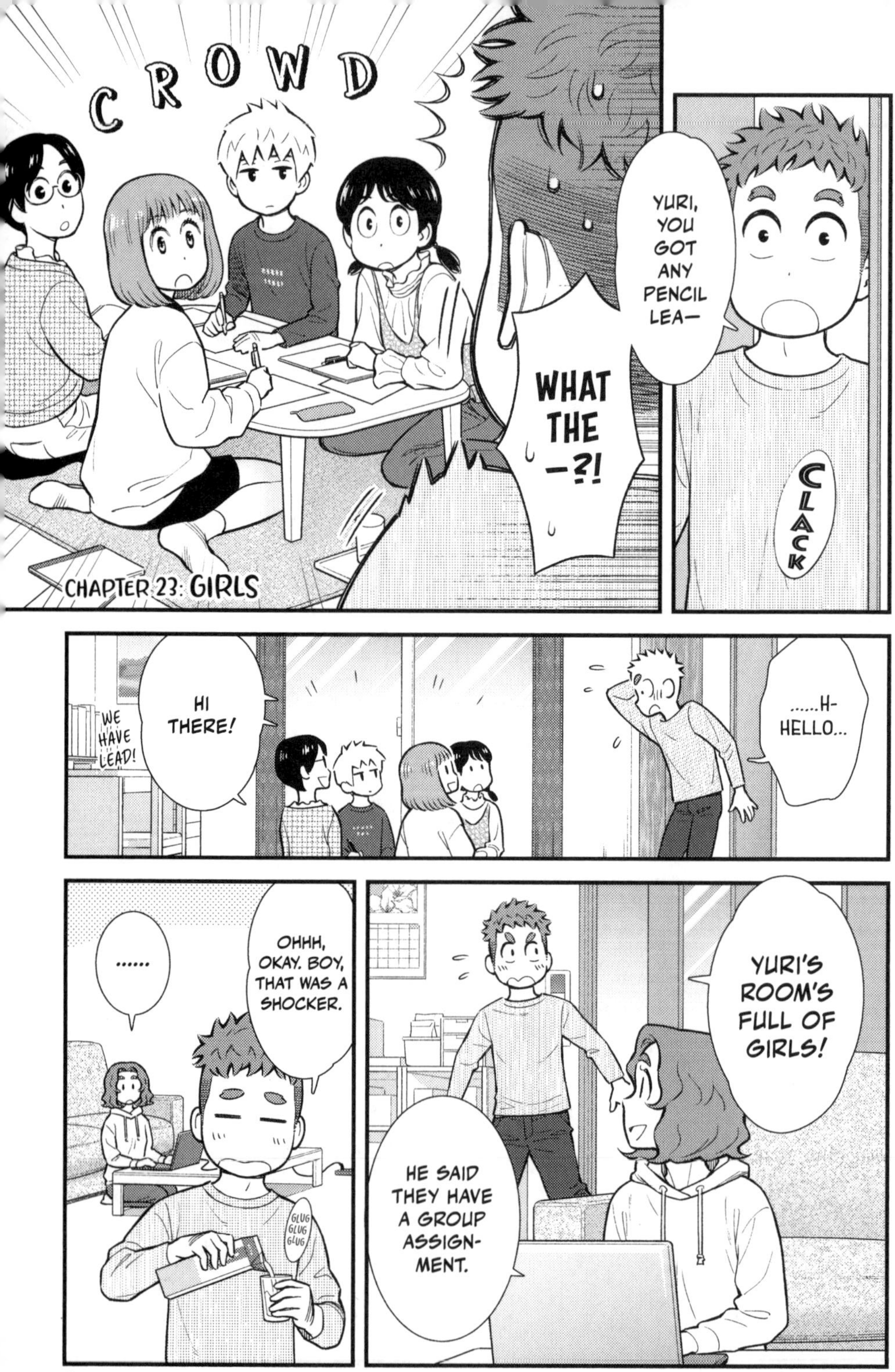
CLACK
YURI, YOU GOT ANY PENCIL LEA—
WHAT THE —?!
CROWD
CHAPTER 23: GIRLS
......H-HELLO...
HI THERE!
WE HAVE LEAD!
YURI'S ROOM'S FULL OF GIRLS!
HE SAID THEY HAVE A GROUP ASSIGN-MENT.
OHHH, OKAY. BOY, THAT WAS A SHOCKER.
......
GLUG GLUG GLUG

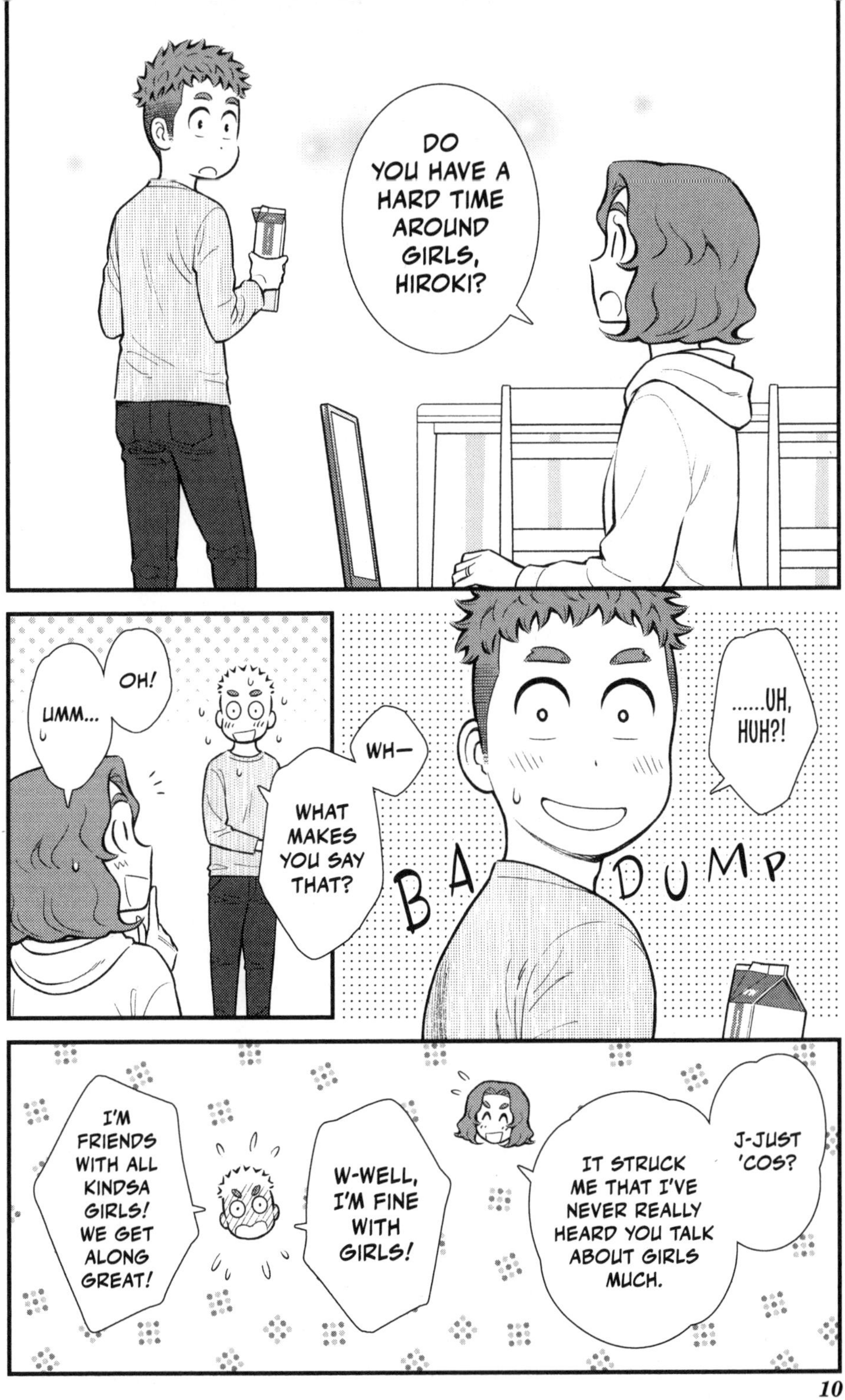
DO YOU HAVE A HARD TIME AROUND GIRLS, HIROKI?
......UH, HUH?!
BA DUMP
WH—
WHAT MAKES YOU SAY THAT?
OH!
UMM...
J-JUST 'COS?
IT STRUCK ME THAT I'VE NEVER REALLY HEARD YOU TALK ABOUT GIRLS MUCH.
W-WELL, I'M FINE WITH GIRLS!
I'M FRIENDS WITH ALL KINDSA GIRLS! WE GET ALONG GREAT!

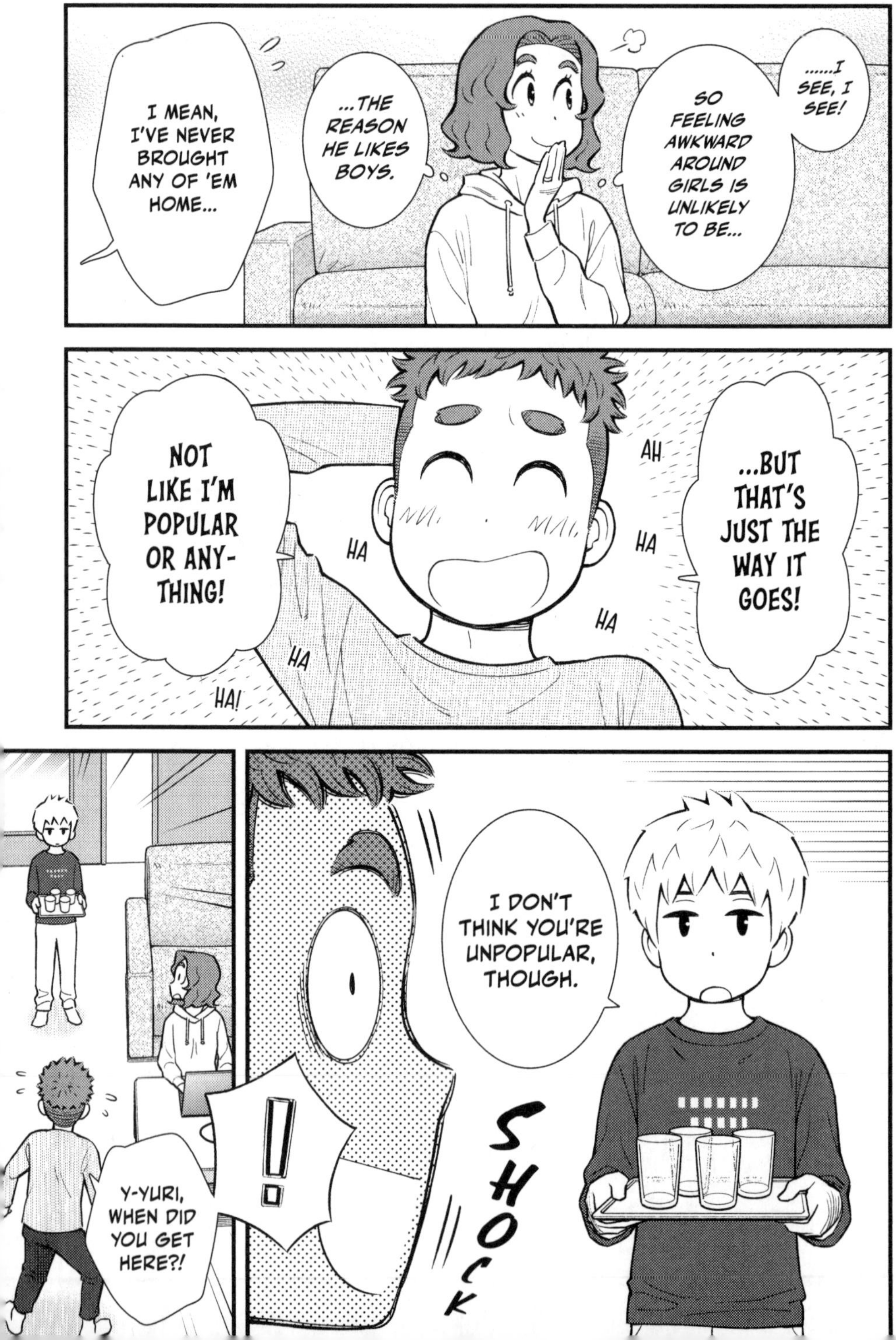
......I SEE, I SEE!
SO FEELING AWKWARD AROUND GIRLS IS UNLIKELY TO BE...
...THE REASON HE LIKES BOYS.
I MEAN, I'VE NEVER BROUGHT ANY OF 'EM HOME...
...BUT THAT'S JUST THE WAY IT GOES!
AH HA HA HA HA HA!
NOT LIKE I'M POPULAR OR ANY-THING!
I DON'T THINK YOU'RE UNPOPULAR, THOUGH.
SHOCK
!!
Y-YURI, WHEN DID YOU GET HERE?!

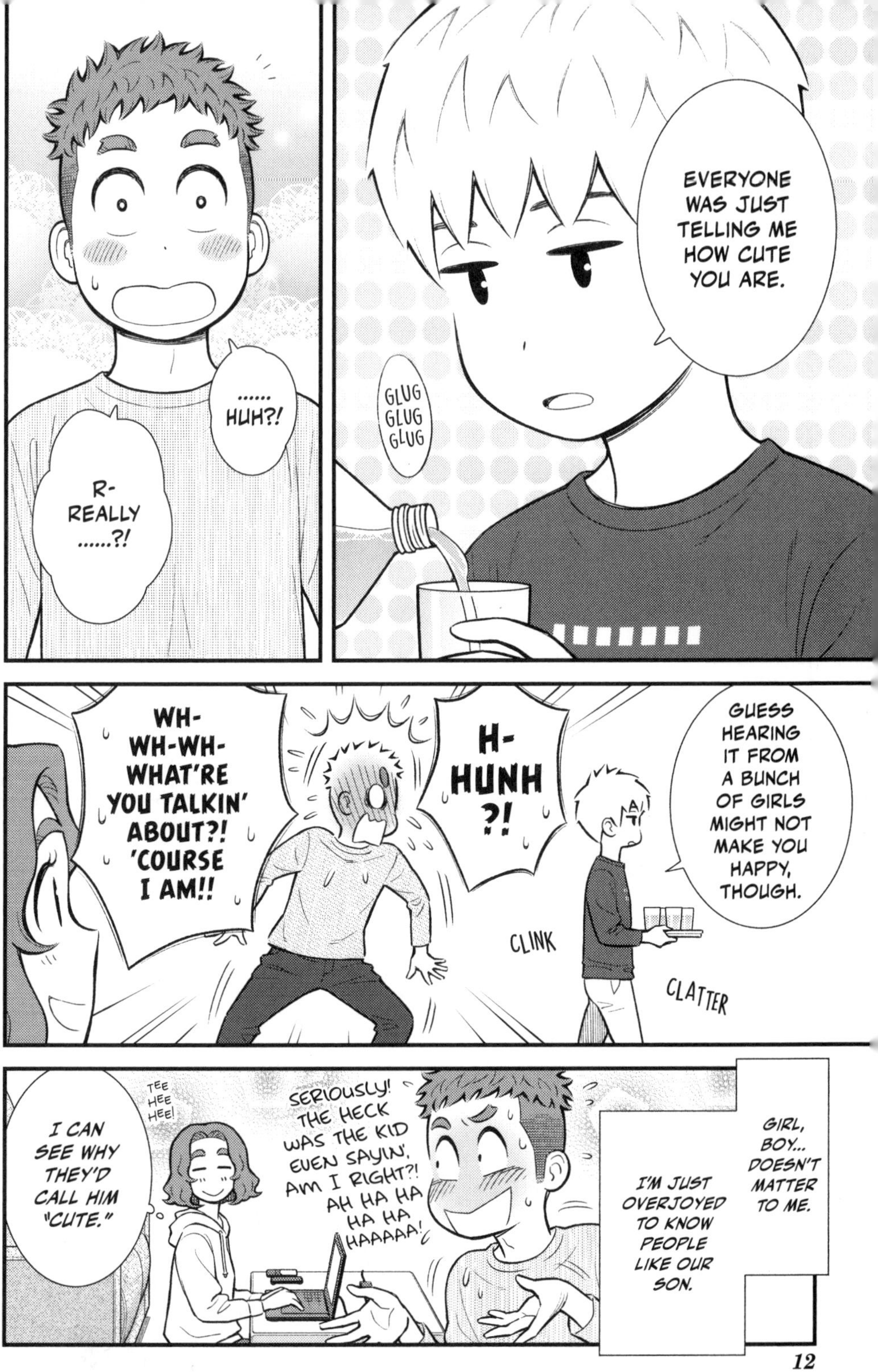
EVERYONE WAS JUST TELLING ME HOW CUTE YOU ARE.
GLUG GLUG GLUG
...... HUH?!
R-REALLY ......?!
GUESS HEARING IT FROM A BUNCH OF GIRLS MIGHT NOT MAKE YOU HAPPY, THOUGH.
CLINK
CLATTER
H-HUNH?!
WH-WH-WH-WHAT'RE YOU TALKIN' ABOUT?! 'COURSE I AM!!
GIRL, BOY... DOESN'T MATTER TO ME.
I'M JUST OVERJOYED TO KNOW PEOPLE LIKE OUR SON.
SERIOUSLY! THE HECK WAS THE KID EVEN SAYIN', AM I RIGHT?! AH HA HA HA HA HAAAAA!
TEE HEE HEE!
I CAN SEE WHY THEY'D CALL HIM "CUTE."

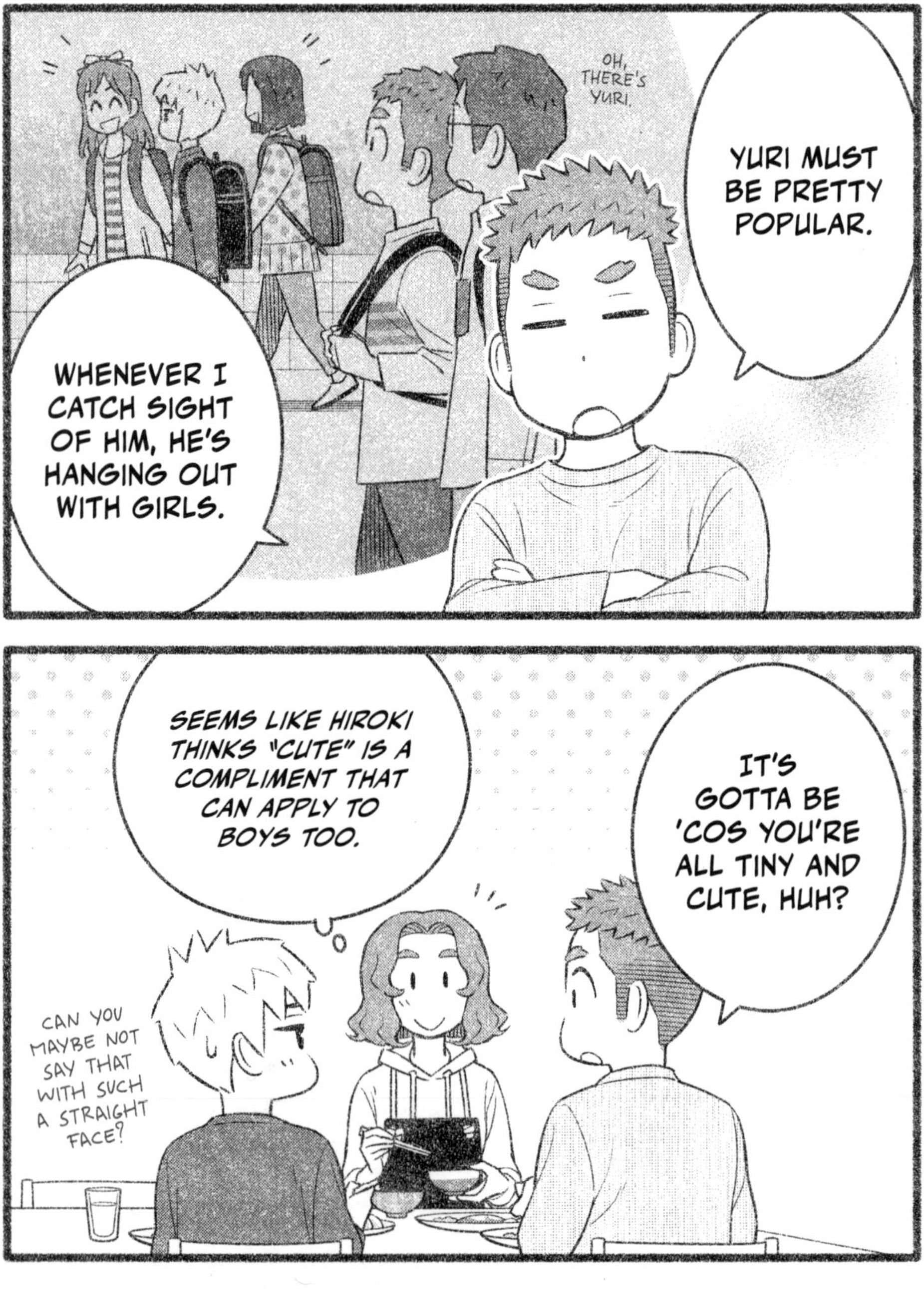
YURI MUST BE PRETTY POPULAR.
OH, THERE'S YURI.
WHENEVER I CATCH SIGHT OF HIM, HE'S HANGING OUT WITH GIRLS.
IT'S GOTTA BE 'COS YOU'RE ALL TINY AND CUTE, HUH?
SEEMS LIKE HIROKI THINKS "CUTE" IS A COMPLIMENT THAT CAN APPLY TO BOYS TOO.
CAN YOU MAYBE NOT SAY THAT WITH SUCH A STRAIGHT FACE?

I Think
Our Son
Is Gay

# CHAPTER 24: ERRAND

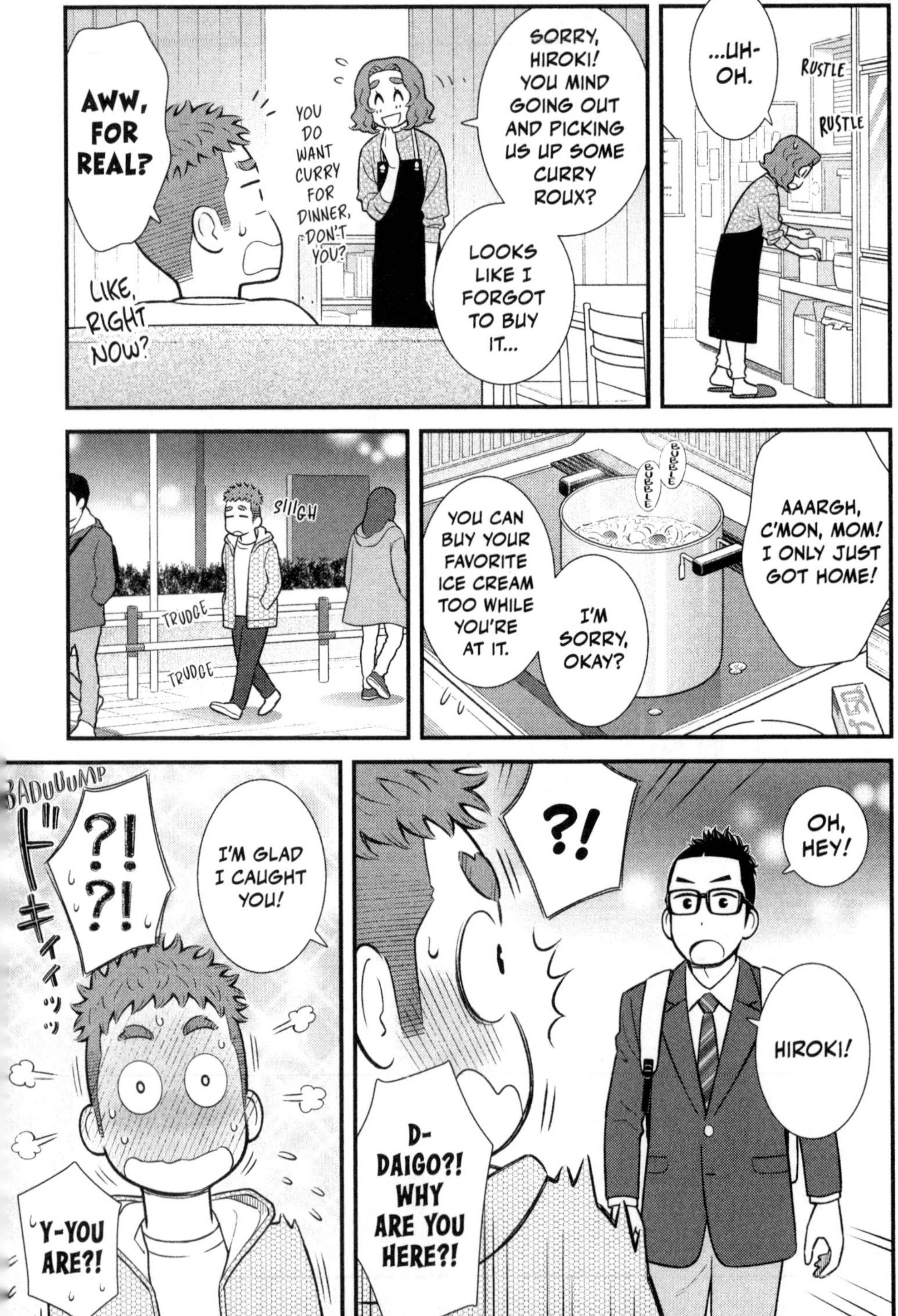

...UH-OH.
RUSTLE
RUSTLE
SORRY, HIROKI! YOU MIND GOING OUT AND PICKING US UP SOME CURRY ROUX?
LOOKS LIKE I FORGOT TO BUY IT...
YOU DO WANT CURRY FOR DINNER, DON'T YOU?
AWW, FOR REAL?
LIKE, RIGHT NOW?
AAARGH, C'MON, MOM! I ONLY JUST GOT HOME!
I'M SORRY, OKAY?
YOU CAN BUY YOUR FAVORITE ICE CREAM TOO WHILE YOU'RE AT IT.
BUBBLE
BUBBLE
SIIIGH
TRUDGE
TRUDGE
OH, HEY!
HIROKI!
?!
D-DAIGO?! WHY ARE YOU HERE?!
I'M GLAD I CAUGHT YOU!
?! ?!
BADUUUMP
ドキイイッッ
Y-YOU ARE?!

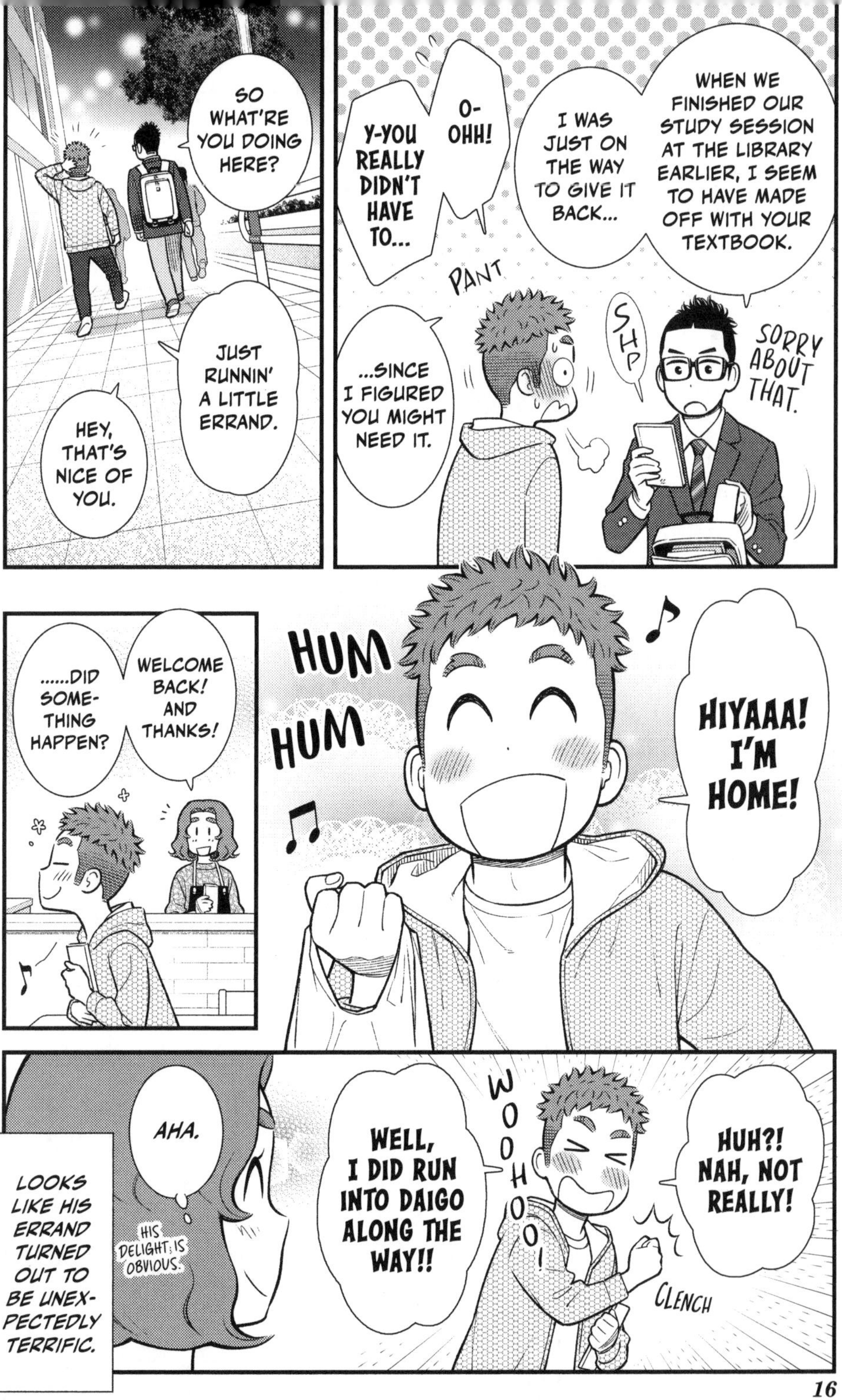
WHEN WE FINISHED OUR STUDY SESSION AT THE LIBRARY EARLIER, I SEEM TO HAVE MADE OFF WITH YOUR TEXTBOOK.
I WAS JUST ON THE WAY TO GIVE IT BACK...
O-OHH!
Y-YOU REALLY DIDN'T HAVE TO...
SORRY ABOUT THAT.
SHP
PANT
...SINCE I FIGURED YOU MIGHT NEED IT.
SO WHAT'RE YOU DOING HERE?
JUST RUNNIN' A LITTLE ERRAND.
HEY, THAT'S NICE OF YOU.
HIYAAA! I'M HOME!
HUM
HUM
WELCOME BACK! AND THANKS!
......DID SOME-THING HAPPEN?
HUH?! NAH, NOT REALLY!
CLENCH
WOOHOO!
WELL, I DID RUN INTO DAIGO ALONG THE WAY!!
AHA.
HIS DELIGHT IS OBVIOUS.
LOOKS LIKE HIS ERRAND TURNED OUT TO BE UNEX-PECTEDLY TERRIFIC.

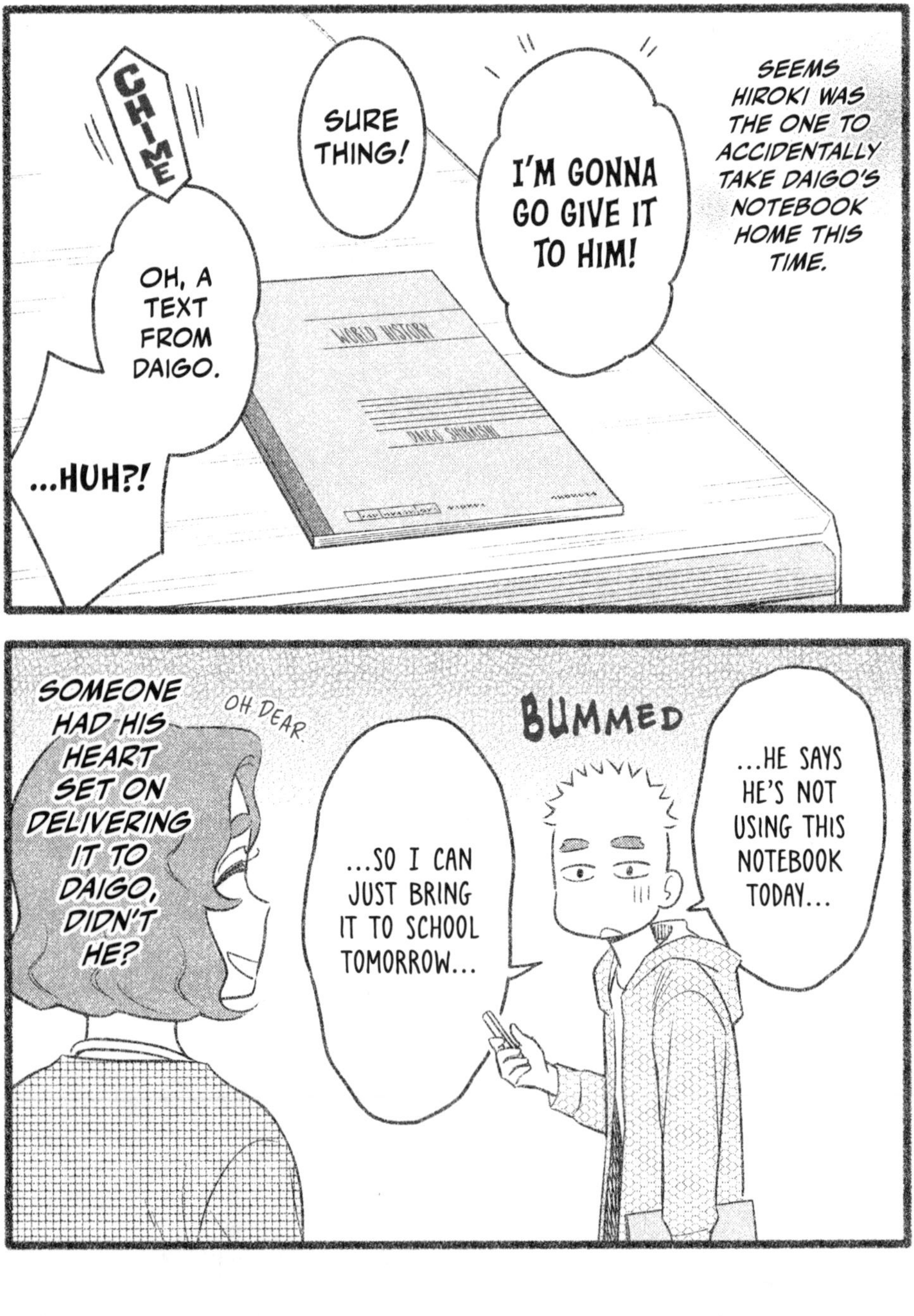
SEEMS HIROKI WAS THE ONE TO ACCIDENTALLY TAKE DAIGO'S NOTEBOOK HOME THIS TIME.
I'M GONNA GO GIVE IT TO HIM!
SURE THING!
CHIME
OH, A TEXT FROM DAIGO.
WORLD HISTORY
...HUH?!
BUMMED
...HE SAYS HE'S NOT USING THIS NOTEBOOK TODAY...
...SO I CAN JUST BRING IT TO SCHOOL TOMORROW...
OH DEAR.
SOMEONE HAD HIS HEART SET ON DELIVERING IT TO DAIGO, DIDN'T HE?

I Think
Our Son
Is Gay

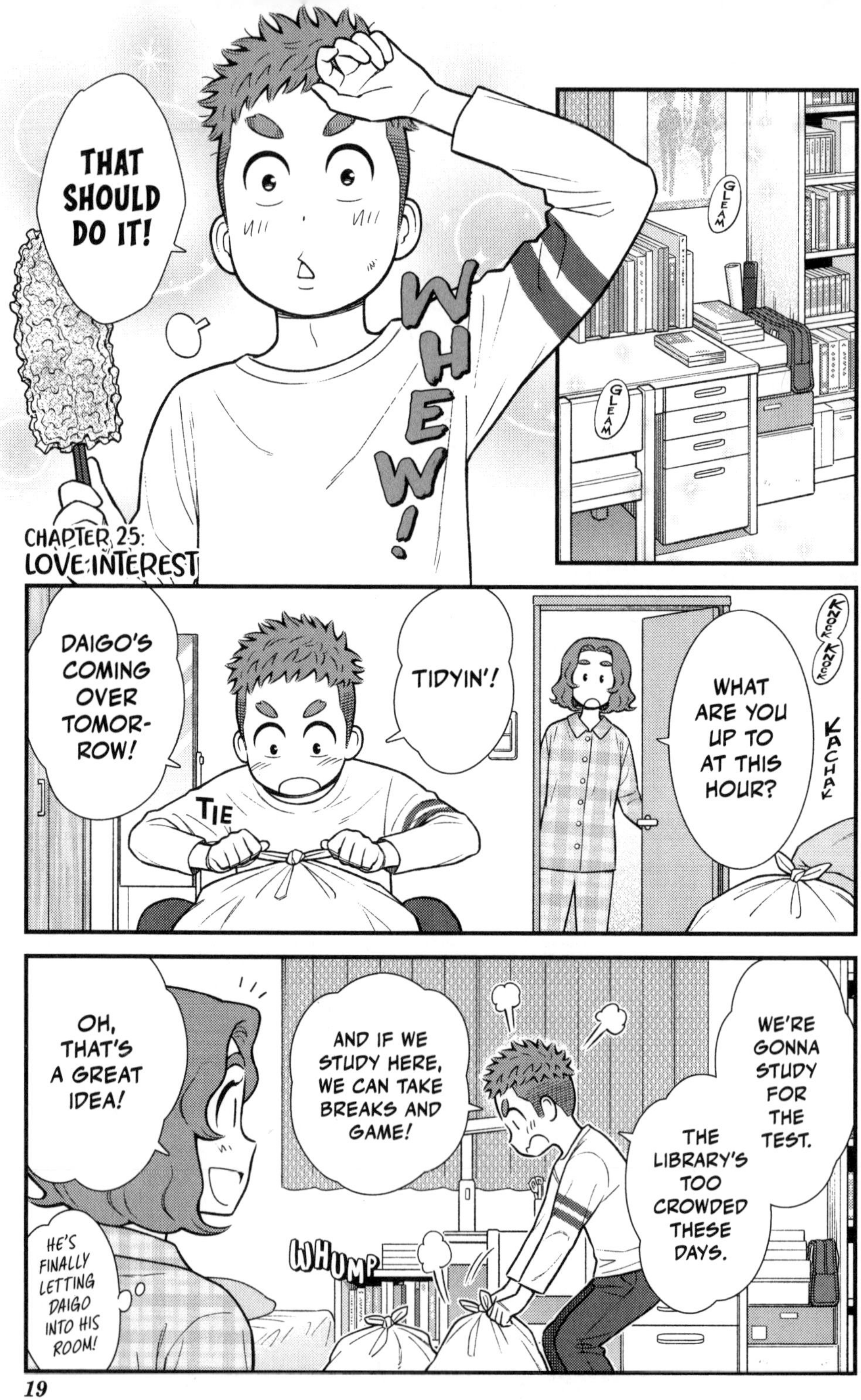
GLEAM
GLEAM
WHEW!
THAT SHOULD DO IT!
CHAPTER 25: LOVE INTEREST
KNOCK KNOCK
KACHAK
WHAT ARE YOU UP TO AT THIS HOUR?
TIDYIN'!
DAIGO'S COMING OVER TOMORROW!
TIE
WE'RE GONNA STUDY FOR THE TEST.
THE LIBRARY'S TOO CROWDED THESE DAYS.
AND IF WE STUDY HERE, WE CAN TAKE BREAKS AND GAME!
OH, THAT'S A GREAT IDEA!
WHUMP
HE'S FINALLY LETTING DAIGO INTO HIS ROOM!

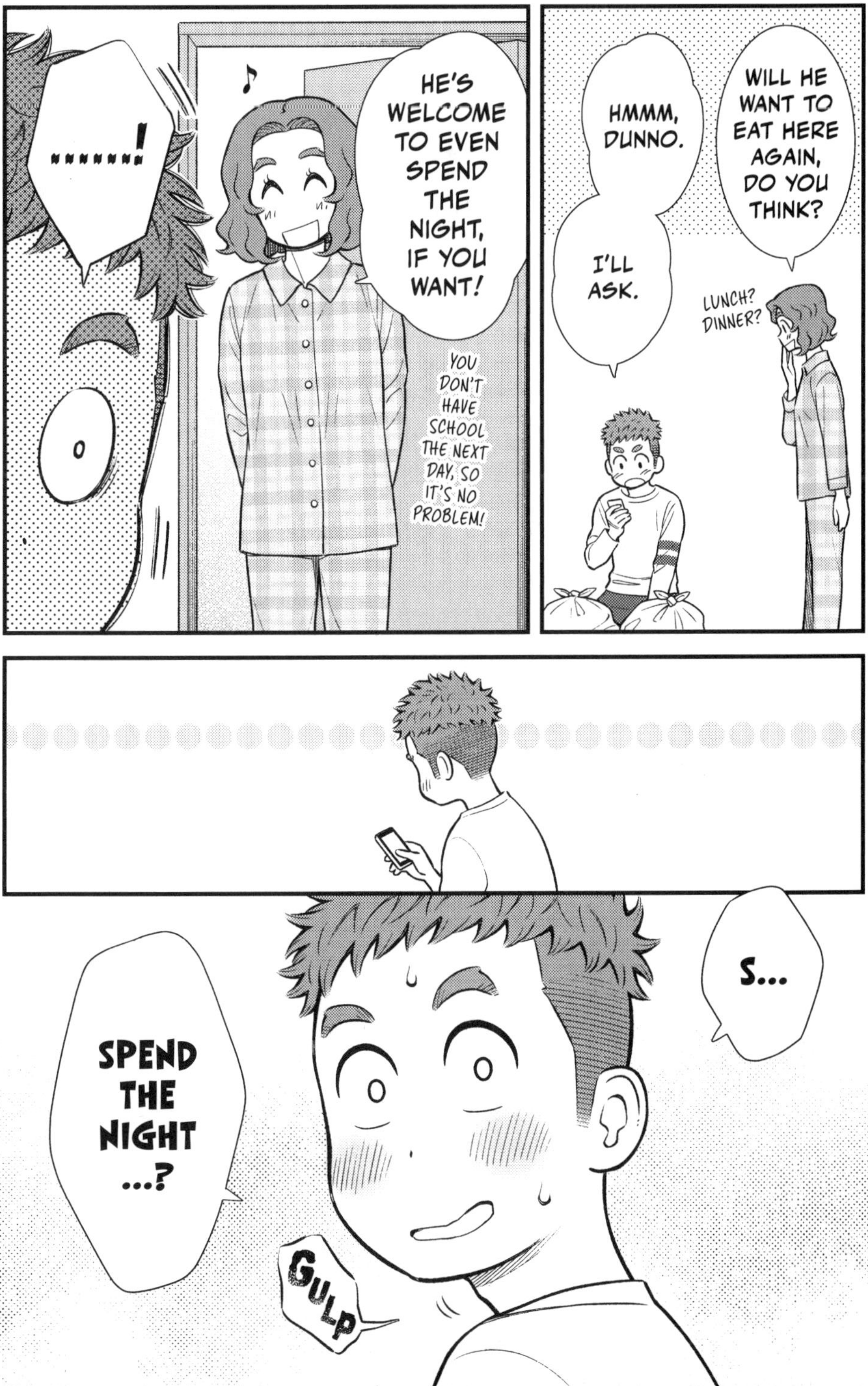
WILL HE WANT TO EAT HERE AGAIN, DO YOU THINK?
HMMM, DUNNO.
I'LL ASK.
LUNCH? DINNER?
HE'S WELCOME TO EVEN SPEND THE NIGHT, IF YOU WANT!
YOU DON'T HAVE SCHOOL THE NEXT DAY, SO IT'S NO PROBLEM!
......!
S...
SPEND THE NIGHT ...?
GULP

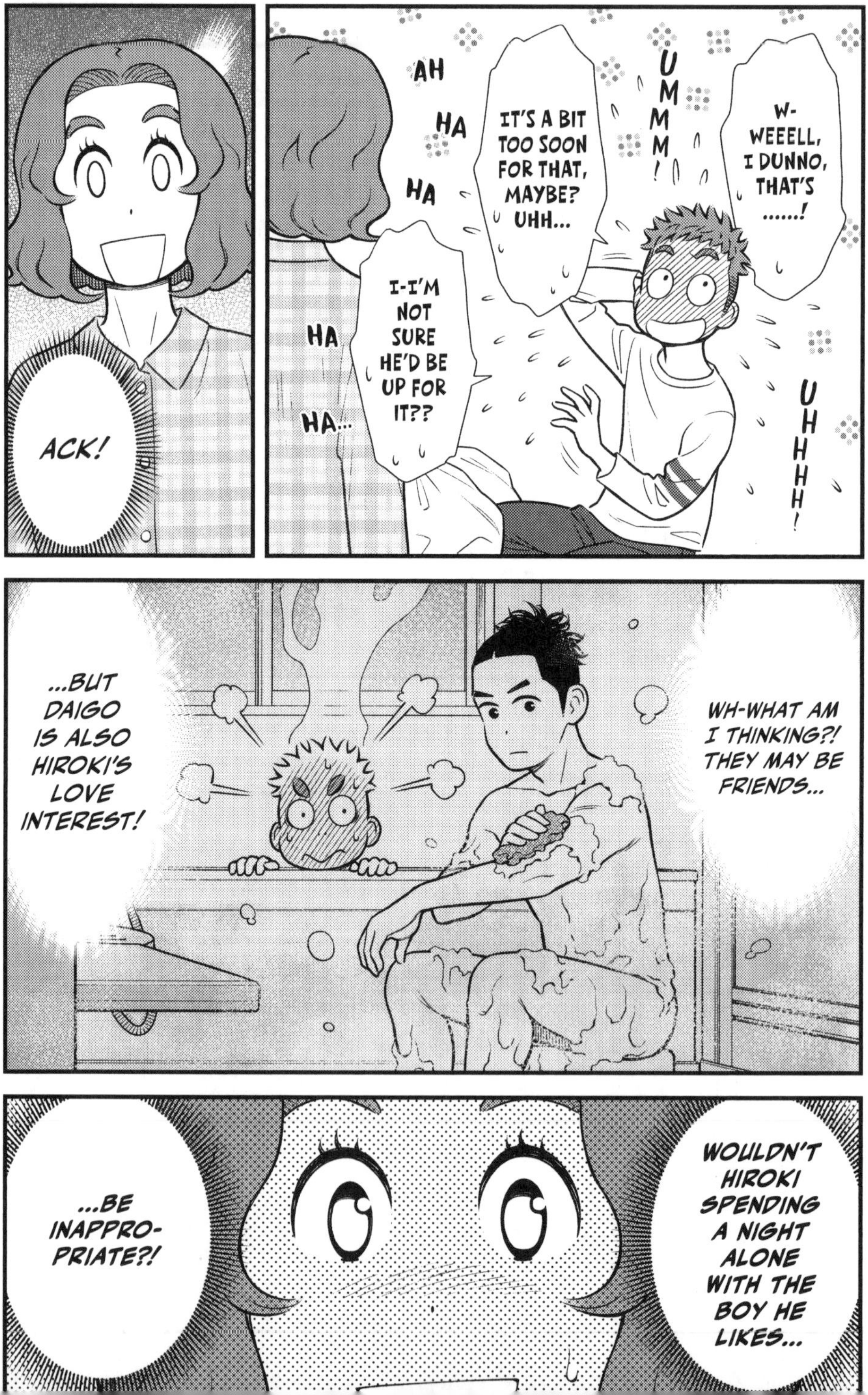
W-WEEELL, I DUNNO, THAT'S ......!
UMMM!
IT'S A BIT TOO SOON FOR THAT, MAYBE? UHH...
AH HA HA
UHHHHH!
I-I'M NOT SURE HE'D BE UP FOR IT??
HA HA...
ACK!
WH-WHAT AM I THINKING?! THEY MAY BE FRIENDS...
...BUT DAIGO IS ALSO HIROKI'S LOVE INTEREST!
WOULDN'T HIROKI SPENDING A NIGHT ALONE WITH THE BOY HE LIKES...
...BE INAPPROPRIATE?!

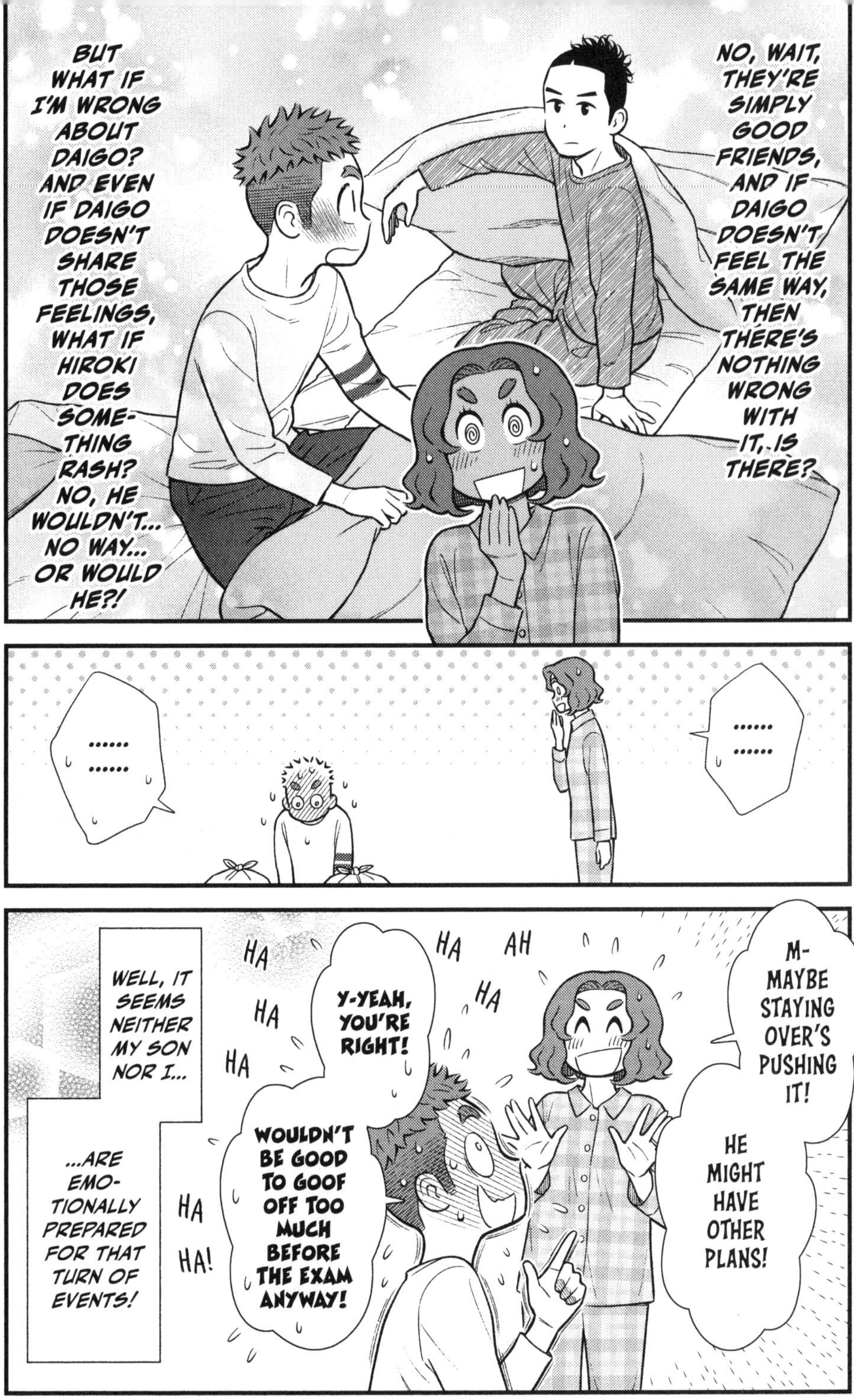
NO, WAIT, THEY'RE SIMPLY GOOD FRIENDS, AND IF DAIGO DOESN'T FEEL THE SAME WAY, THEN THERE'S NOTHING WRONG WITH IT, IS THERE?
BUT WHAT IF I'M WRONG ABOUT DAIGO? AND EVEN IF DAIGO DOESN'T SHARE THOSE FEELINGS, WHAT IF HIROKI DOES SOME-THING RASH? NO, HE WOULDN'T... NO WAY... OR WOULD HE?!
...... ......
...... ......
M-MAYBE STAYING OVER'S PUSHING IT!
HE MIGHT HAVE OTHER PLANS!
AH HA
HA
Y-YEAH, YOU'RE RIGHT!
WOULDN'T BE GOOD TO GOOF OFF TOO MUCH BEFORE THE EXAM ANYWAY!
HA HA HA HA HA HA!
WELL, IT SEEMS NEITHER MY SON NOR I...
...ARE EMOTIONALLY PREPARED FOR THAT TURN OF EVENTS!

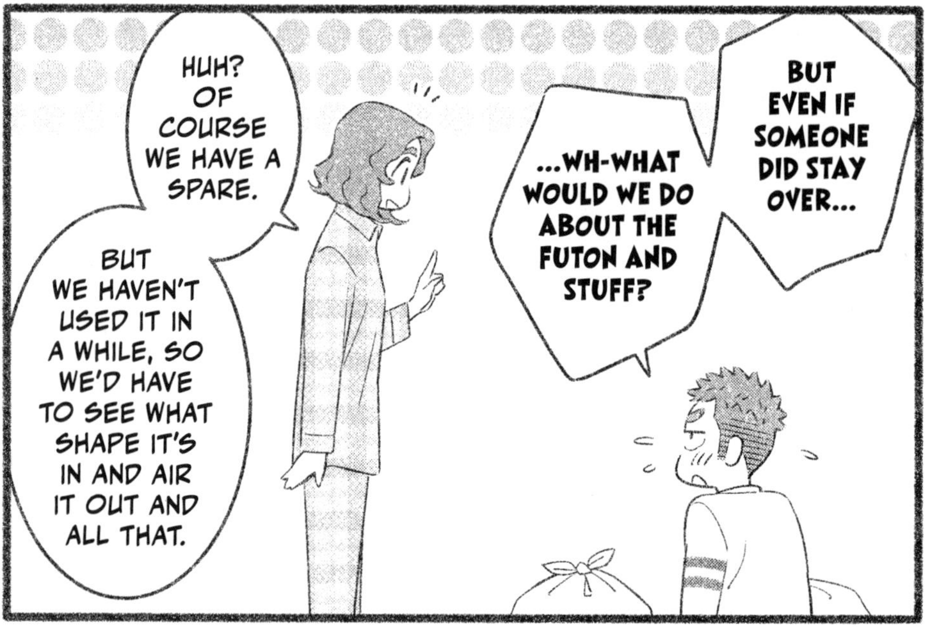
BUT EVEN IF SOMEONE DID STAY OVER...
...WH-WHAT WOULD WE DO ABOUT THE FUTON AND STUFF?
HUH? OF COURSE WE HAVE A SPARE.
BUT WE HAVEN'T USED IT IN A WHILE, SO WE'D HAVE TO SEE WHAT SHAPE IT'S IN AND AIR IT OUT AND ALL THAT.

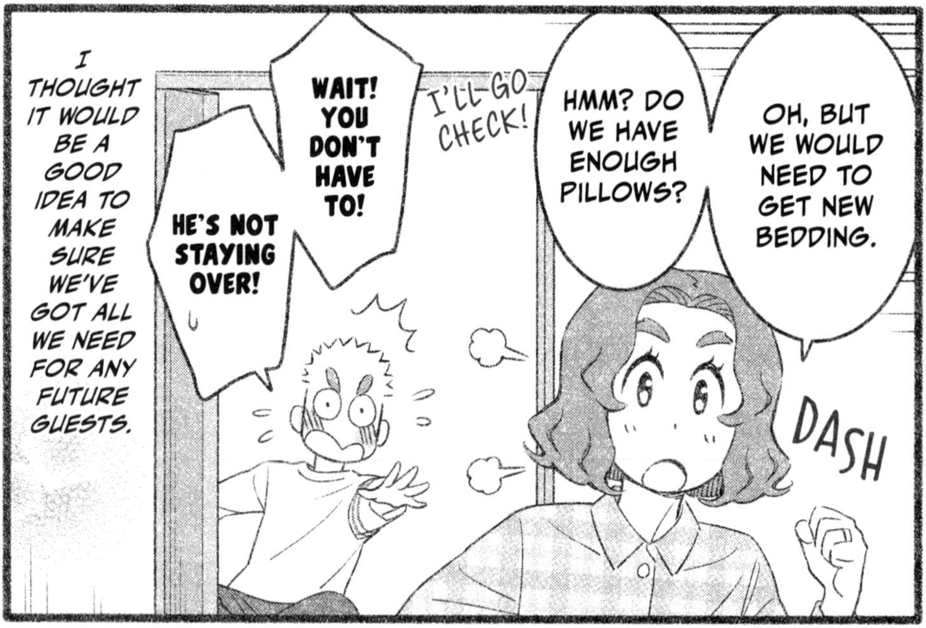
OH, BUT WE WOULD NEED TO GET NEW BEDDING.
HMM? DO WE HAVE ENOUGH PILLOWS?
DASH
I'LL GO CHECK!
WAIT! YOU DON'T HAVE TO!
HE'S NOT STAYING OVER!
I THOUGHT IT WOULD BE A GOOD IDEA TO MAKE SURE WE'VE GOT ALL WE NEED FOR ANY FUTURE GUESTS.

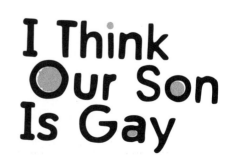

I Think
Our Son
Is Gay

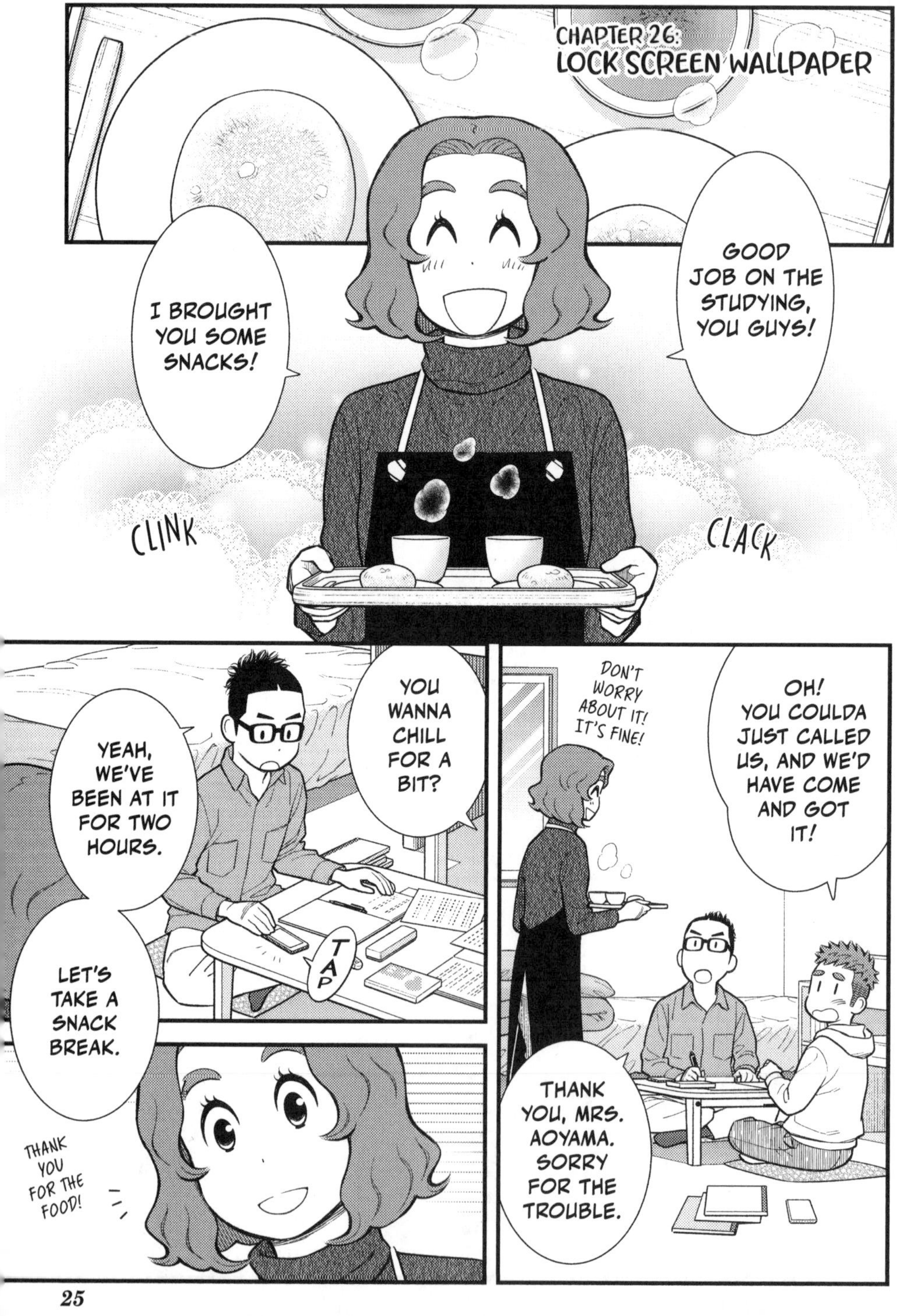
CHAPTER 26:
LOCK SCREEN WALLPAPER
GOOD JOB ON THE STUDYING, YOU GUYS!
I BROUGHT YOU SOME SNACKS!
CLACK
CLINK
OH! YOU COULDA JUST CALLED US, AND WE'D HAVE COME AND GOT IT!
DON'T WORRY ABOUT IT! IT'S FINE!
THANK YOU, MRS. AOYAMA. SORRY FOR THE TROUBLE.
YOU WANNA CHILL FOR A BIT?
YEAH, WE'VE BEEN AT IT FOR TWO HOURS.
TAP
LET'S TAKE A SNACK BREAK.
THANK YOU FOR THE FOOD!

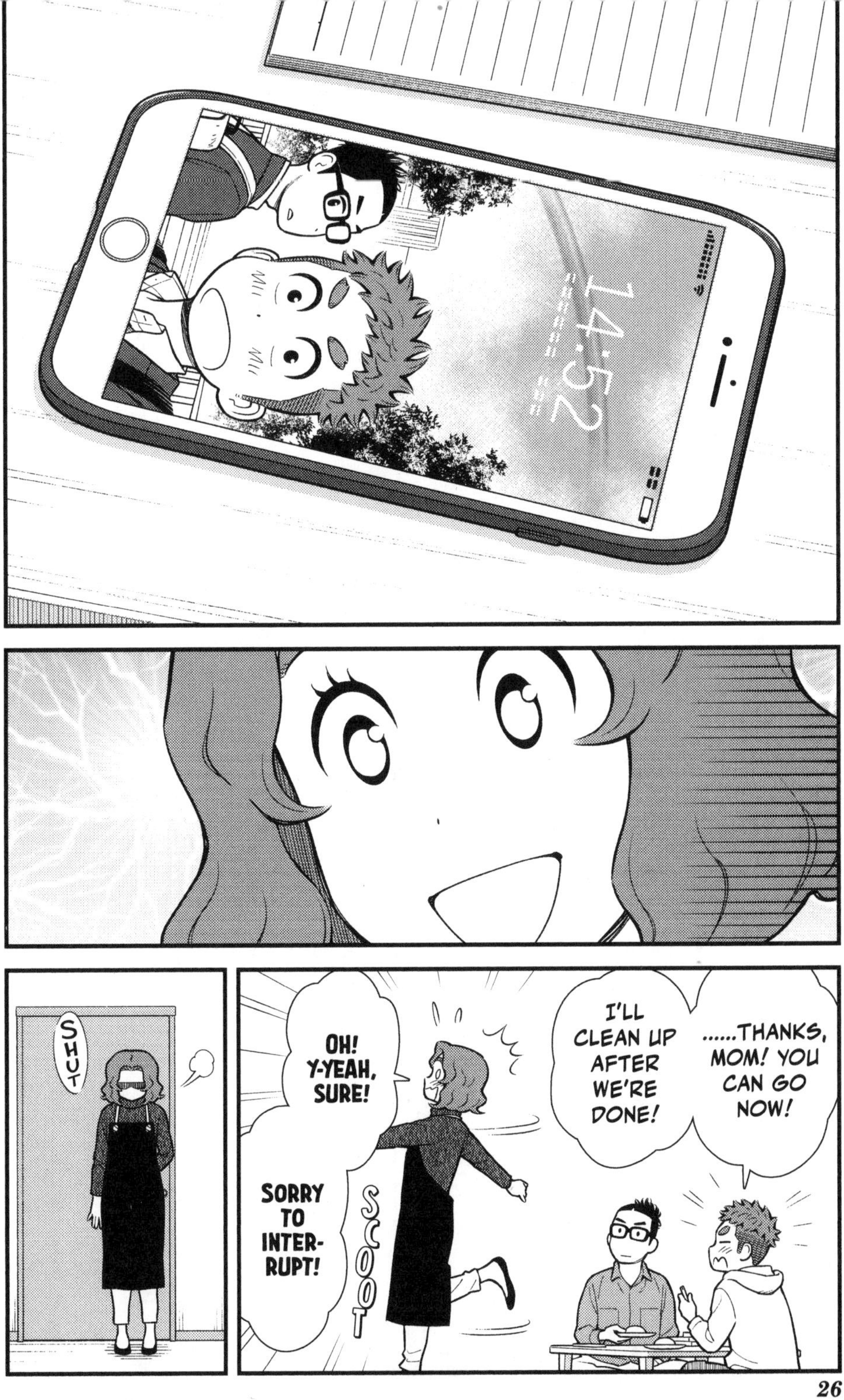
14:52
......THANKS, MOM! YOU CAN GO NOW!
I'LL CLEAN UP AFTER WE'RE DONE!
OH! Y-YEAH, SURE!
SCOOT
SORRY TO INTERRUPT!
SHUT

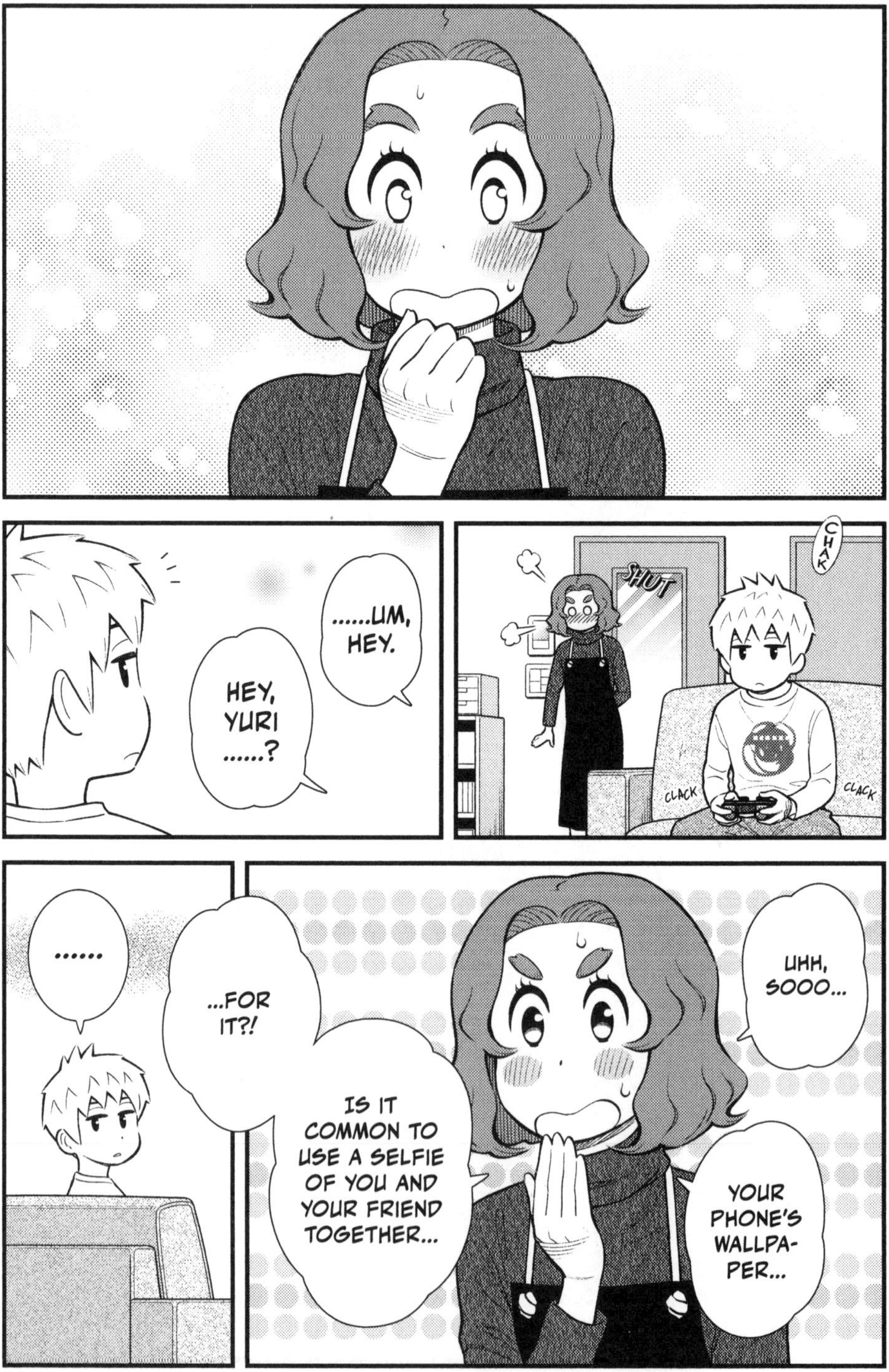
CHAK
SHUT
CLACK
CLACK
......UM, HEY.
HEY, YURI ......?
UHH, SOOO...
YOUR PHONE'S WALLPA-PER...
IS IT COMMON TO USE A SELFIE OF YOU AND YOUR FRIEND TOGETHER...
...FOR IT?!
......

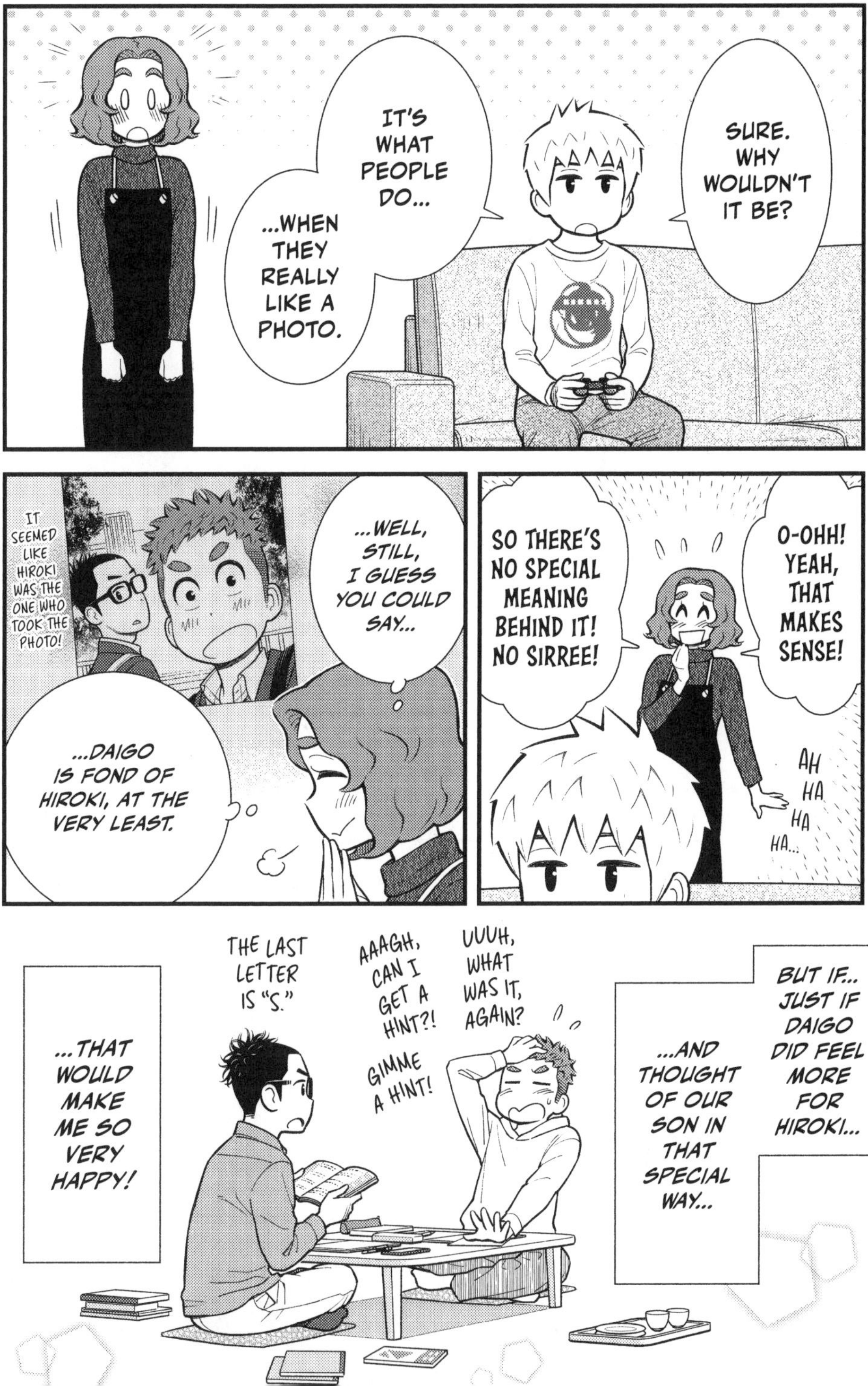
SURE. WHY WOULDN'T IT BE?
IT'S WHAT PEOPLE DO...
...WHEN THEY REALLY LIKE A PHOTO.
O-OHH! YEAH, THAT MAKES SENSE!
SO THERE'S NO SPECIAL MEANING BEHIND IT! NO SIRREE!
AH HA HA HA...
...WELL, STILL, I GUESS YOU COULD SAY...
IT SEEMED LIKE HIROKI WAS THE ONE WHO TOOK THE PHOTO!
...DAIGO IS FOND OF HIROKI, AT THE VERY LEAST.
BUT IF... JUST IF DAIGO DID FEEL MORE FOR HIROKI...
...AND THOUGHT OF OUR SON IN THAT SPECIAL WAY...
UUUH, WHAT WAS IT, AGAIN?
AAAGH, CAN I GET A HINT?!
GIMME A HINT!
THE LAST LETTER IS "S."
...THAT WOULD MAKE ME SO VERY HAPPY!

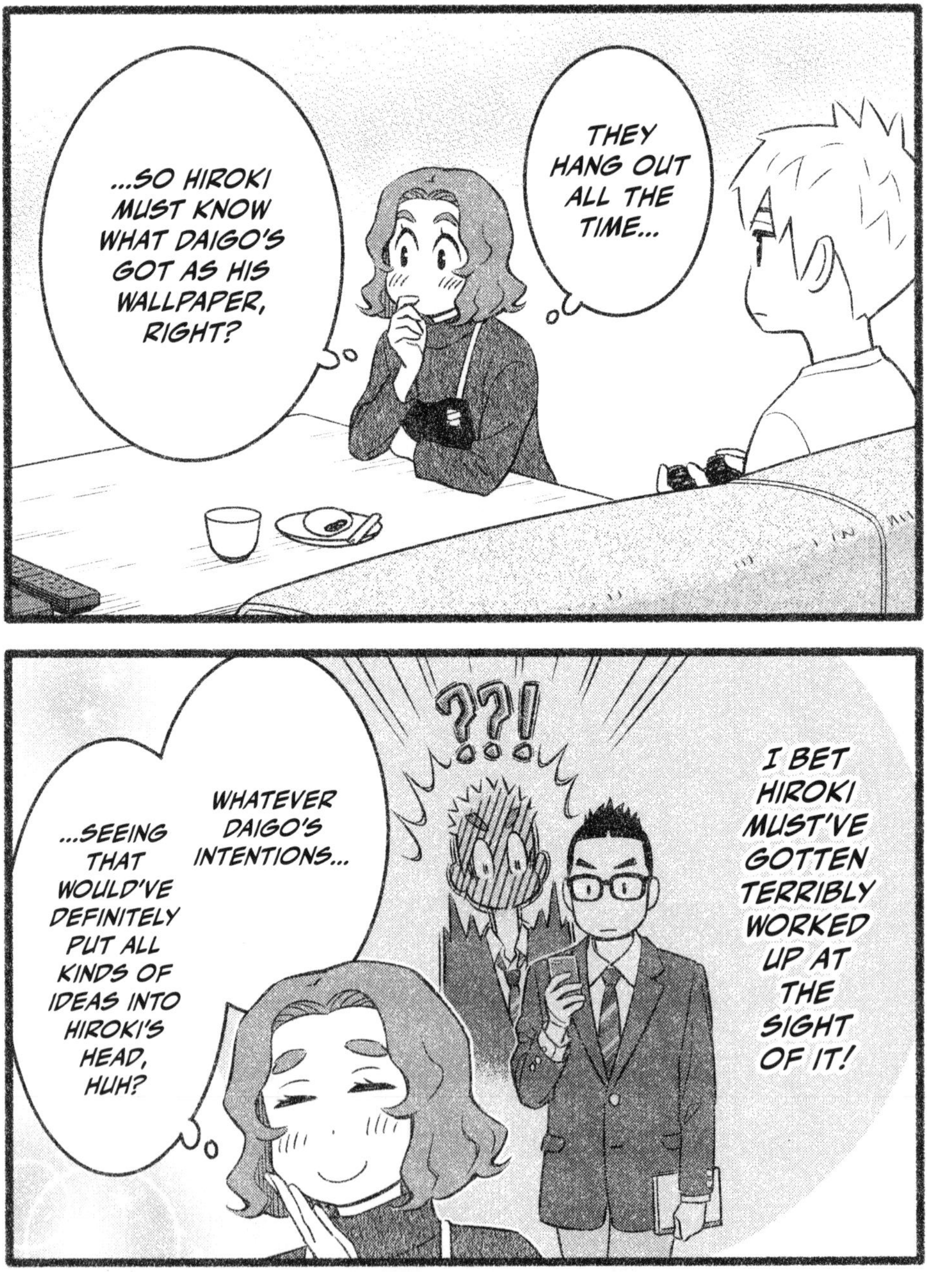
THEY HANG OUT ALL THE TIME...
...SO HIROKI MUST KNOW WHAT DAIGO'S GOT AS HIS WALLPAPER, RIGHT?
I BET HIROKI MUST'VE GOTTEN TERRIBLY WORKED UP AT THE SIGHT OF IT!
??!
WHATEVER DAIGO'S INTENTIONS...
...SEEING THAT WOULD'VE DEFINITELY PUT ALL KINDS OF IDEAS INTO HIROKI'S HEAD, HUH?

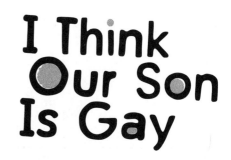

I Think
Our Son
Is Gay

CHAPTER 27: CLASS PRESIDENT

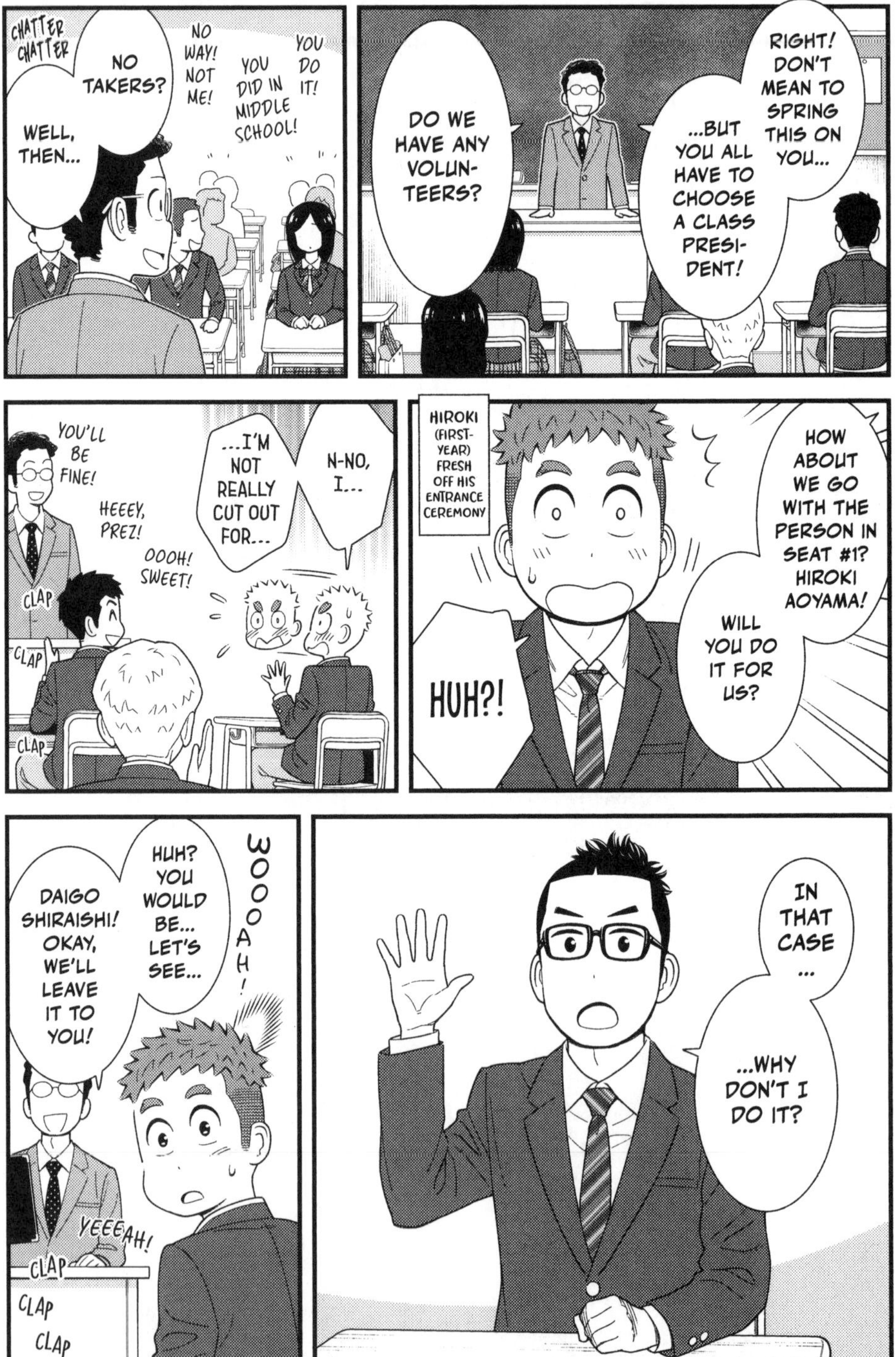
RIGHT! DON'T MEAN TO SPRING THIS ON YOU...
...BUT YOU ALL HAVE TO CHOOSE A CLASS PRESIDENT!
DO WE HAVE ANY VOLUNTEERS?
YOU DO IT!
YOU DID IN MIDDLE SCHOOL!
NO WAY! NOT ME!
NO TAKERS?
CHATTER CHATTER
WELL, THEN...
HOW ABOUT WE GO WITH THE PERSON IN SEAT #1? HIROKI AOYAMA!
WILL YOU DO IT FOR US?
HIROKI (FIRST-YEAR) FRESH OFF HIS ENTRANCE CEREMONY
HUH?!
N-NO, I...
...I'M NOT REALLY CUT OUT FOR...
OOOH! SWEET!
HEEEY, PREZ!
YOU'LL BE FINE!
CLAP
CLAP
CLAP
IN THAT CASE...
...WHY DON'T I DO IT?
WOOOAH!
HUH? YOU WOULD BE... LET'S SEE...
DAIGO SHIRAISHI! OKAY, WE'LL LEAVE IT TO YOU!
YEEEAH!
CLAP
CLAP
CLAP

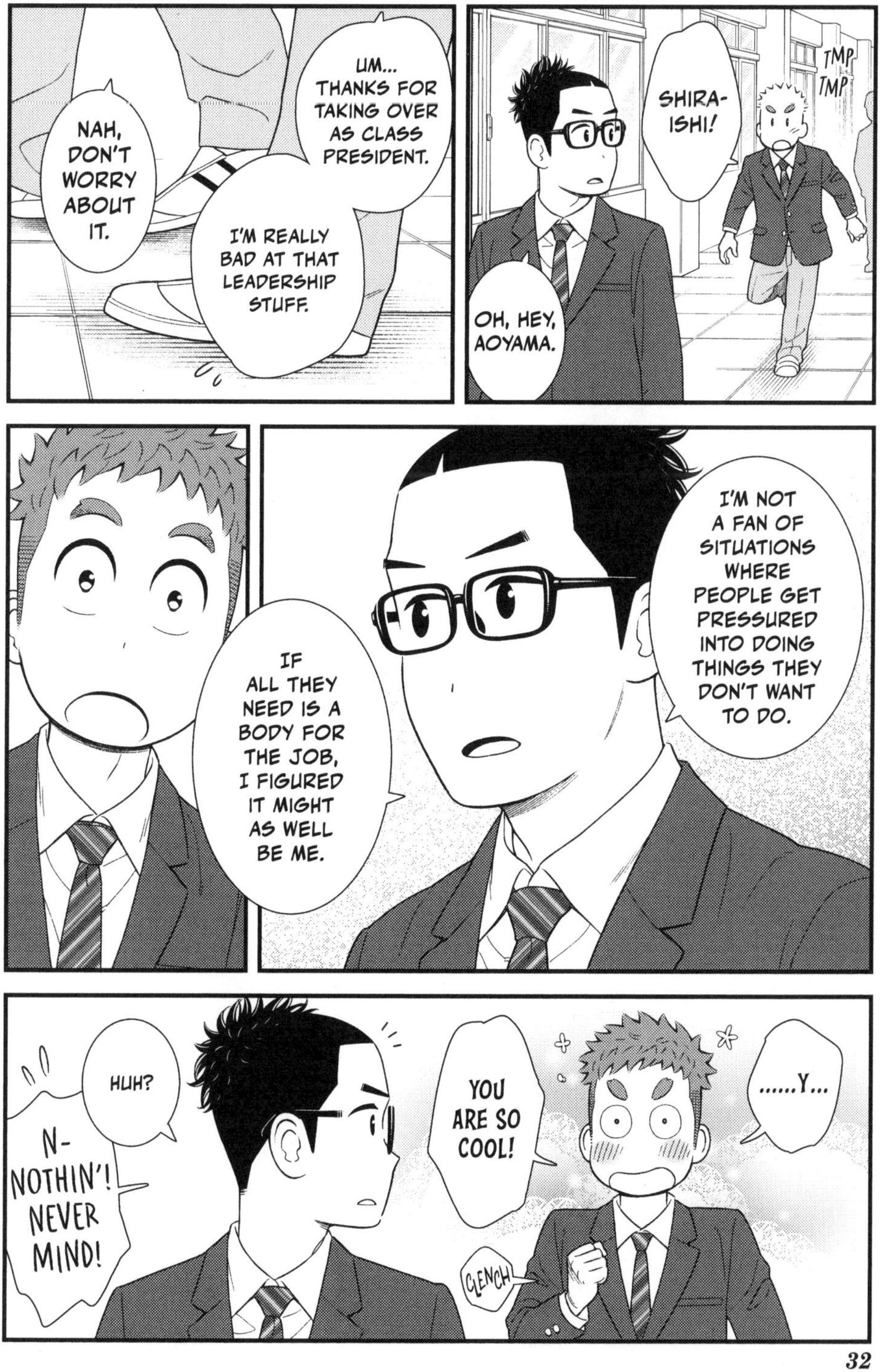
TMP TMP
SHIRA-ISHI!
OH, HEY, AOYAMA.
UM... THANKS FOR TAKING OVER AS CLASS PRESIDENT.
I'M REALLY BAD AT THAT LEADERSHIP STUFF.
NAH, DON'T WORRY ABOUT IT.
I'M NOT A FAN OF SITUATIONS WHERE PEOPLE GET PRESSURED INTO DOING THINGS THEY DON'T WANT TO DO.
IF ALL THEY NEED IS A BODY FOR THE JOB, I FIGURED IT MIGHT AS WELL BE ME.
......Y...
YOU ARE SO COOL!
CLENCH
HUH?
N-NOTHIN'! NEVER MIND!

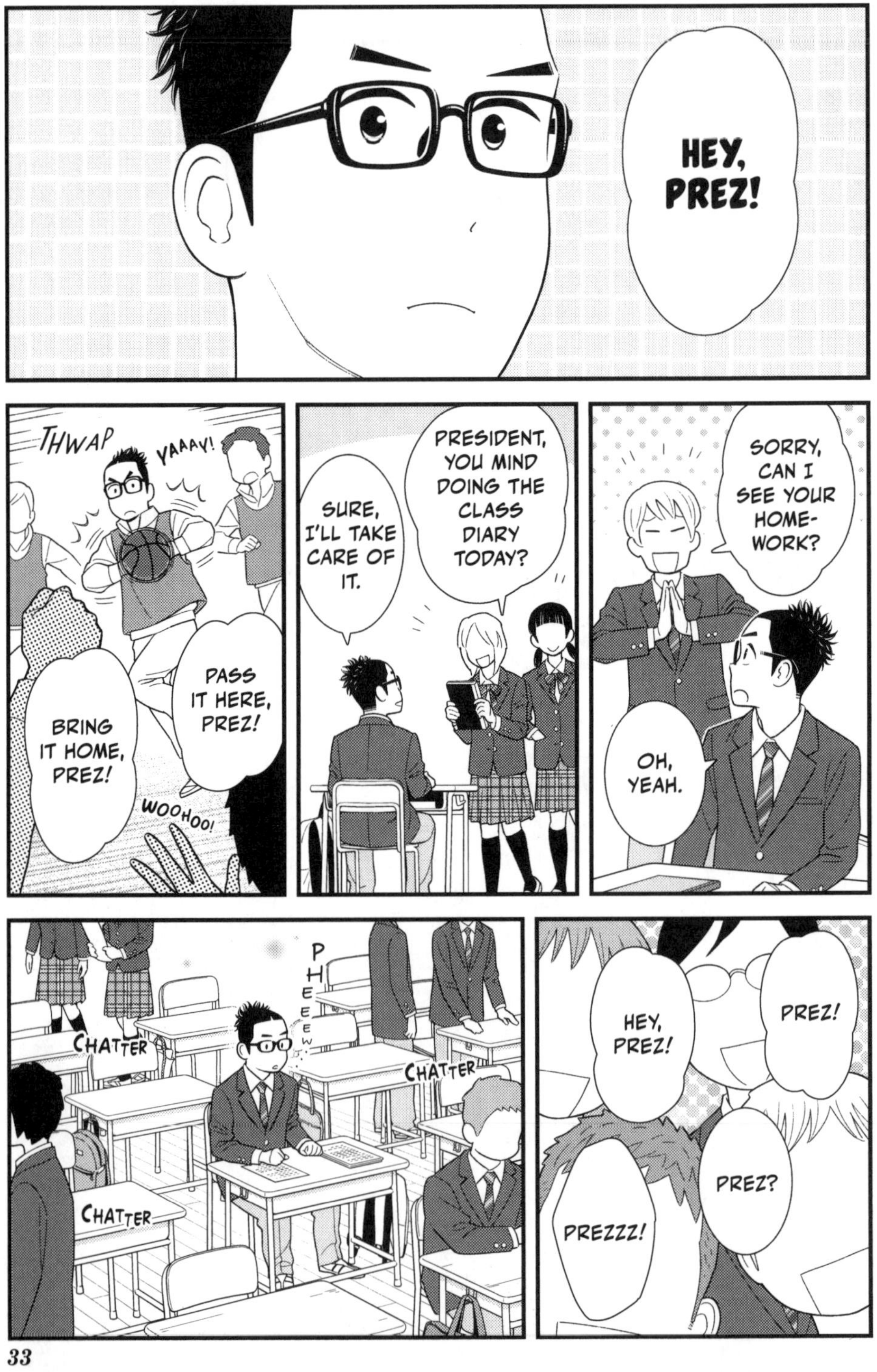
HEY, PREZ!
SORRY, CAN I SEE YOUR HOME-WORK?
OH, YEAH.
PRESIDENT, YOU MIND DOING THE CLASS DIARY TODAY?
SURE, I'LL TAKE CARE OF IT.
THWAP
YAAAY!
PASS IT HERE, PREZ!
BRING IT HOME, PREZ!
WOOHOO!
PREZ!
HEY, PREZ!
PREZ?
PREZZZ!
PHEEEEW
CHATTER
CHATTER
CHATTER

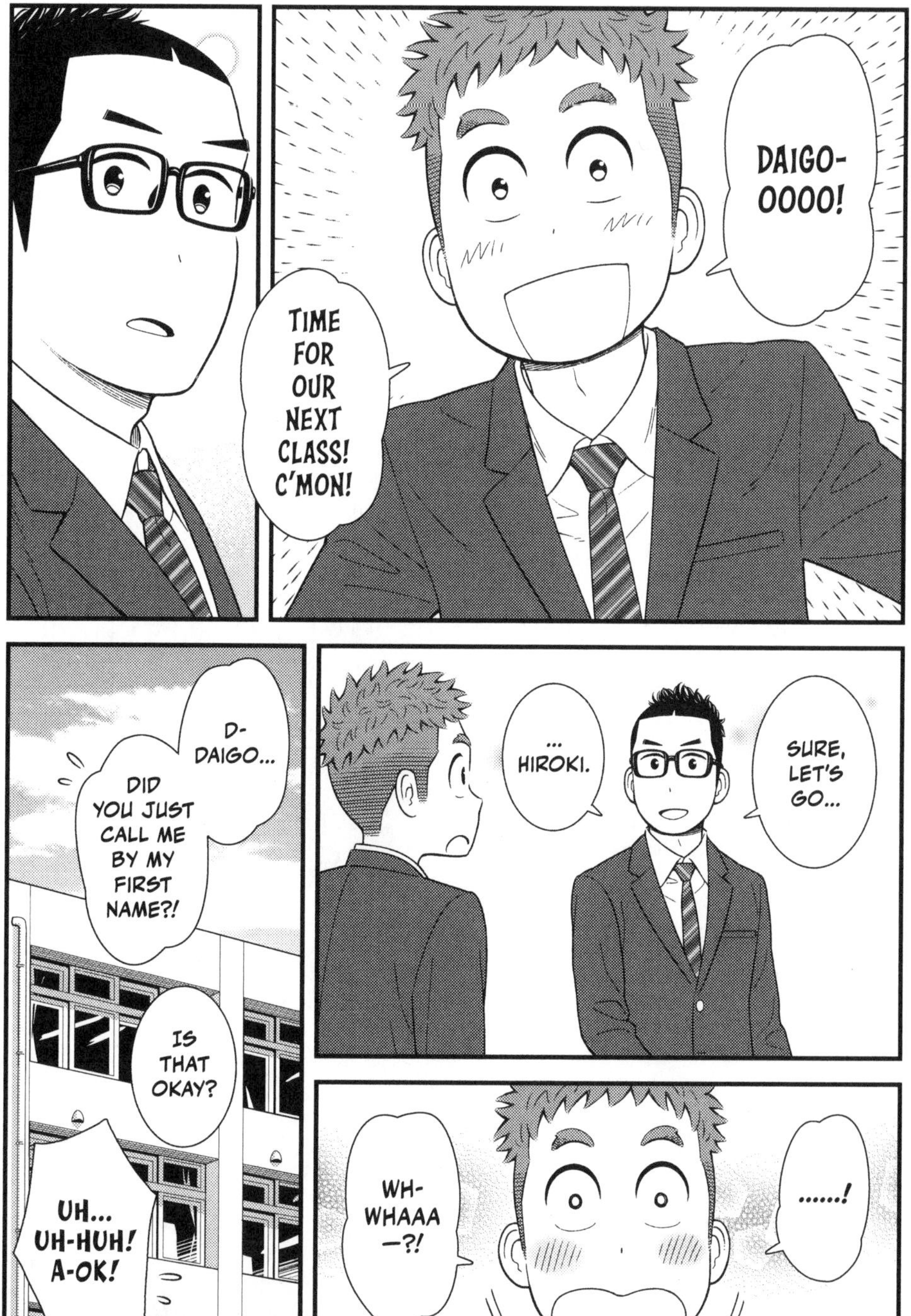
DAIGO-OOOO!
TIME FOR OUR NEXT CLASS! C'MON!
SURE, LET'S GO...
... HIROKI.
......!
WH-WHAAA—?!
D-DAIGO...
DID YOU JUST CALL ME BY MY FIRST NAME?!
IS THAT OKAY?
UH... UH-HUH! A-OK!

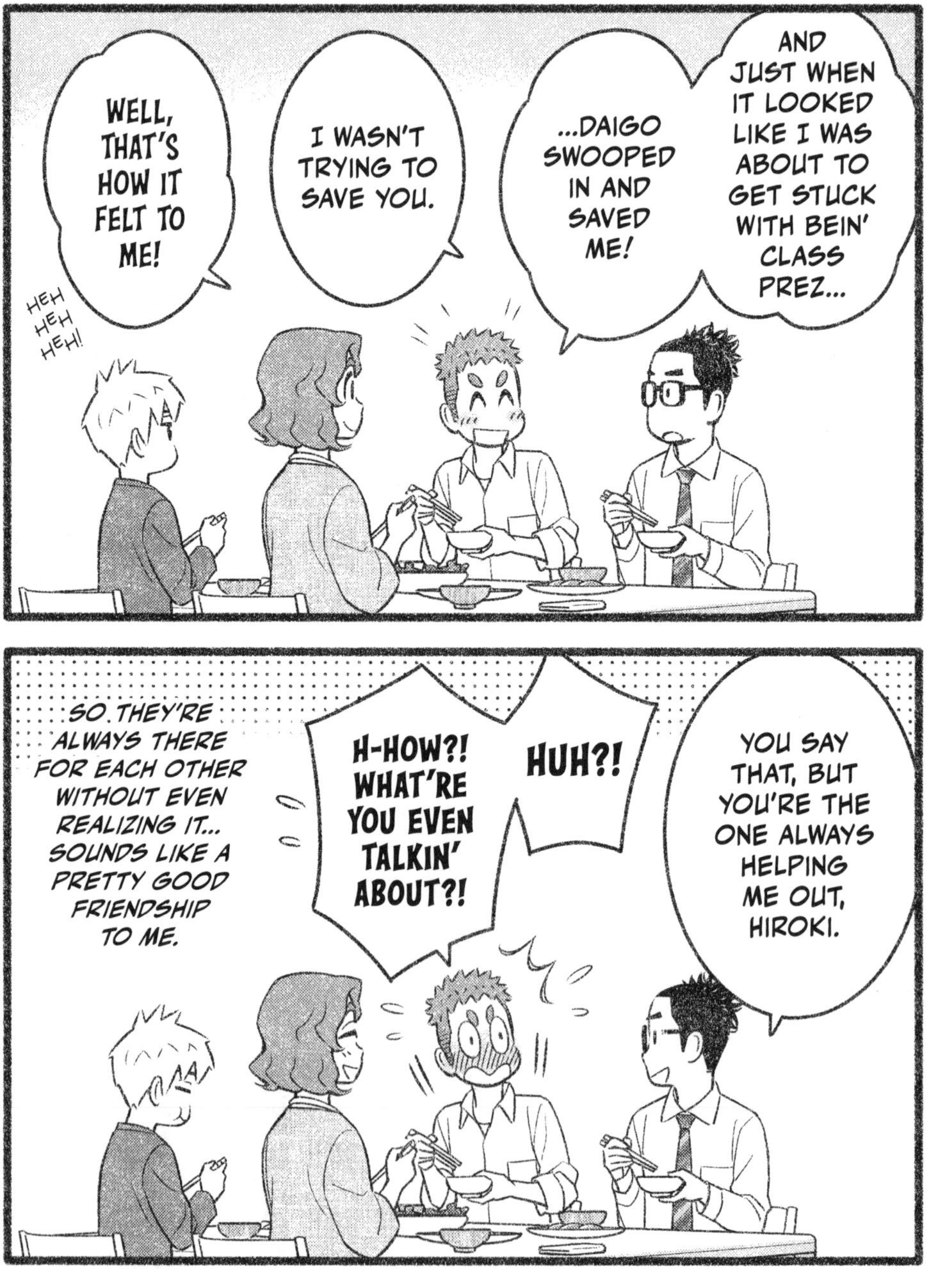
AND JUST WHEN IT LOOKED LIKE I WAS ABOUT TO GET STUCK WITH BEIN' CLASS PREZ...
...DAIGO SWOOPED IN AND SAVED ME!
I WASN'T TRYING TO SAVE YOU.
WELL, THAT'S HOW IT FELT TO ME!
HEH HEH HEH!
YOU SAY THAT, BUT YOU'RE THE ONE ALWAYS HELPING ME OUT, HIROKI.
HUH?!
H-HOW?! WHAT'RE YOU EVEN TALKIN' ABOUT?!
SO THEY'RE ALWAYS THERE FOR EACH OTHER WITHOUT EVEN REALIZING IT... SOUNDS LIKE A PRETTY GOOD FRIENDSHIP TO ME.

# I Think
## Our Son
### Is Gay

CHAPTER 28: CRUSH TALK

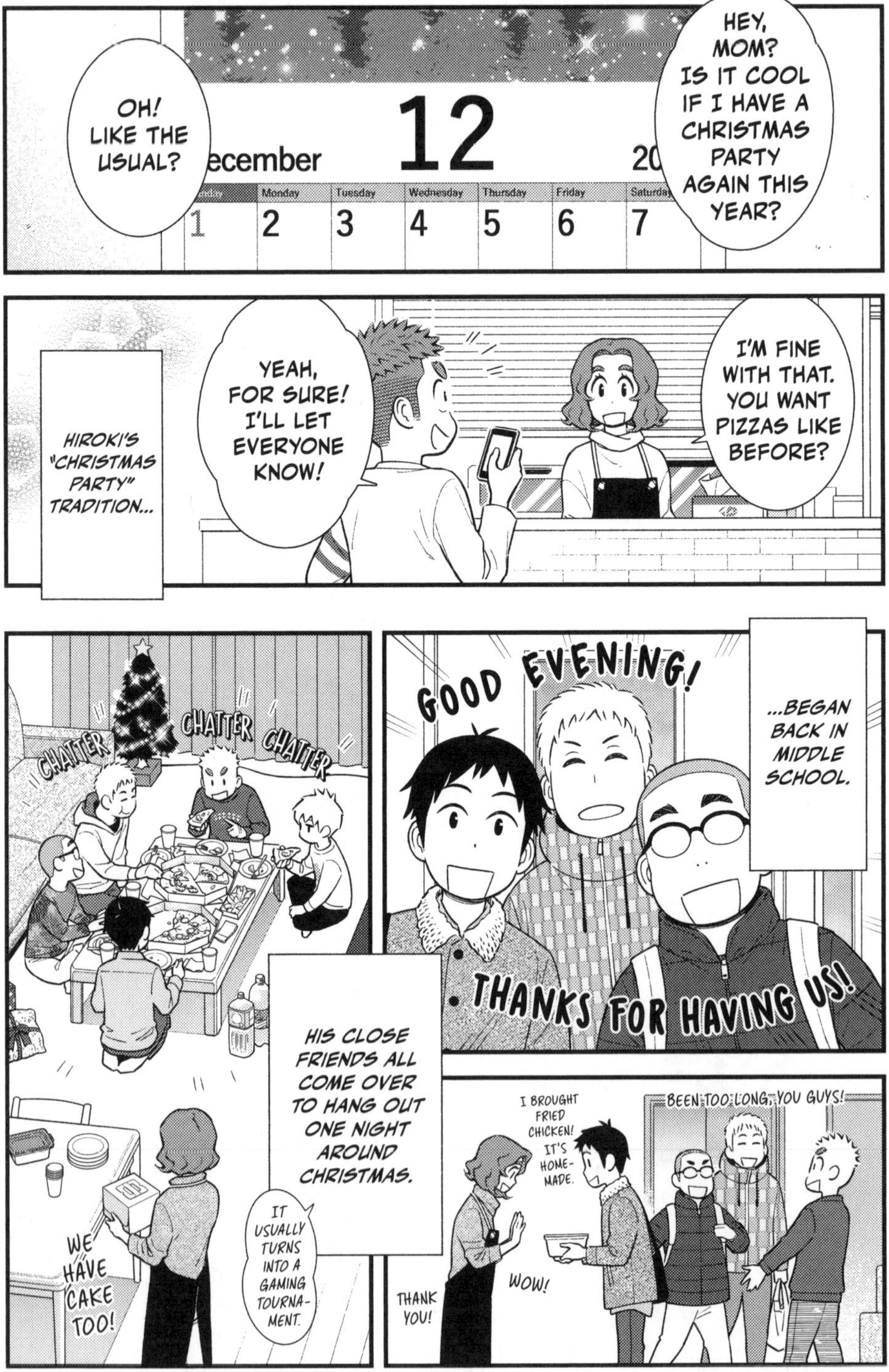
HEY, MOM? IS IT COOL IF I HAVE A CHRISTMAS PARTY AGAIN THIS YEAR?
OH! LIKE THE USUAL?
I'M FINE WITH THAT. YOU WANT PIZZAS LIKE BEFORE?
YEAH, FOR SURE! I'LL LET EVERYONE KNOW!
HIROKI'S "CHRISTMAS PARTY" TRADITION...
...BEGAN BACK IN MIDDLE SCHOOL.
GOOD EVENING!
THANKS FOR HAVING US!
BEEN TOO LONG, YOU GUYS!
I BROUGHT FRIED CHICKEN! IT'S HOME-MADE.
WOW!
THANK YOU!
HIS CLOSE FRIENDS ALL COME OVER TO HANG OUT ONE NIGHT AROUND CHRISTMAS.
CHATTER CHATTER
CHATTER
IT USUALLY TURNS INTO A GAMING TOURNA-MENT.
WE HAVE CAKE TOO!

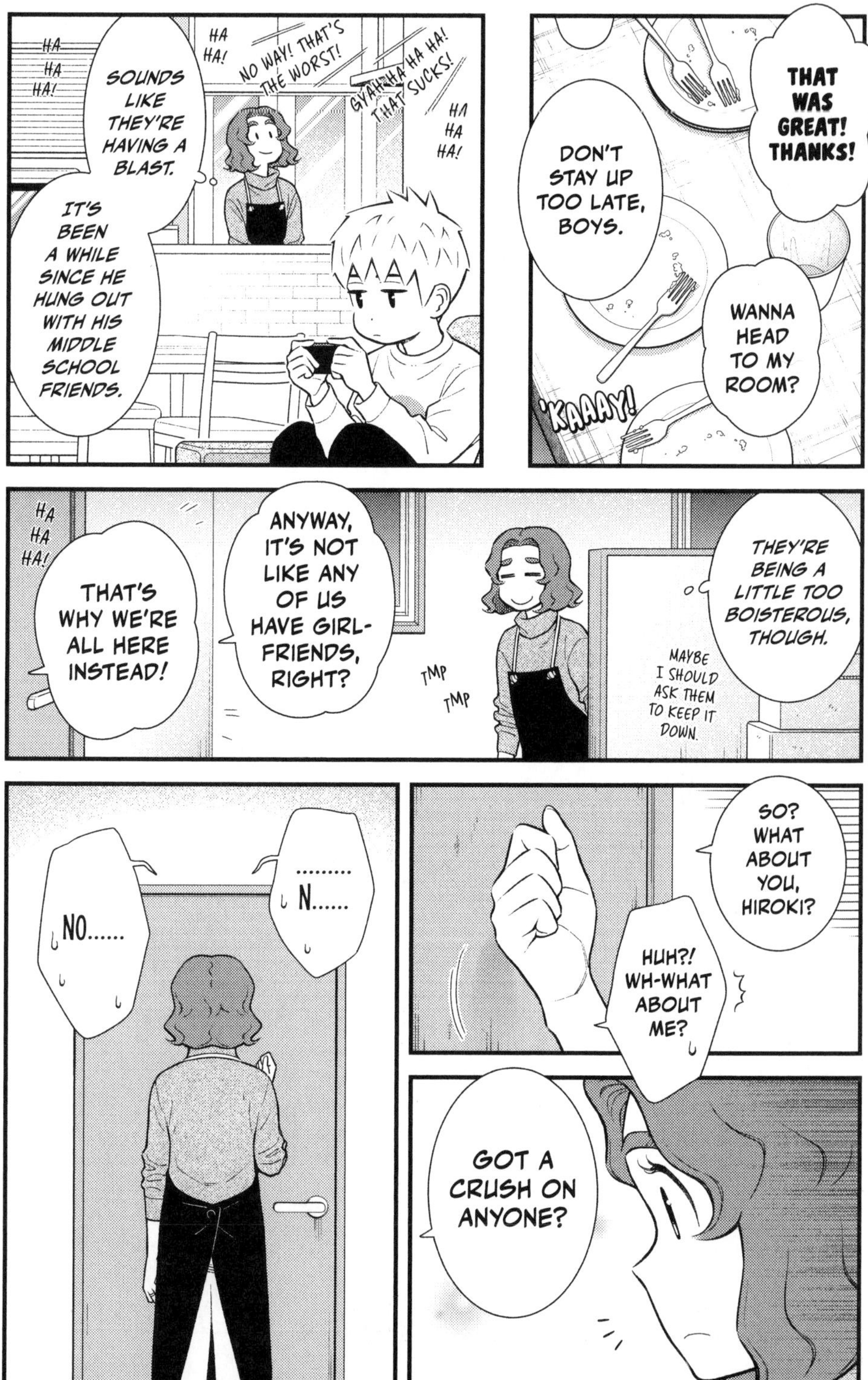
THAT WAS GREAT! THANKS!
DON'T STAY UP TOO LATE, BOYS.
WANNA HEAD TO MY ROOM?
'KAAAY!
HA HA!
NO WAY! THAT'S THE WORST!
GYAH HA HA HA! THAT SUCKS!
HA HA HA!
SOUNDS LIKE THEY'RE HAVING A BLAST.
HA HA HA!
IT'S BEEN A WHILE SINCE HE HUNG OUT WITH HIS MIDDLE SCHOOL FRIENDS.
THEY'RE BEING A LITTLE TOO BOISTEROUS, THOUGH.
MAYBE I SHOULD ASK THEM TO KEEP IT DOWN.
TMP TMP
ANYWAY, IT'S NOT LIKE ANY OF US HAVE GIRL-FRIENDS, RIGHT?
THAT'S WHY WE'RE ALL HERE INSTEAD!
HA HA HA!
SO? WHAT ABOUT YOU, HIROKI?
HUH?! WH-WHAT ABOUT ME?
GOT A CRUSH ON ANYONE?
......... N......
NO......

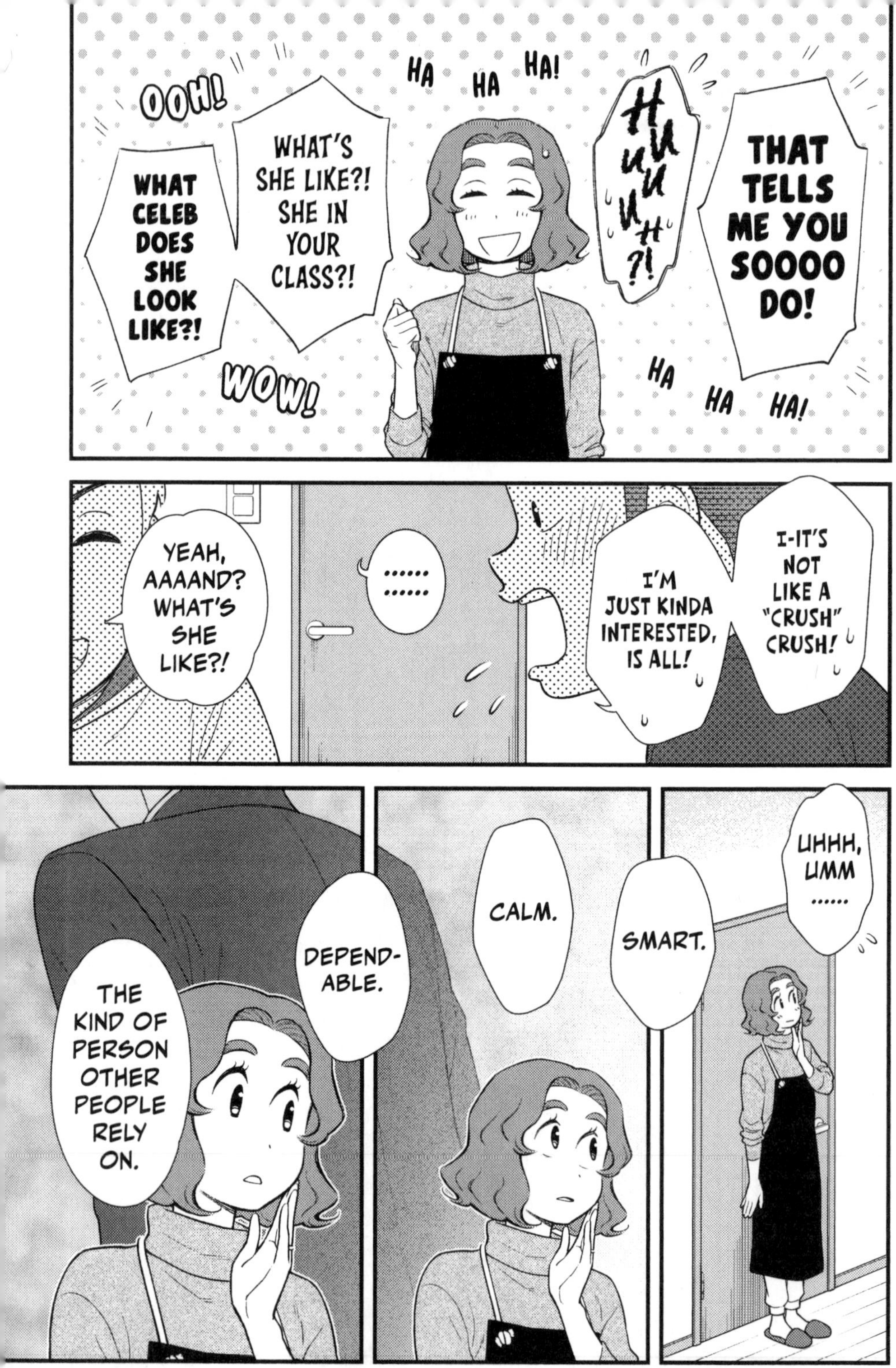

THAT TELLS ME YOU SOOOO DO!
HA HA HA!
HUUUUH?!
HA HA HA!
WHAT'S SHE LIKE?! SHE IN YOUR CLASS?!
OOH!
WHAT CELEB DOES SHE LOOK LIKE?!
WOW!
I-IT'S NOT LIKE A "CRUSH" CRUSH!
I'M JUST KINDA INTERESTED, IS ALL!
............
YEAH, AAAAND? WHAT'S SHE LIKE?!
UHHH, UMM ......
SMART.
CALM.
DEPEND-ABLE.
THE KIND OF PERSON OTHER PEOPLE RELY ON.

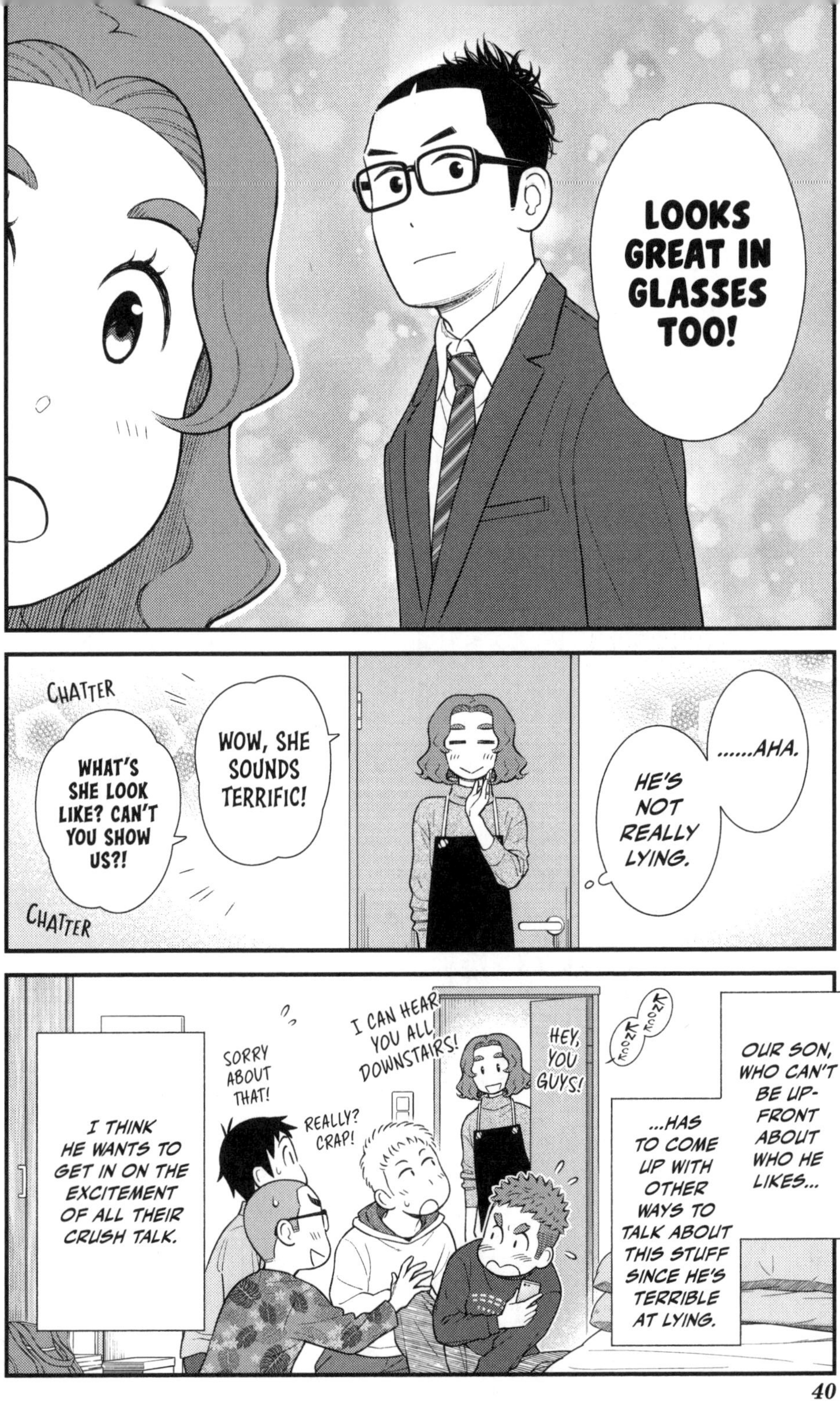
LOOKS GREAT IN GLASSES TOO!
......AHA.
HE'S NOT REALLY LYING.
WOW, SHE SOUNDS TERRIFIC!
WHAT'S SHE LOOK LIKE? CAN'T YOU SHOW US?!
CHATTER
CHATTER
OUR SON, WHO CAN'T BE UP-FRONT ABOUT WHO HE LIKES...
...HAS TO COME UP WITH OTHER WAYS TO TALK ABOUT THIS STUFF SINCE HE'S TERRIBLE AT LYING.
KNOCK KNOCK
HEY, YOU GUYS!
I CAN HEAR YOU ALL DOWNSTAIRS!
SORRY ABOUT THAT!
REALLY? CRAP!
I THINK HE WANTS TO GET IN ON THE EXCITEMENT OF ALL THEIR CRUSH TALK.

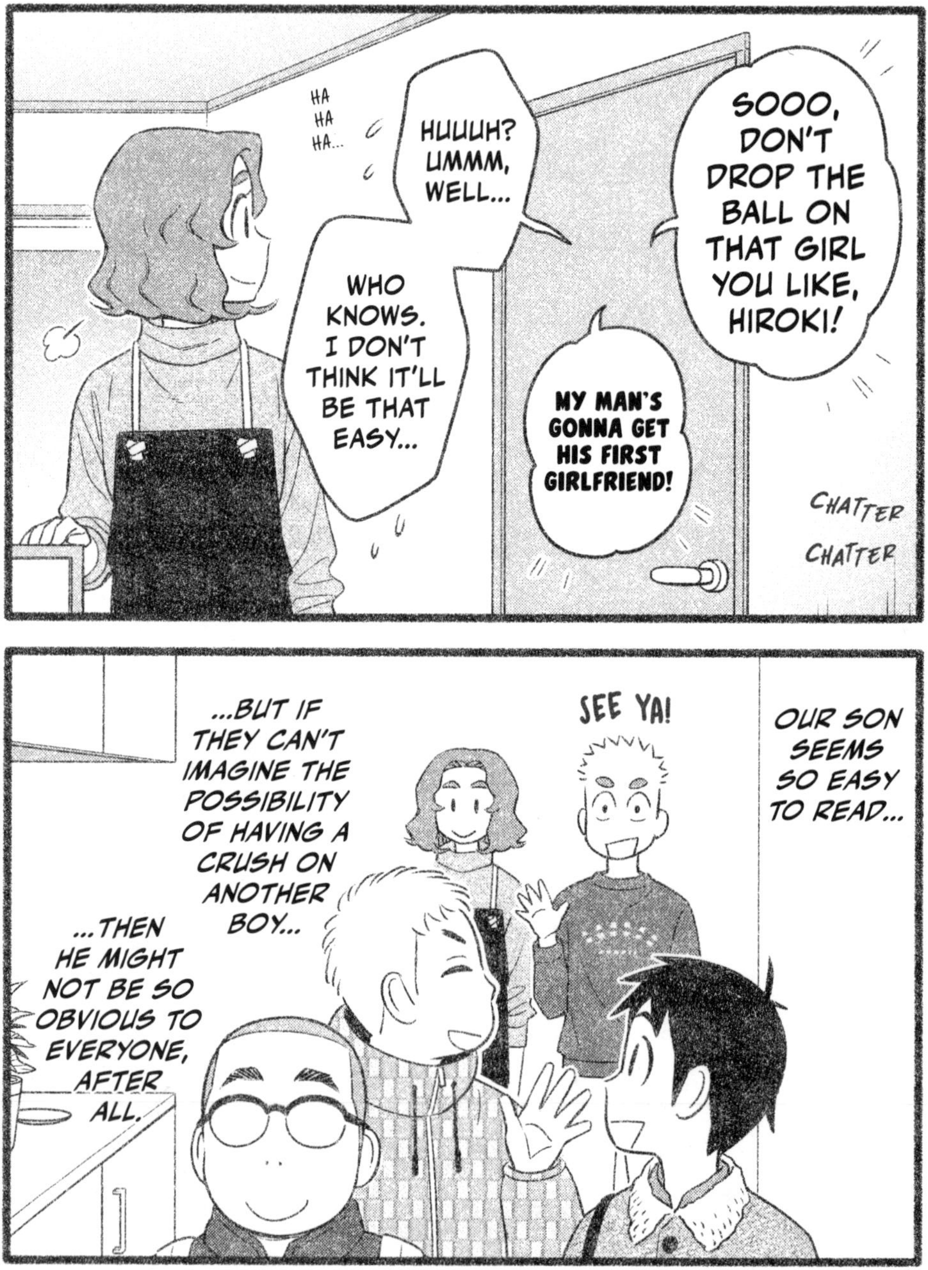
SOOO, DON'T DROP THE BALL ON THAT GIRL YOU LIKE, HIROKI!
MY MAN'S GONNA GET HIS FIRST GIRLFRIEND!
CHATTER
CHATTER
HUUUH? UMMM, WELL...
HA HA HA...
WHO KNOWS. I DON'T THINK IT'LL BE THAT EASY...
OUR SON SEEMS SO EASY TO READ...
SEE YA!
...BUT IF THEY CAN'T IMAGINE THE POSSIBILITY OF HAVING A CRUSH ON ANOTHER BOY...
...THEN HE MIGHT NOT BE SO OBVIOUS TO EVERYONE, AFTER ALL.

# I Think
# Our Son
# Is Gay

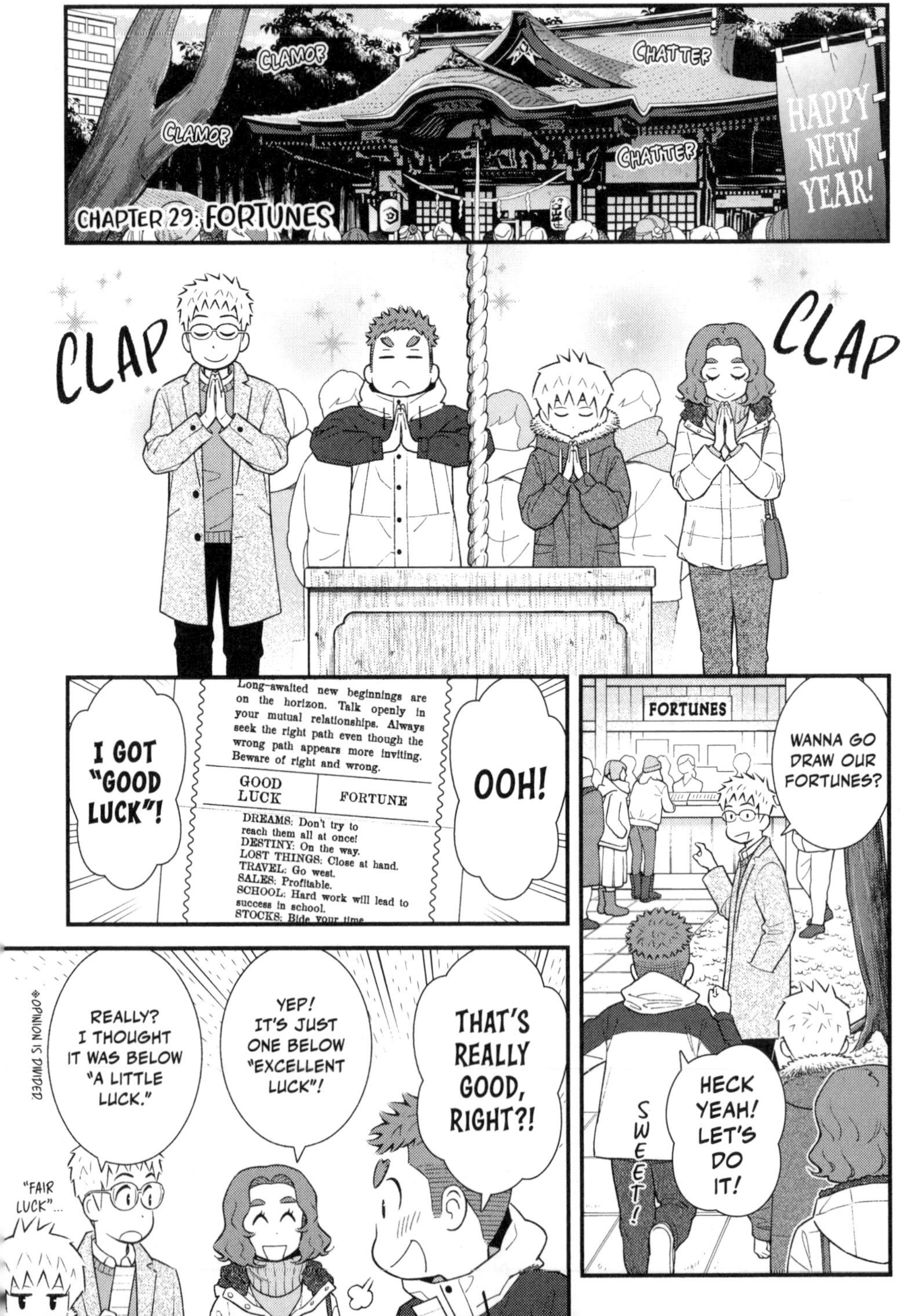
HAPPY NEW YEAR!
CHATTER
CHATTER
CLAMOR
CLAMOR
CHAPTER 29: FORTUNES
CLAP
CLAP
FORTUNES
WANNA GO DRAW OUR FORTUNES?
HECK YEAH! LET'S DO IT!
SWEET!
OOH!
Long-awaited new beginnings are on the horizon. Talk openly in your mutual relationships. Always seek the right path even though the wrong path appears more inviting. Beware of right and wrong.
GOOD LUCK
FORTUNE
DREAMS: Don't try to reach them all at once!
DESTINY: On the way.
LOST THINGS: Close at hand.
TRAVEL: Go west.
SALES: Profitable.
SCHOOL: Hard work will lead to success in school.
STOCKS: Bide your time.
I GOT "GOOD LUCK"!
THAT'S REALLY GOOD, RIGHT?!
YEP! IT'S JUST ONE BELOW "EXCELLENT LUCK"!
REALLY? I THOUGHT IT WAS BELOW "A LITTLE LUCK."
"FAIR LUCK"...
※OPINION IS DIVIDED.

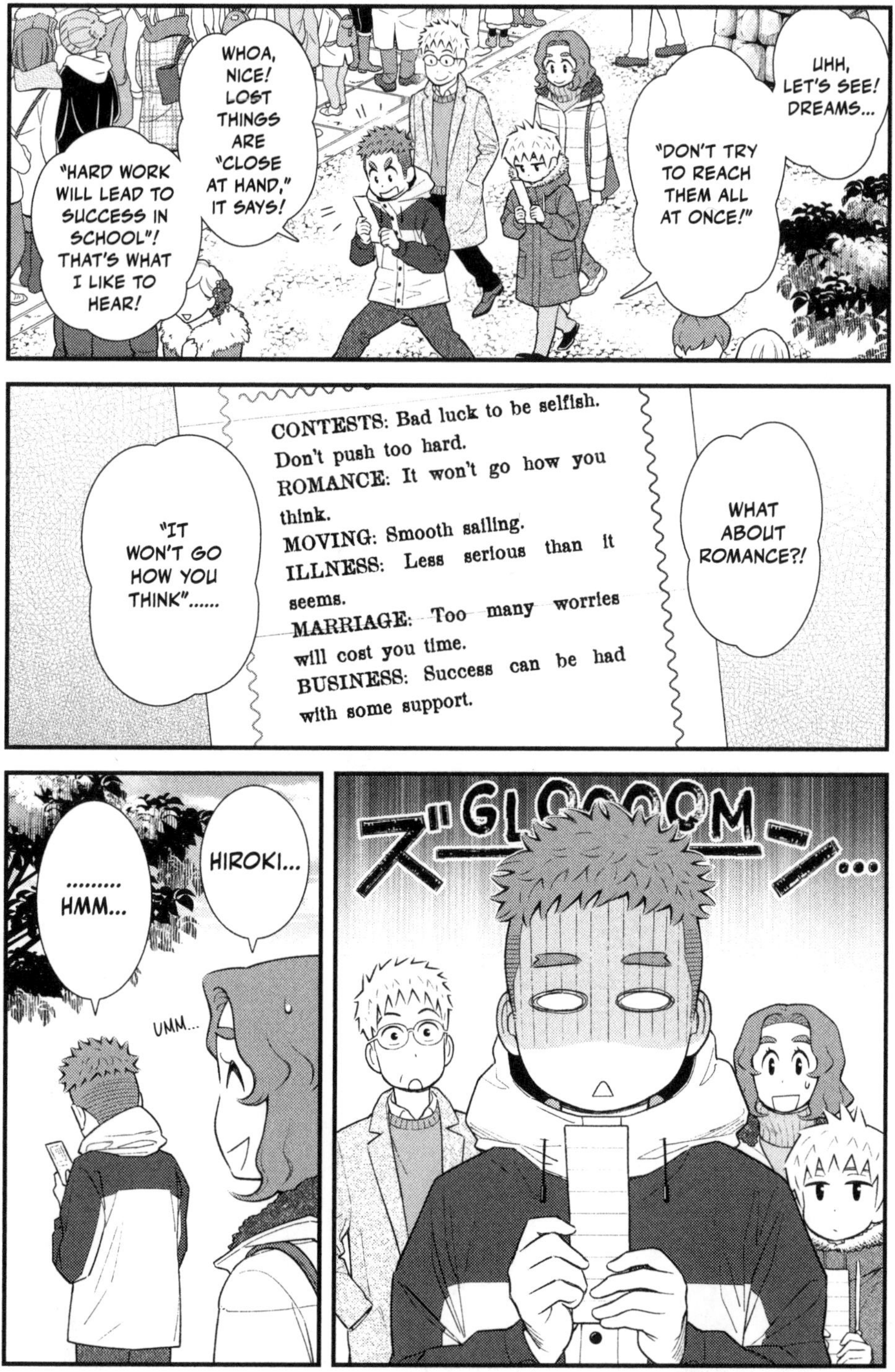
UHH, LET'S SEE! DREAMS...
"DON'T TRY TO REACH THEM ALL AT ONCE!"
WHOA, NICE! LOST THINGS ARE "CLOSE AT HAND," IT SAYS!
"HARD WORK WILL LEAD TO SUCCESS IN SCHOOL"! THAT'S WHAT I LIKE TO HEAR!
WHAT ABOUT ROMANCE?!
CONTESTS: Bad luck to be selfish. Don't push too hard.
ROMANCE: It won't go how you think.
MOVING: Smooth sailing.
ILLNESS: Less serious than it seems.
MARRIAGE: Too many worries will cost you time.
BUSINESS: Success can be had with some support.
"IT WON'T GO HOW YOU THINK"......
GLOOOOM...
HIROKI...
......... HMM...
UMM...

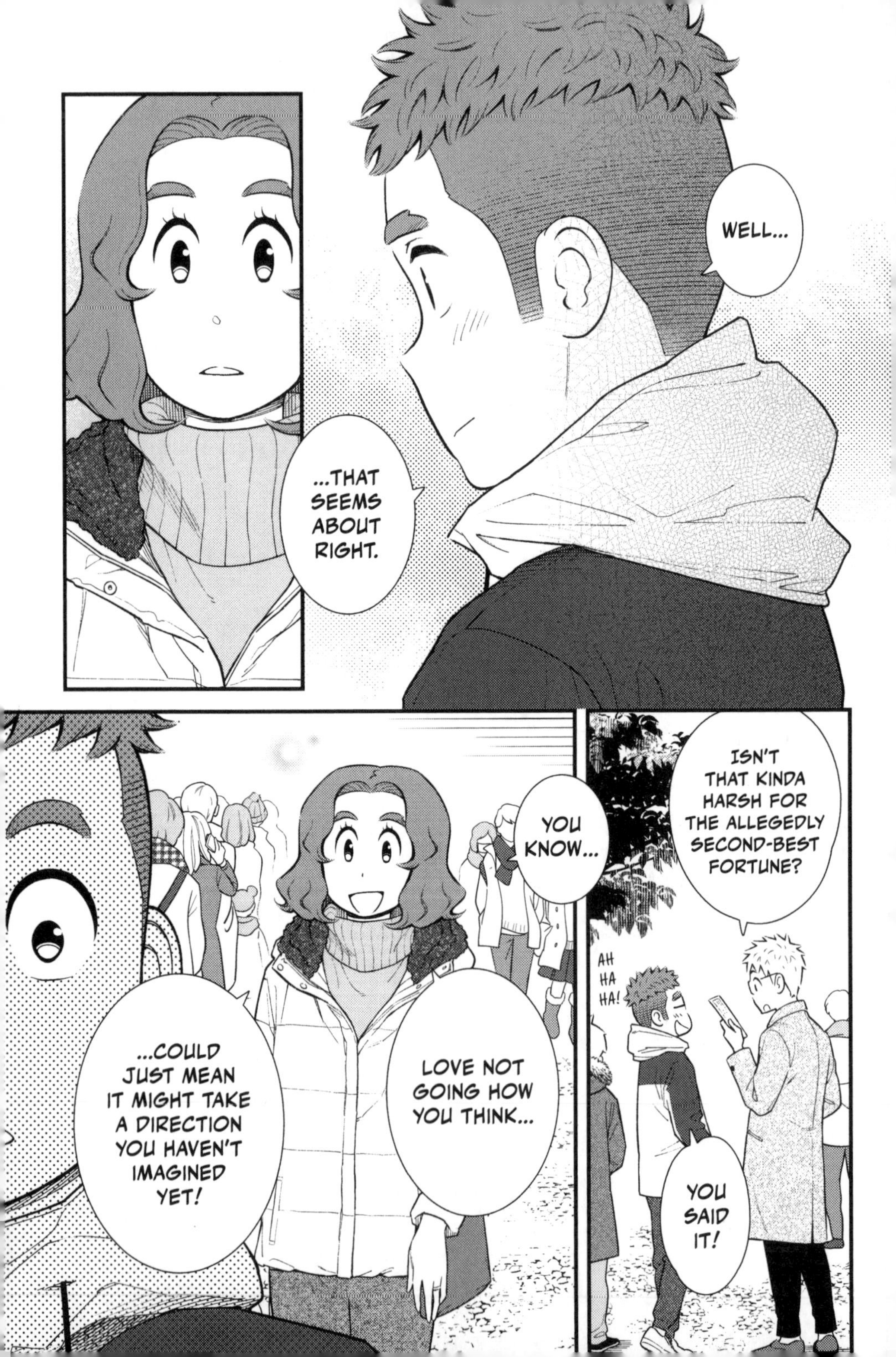
WELL...
...THAT SEEMS ABOUT RIGHT.
ISN'T THAT KINDA HARSH FOR THE ALLEGEDLY SECOND-BEST FORTUNE?
AH HA HA!
YOU SAID IT!
YOU KNOW...
LOVE NOT GOING HOW YOU THINK...
...COULD JUST MEAN IT MIGHT TAKE A DIRECTION YOU HAVEN'T IMAGINED YET!

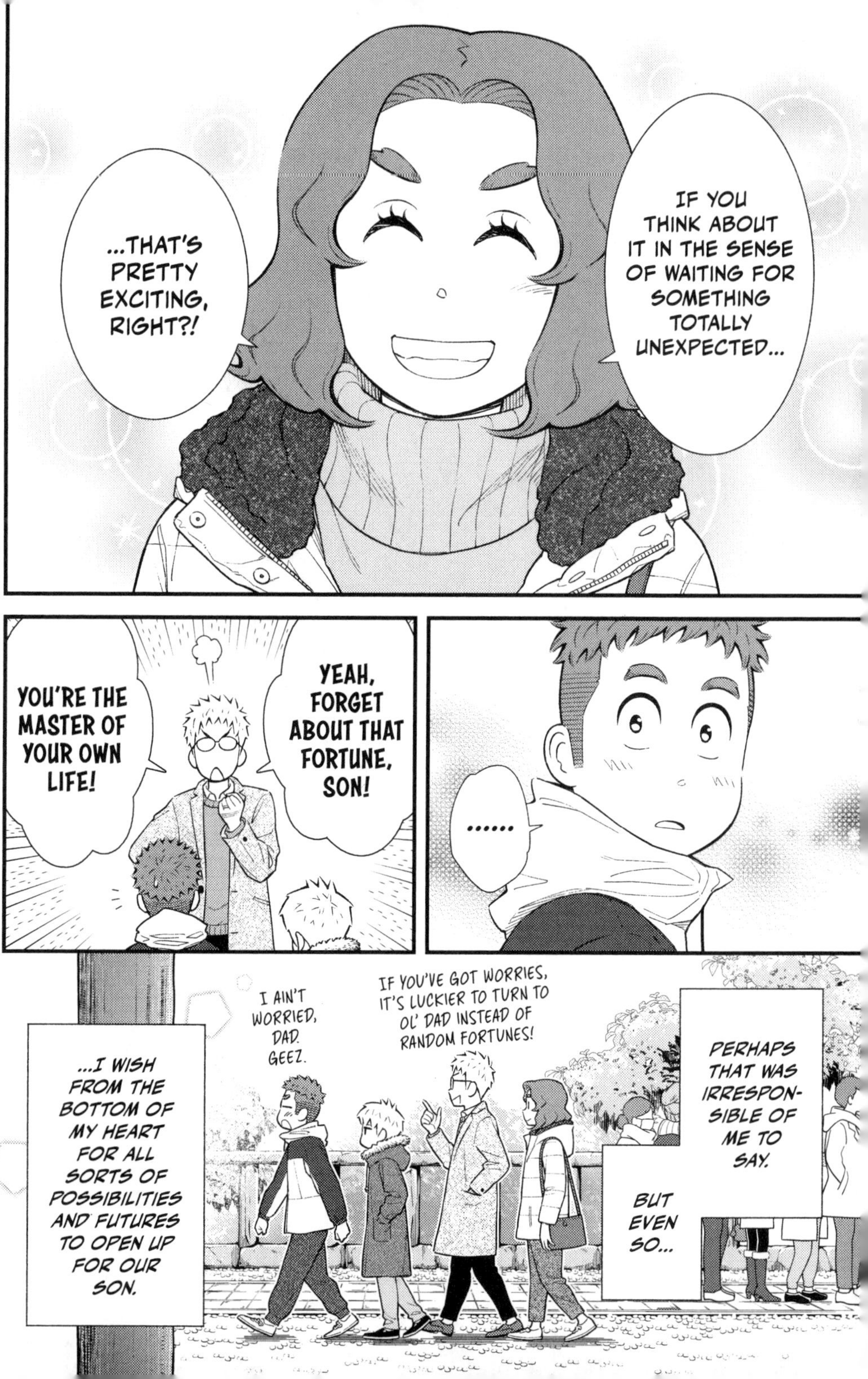
IF YOU THINK ABOUT IT IN THE SENSE OF WAITING FOR SOMETHING TOTALLY UNEXPECTED...
...THAT'S PRETTY EXCITING, RIGHT?!
......
YEAH, FORGET ABOUT THAT FORTUNE, SON!
YOU'RE THE MASTER OF YOUR OWN LIFE!
PERHAPS THAT WAS IRRESPONSIBLE OF ME TO SAY.
BUT EVEN SO...
IF YOU'VE GOT WORRIES, IT'S LUCKIER TO TURN TO OL' DAD INSTEAD OF RANDOM FORTUNES!
I AIN'T WORRIED, DAD. GEEZ.
...I WISH FROM THE BOTTOM OF MY HEART FOR ALL SORTS OF POSSIBILITIES AND FUTURES TO OPEN UP FOR OUR SON.

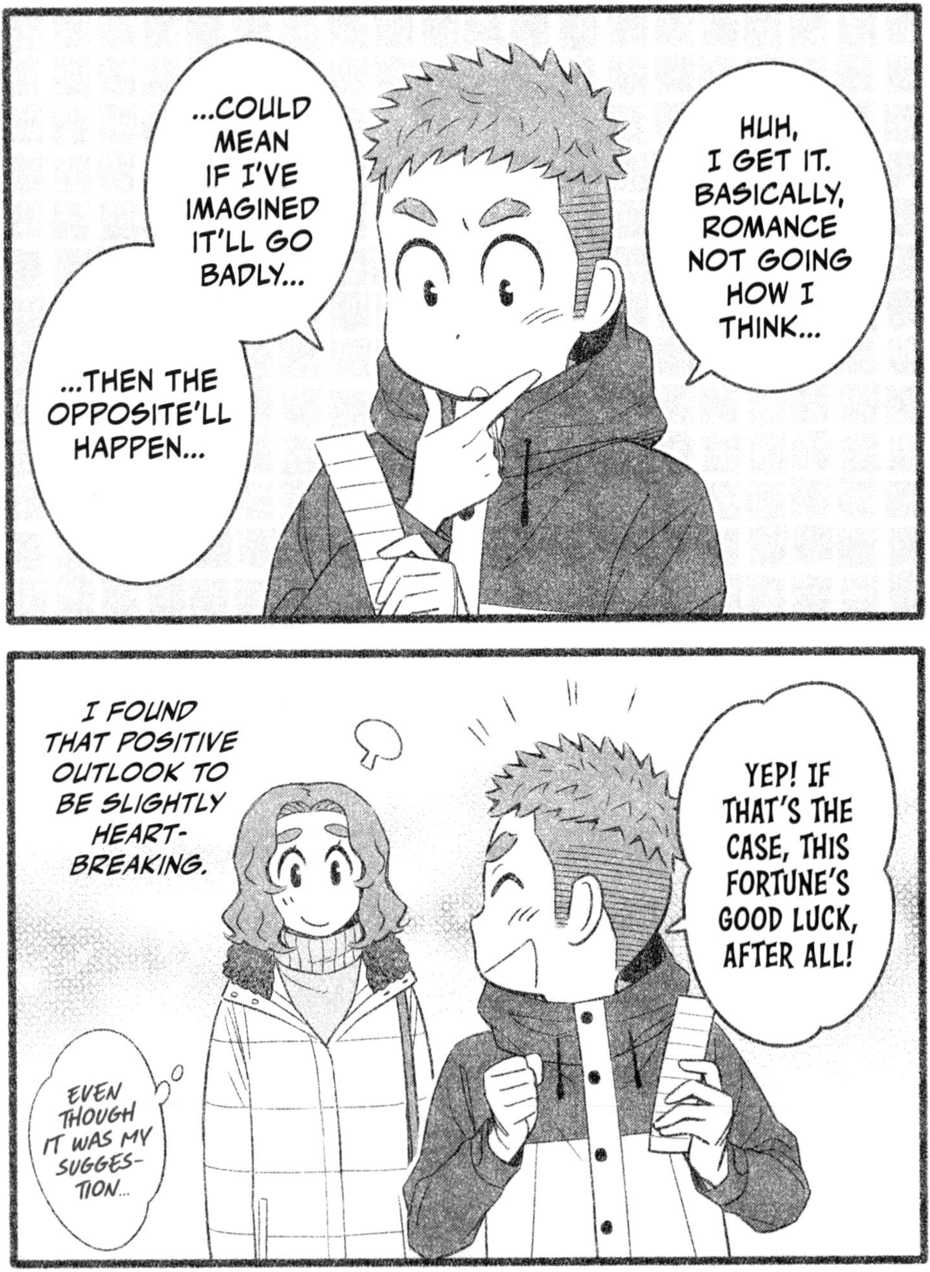
HUH, I GET IT. BASICALLY, ROMANCE NOT GOING HOW I THINK...
...COULD MEAN IF I'VE IMAGINED IT'LL GO BADLY...
...THEN THE OPPOSITE'LL HAPPEN...
YEP! IF THAT'S THE CASE, THIS FORTUNE'S GOOD LUCK, AFTER ALL!
I FOUND THAT POSITIVE OUTLOOK TO BE SLIGHTLY HEART-BREAKING.
EVEN THOUGH IT WAS MY SUGGES-TION...

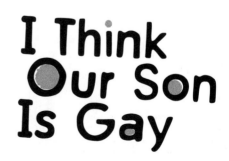

I Think
Our Son
Is Gay

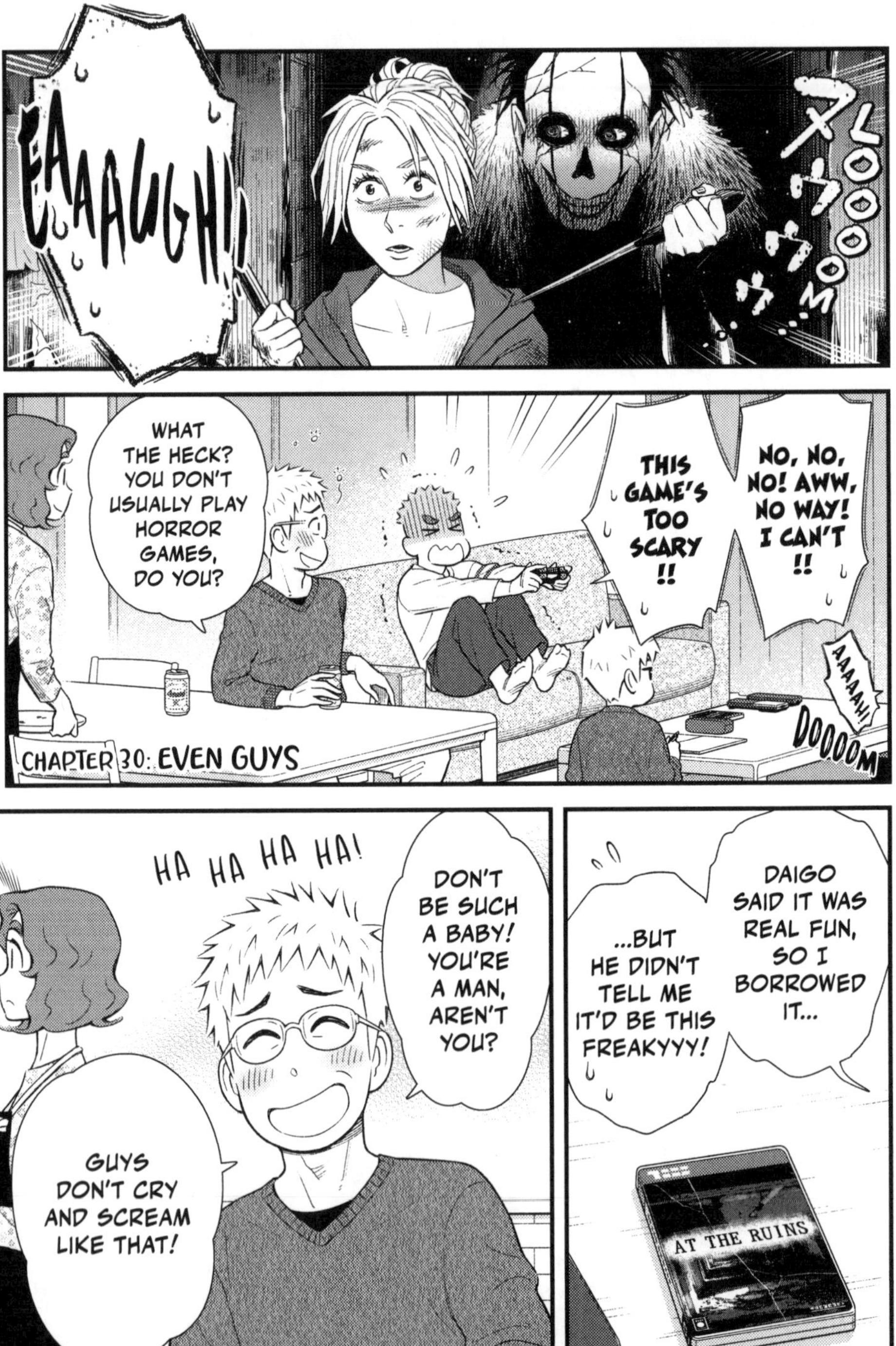
VLOOOOOM
EAAAUGH!!
NO, NO, NO! AWW, NO WAY! I CAN'T!!
THIS GAME'S TOO SCARY!!
AAAAAH!
DOOOOM
WHAT THE HECK? YOU DON'T USUALLY PLAY HORROR GAMES, DO YOU?
CHAPTER 30: EVEN GUYS
DAIGO SAID IT WAS REAL FUN, SO I BORROWED IT...
...BUT HE DIDN'T TELL ME IT'D BE THIS FREAKYYY!
AT THE RUINS
DON'T BE SUCH A BABY! YOU'RE A MAN, AREN'T YOU?
HA HA HA HA HA!
GUYS DON'T CRY AND SCREAM LIKE THAT!

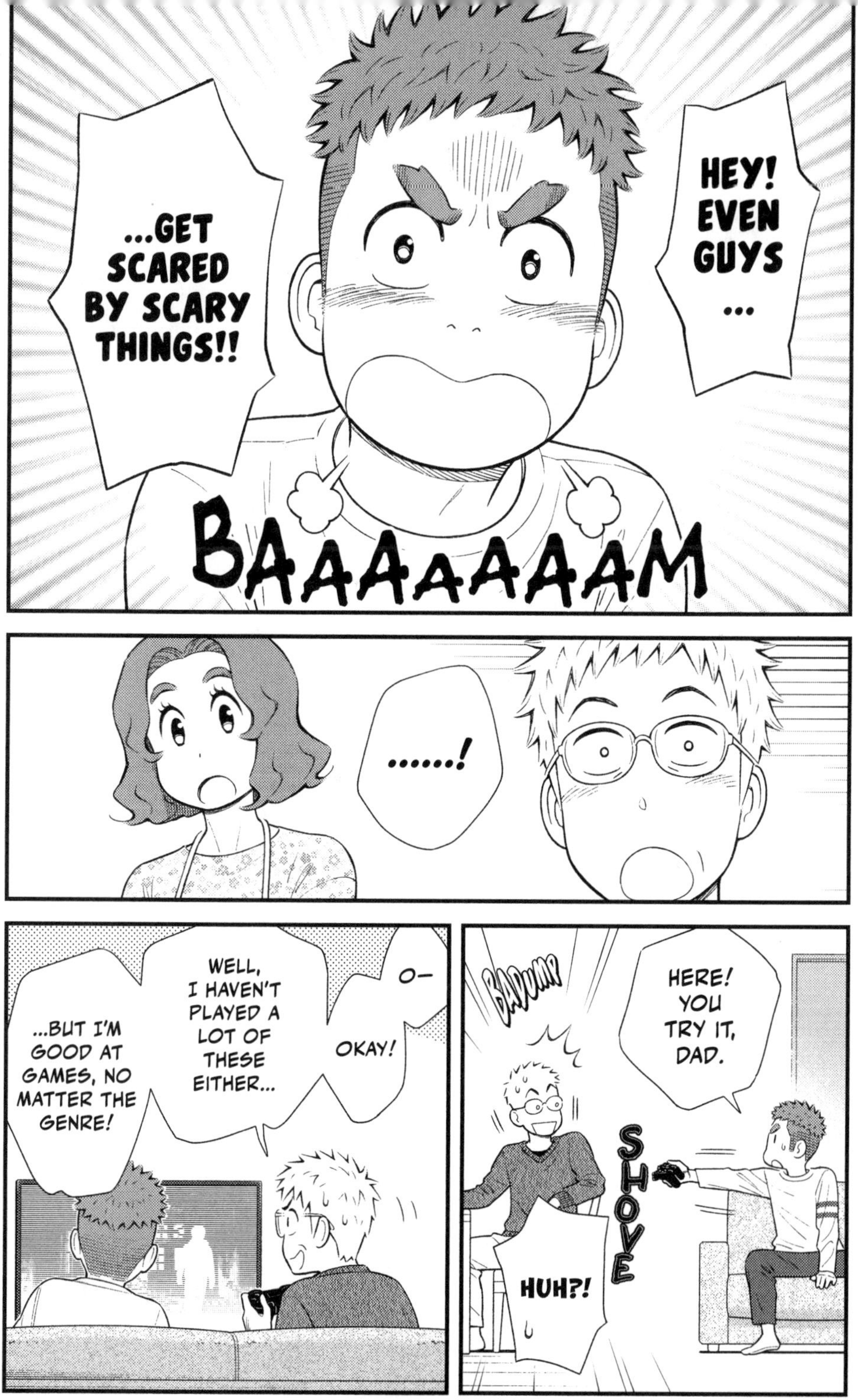
HEY! EVEN GUYS ...
...GET SCARED BY SCARY THINGS!!
BAAAAAAAM
......!
BADUMP
HERE! YOU TRY IT, DAD.
SHOVE
HUH?!
O— OKAY!
WELL, I HAVEN'T PLAYED A LOT OF THESE EITHER...
...BUT I'M GOOD AT GAMES, NO MATTER THE GENRE!

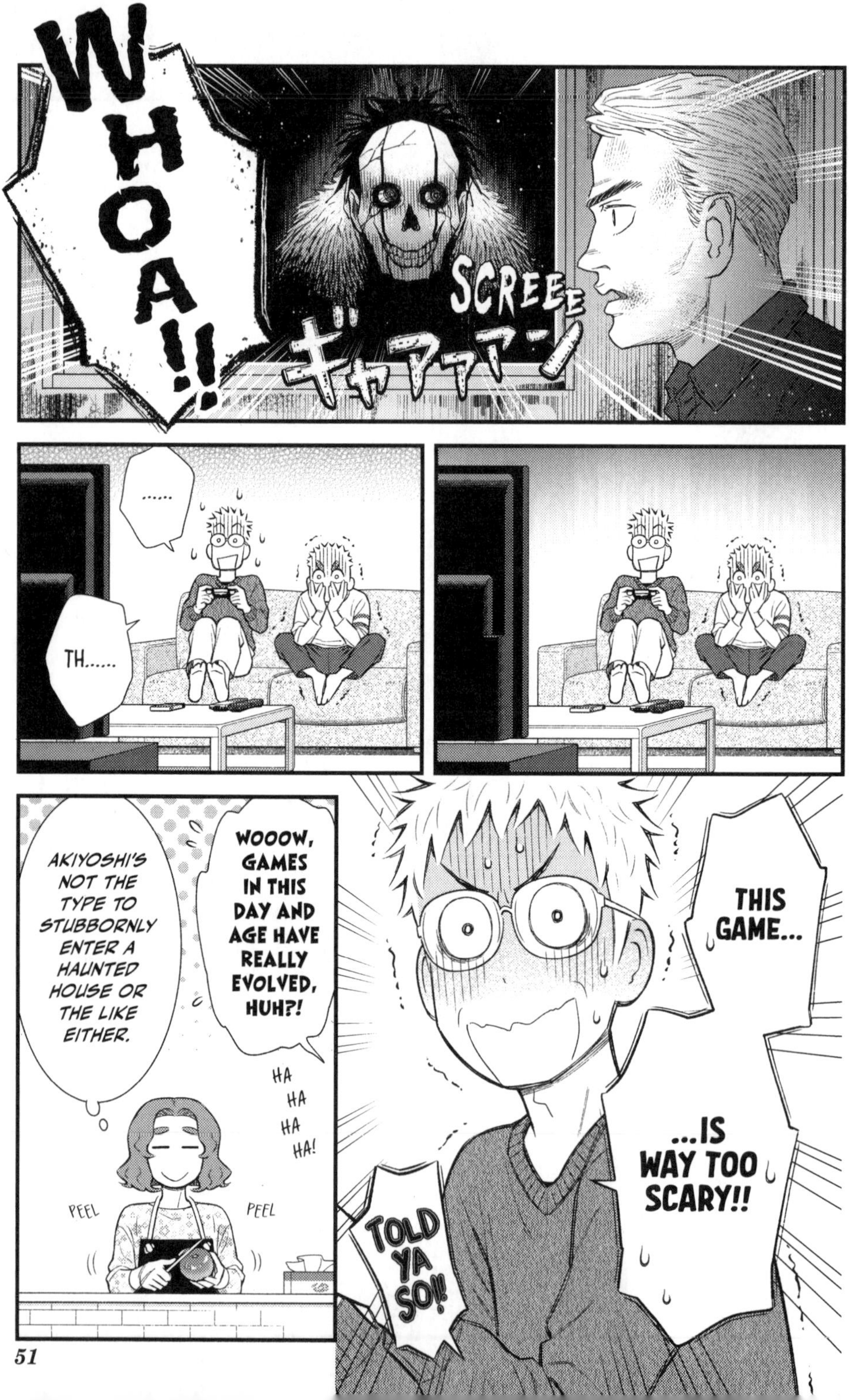
WHOA!!
SCREEEE
ギャアアアーン
......
TH......
THIS GAME...
...IS WAY TOO SCARY!!
TOLD YA SO!!
WOOOW, GAMES IN THIS DAY AND AGE HAVE REALLY EVOLVED, HUH?!
HA HA HA HA!
AKIYOSHI'S NOT THE TYPE TO STUBBORNLY ENTER A HAUNTED HOUSE OR THE LIKE EITHER.
PEEL
PEEL

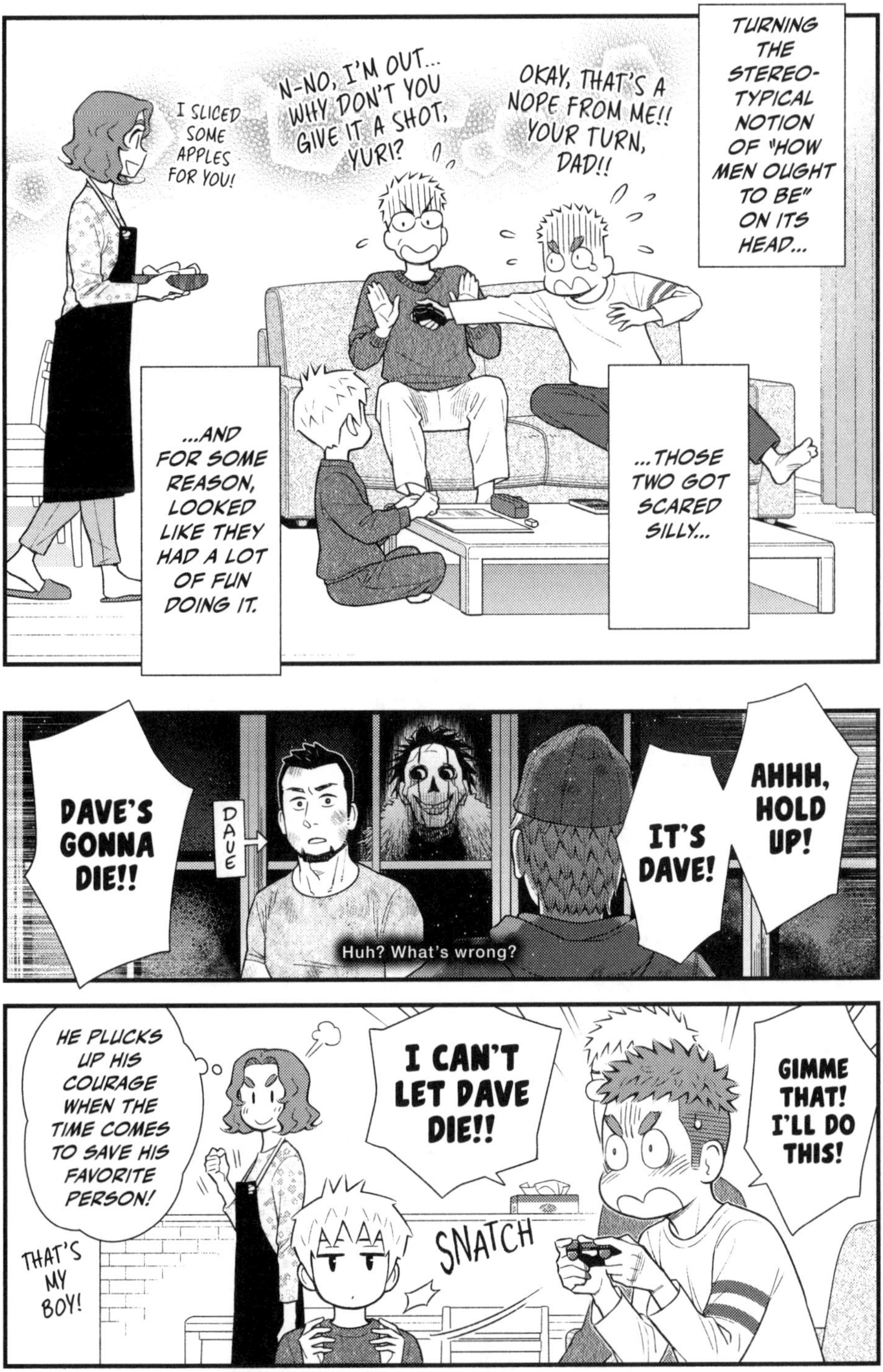

TURNING THE STEREOTYPICAL NOTION OF "HOW MEN OUGHT TO BE" ON ITS HEAD...
OKAY, THAT'S A NOPE FROM ME!! YOUR TURN, DAD!!
N-NO, I'M OUT... WHY DON'T YOU GIVE IT A SHOT, YURI?
I SLICED SOME APPLES FOR YOU!
...THOSE TWO GOT SCARED SILLY...
...AND FOR SOME REASON, LOOKED LIKE THEY HAD A LOT OF FUN DOING IT.
AHHH, HOLD UP!
IT'S DAVE!
DAUE
Huh? What's wrong?
DAVE'S GONNA DIE!!
GIMME THAT! I'LL DO THIS!
I CAN'T LET DAVE DIE!!
SNATCH
HE PLUCKS UP HIS COURAGE WHEN THE TIME COMES TO SAVE HIS FAVORITE PERSON!
THAT'S MY BOY!

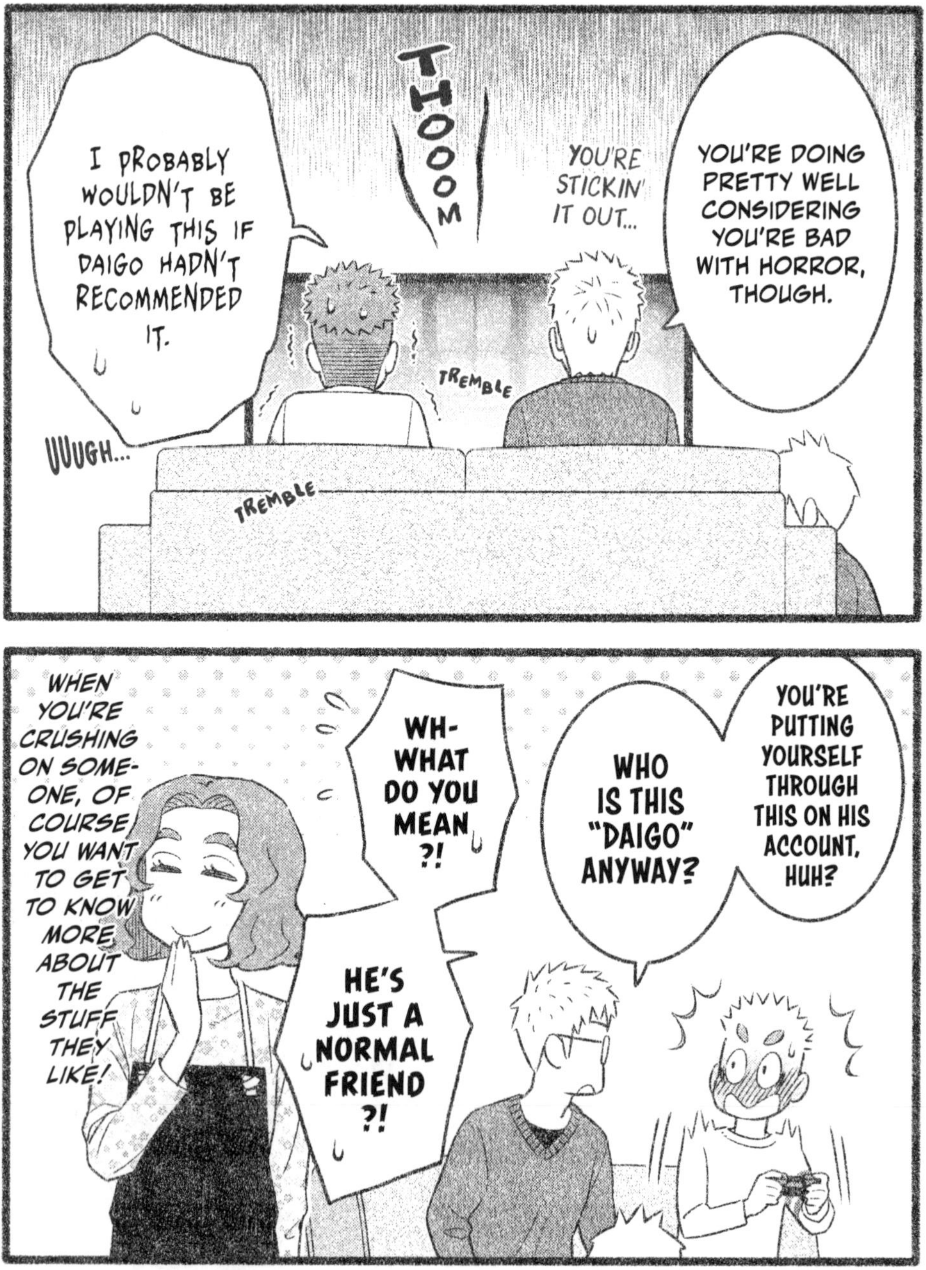
YOU'RE DOING PRETTY WELL CONSIDERING YOU'RE BAD WITH HORROR, THOUGH.
YOU'RE STICKIN' IT OUT...
THOOOM
I PROBABLY WOULDN'T BE PLAYING THIS IF DAIGO HADN'T RECOMMENDED IT.
TREMBLE
UUUGH...
TREMBLE
YOU'RE PUTTING YOURSELF THROUGH THIS ON HIS ACCOUNT, HUH?
WHO IS THIS "DAIGO" ANYWAY?
WH-WHAT DO YOU MEAN?!
HE'S JUST A NORMAL FRIEND?!
WHEN YOU'RE CRUSHING ON SOME-ONE, OF COURSE YOU WANT TO GET TO KNOW MORE ABOUT THE STUFF THEY LIKE!

# I Think Our Son Is Gay

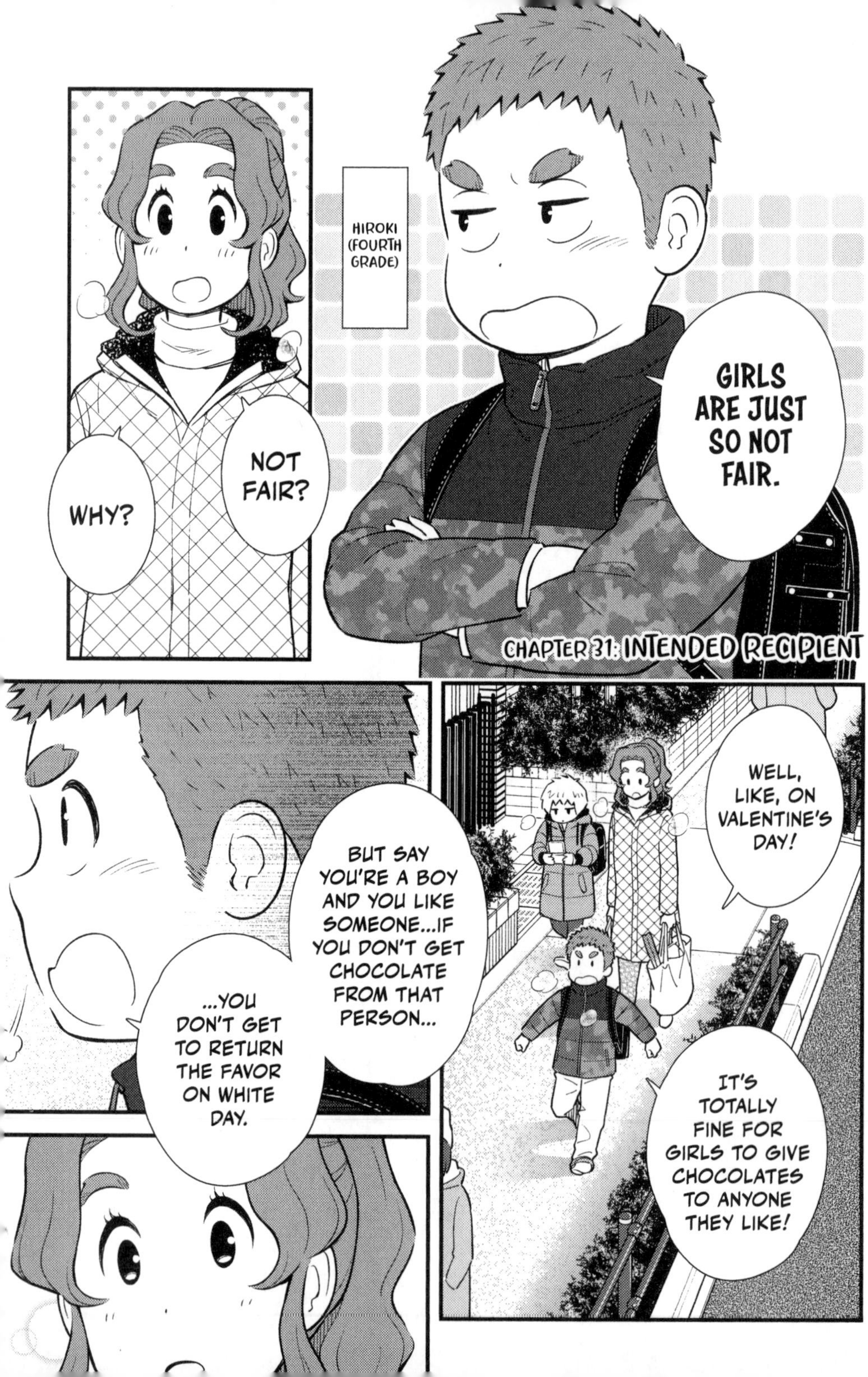
HIROKI (FOURTH GRADE)
GIRLS ARE JUST SO NOT FAIR.
CHAPTER 31: INTENDED RECIPIENT
NOT FAIR?
WHY?
WELL, LIKE, ON VALENTINE'S DAY!
IT'S TOTALLY FINE FOR GIRLS TO GIVE CHOCOLATES TO ANYONE THEY LIKE!
BUT SAY YOU'RE A BOY AND YOU LIKE SOMEONE...IF YOU DON'T GET CHOCOLATE FROM THAT PERSON...
...YOU DON'T GET TO RETURN THE FAVOR ON WHITE DAY.

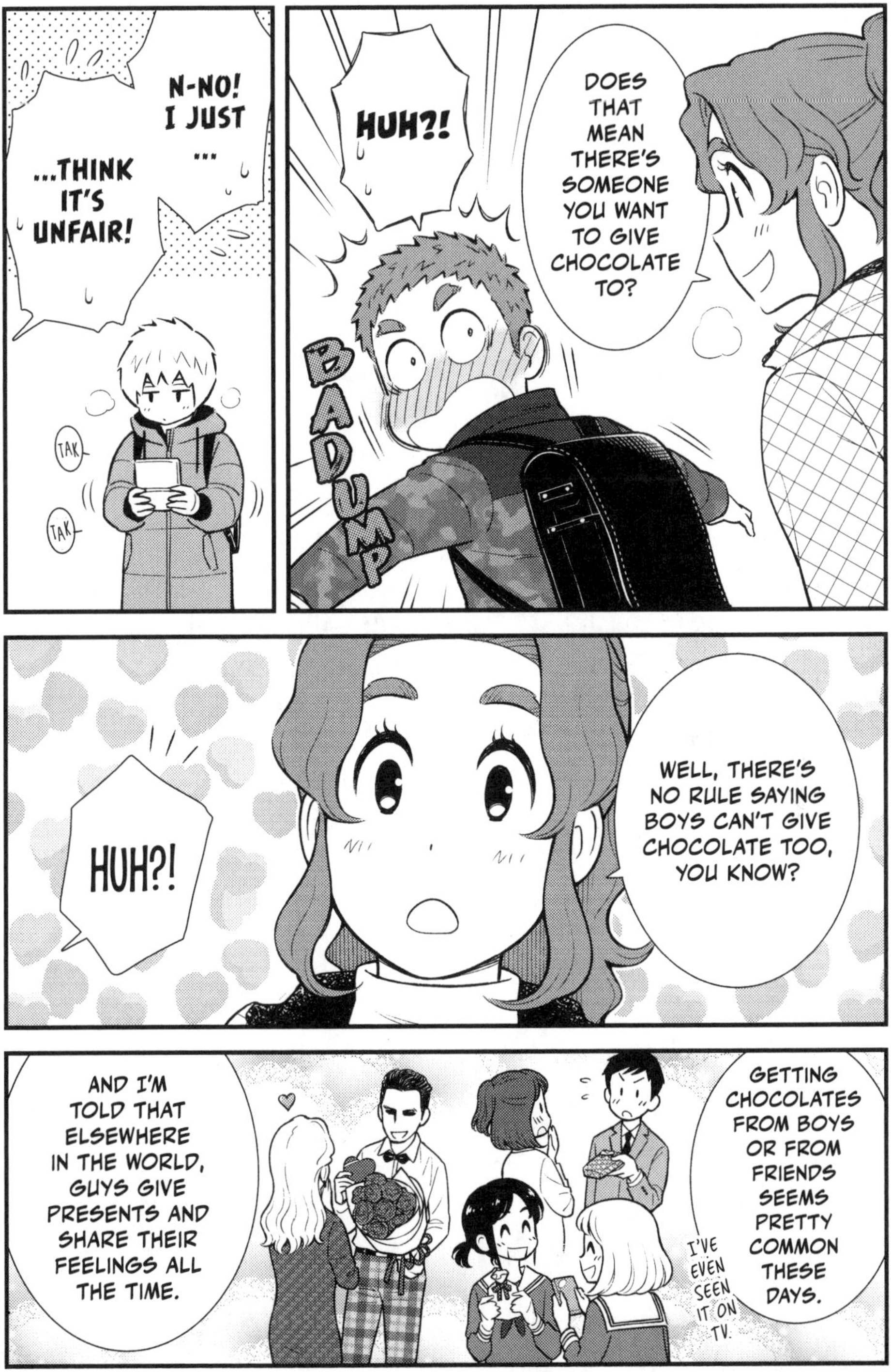
DOES THAT MEAN THERE'S SOMEONE YOU WANT TO GIVE CHOCOLATE TO?
HUH?!
BADUMP
N-NO! I JUST ...
...THINK IT'S UNFAIR!
TAK
TAK
WELL, THERE'S NO RULE SAYING BOYS CAN'T GIVE CHOCOLATE TOO, YOU KNOW?
HUH?!
GETTING CHOCOLATES FROM BOYS OR FROM FRIENDS SEEMS PRETTY COMMON THESE DAYS.
I'VE EVEN SEEN IT ON TV.
AND I'M TOLD THAT ELSEWHERE IN THE WORLD, GUYS GIVE PRESENTS AND SHARE THEIR FEELINGS ALL THE TIME.

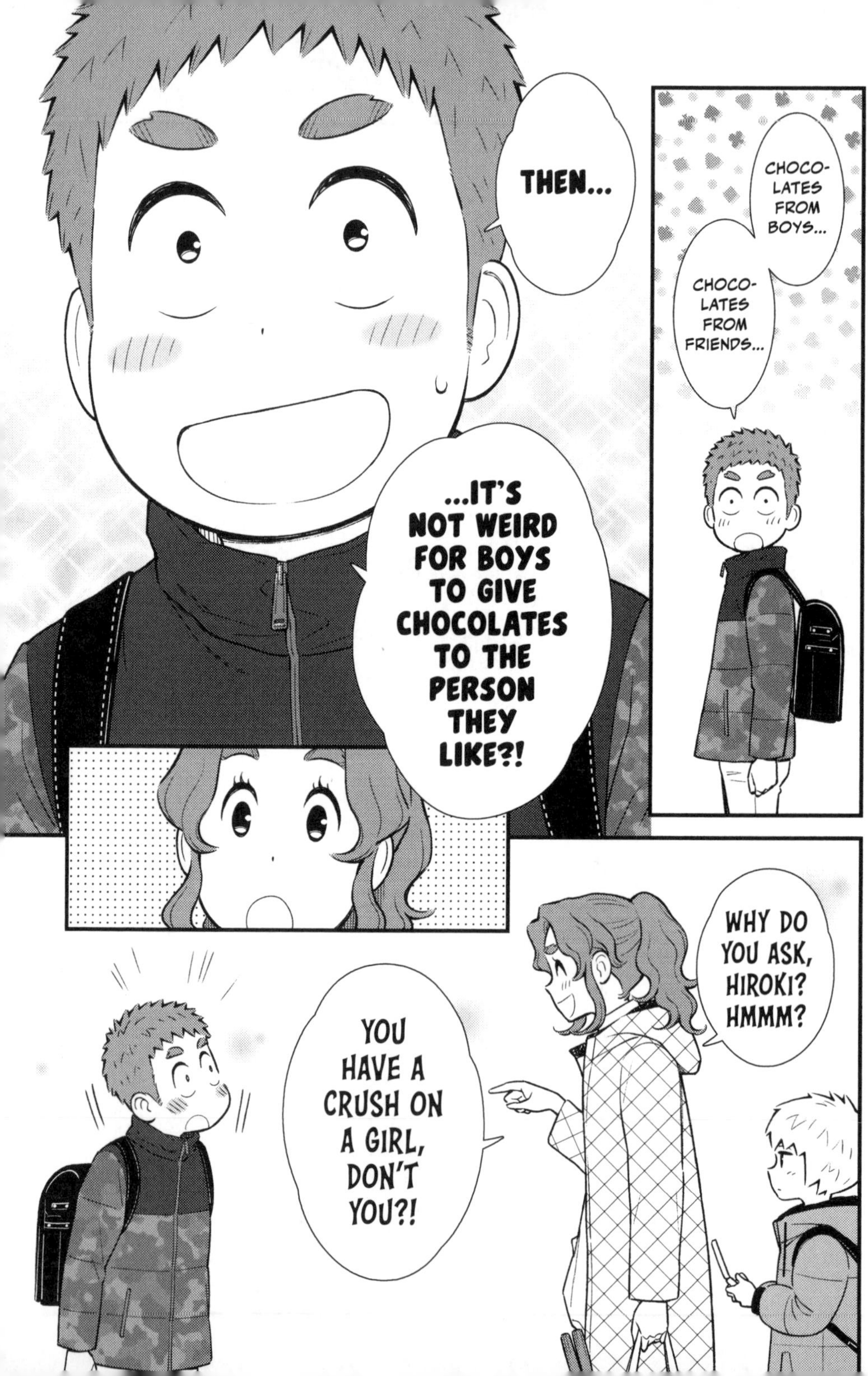

CHOCO-LATES FROM BOYS...
CHOCO-LATES FROM FRIENDS...
THEN...
...IT'S NOT WEIRD FOR BOYS TO GIVE CHOCOLATES TO THE PERSON THEY LIKE?!
WHY DO YOU ASK, HIROKI? HMMM?
YOU HAVE A CRUSH ON A GIRL, DON'T YOU?!

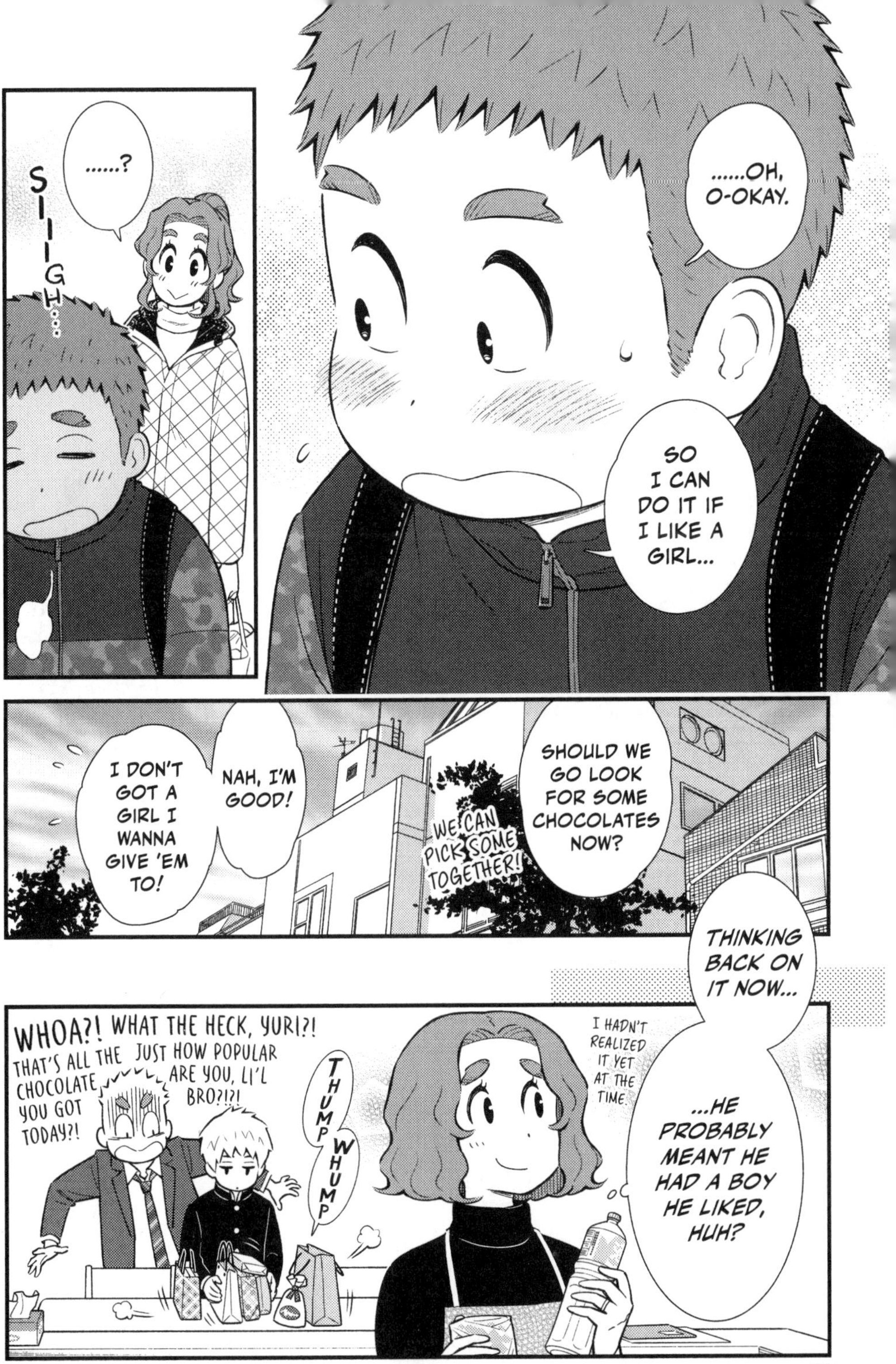
......OH, O-OKAY.
SO I CAN DO IT IF I LIKE A GIRL...
......?
SIIIGH...
SHOULD WE GO LOOK FOR SOME CHOCOLATES NOW?
WE CAN PICK SOME TOGETHER!
NAH, I'M GOOD!
I DON'T GOT A GIRL I WANNA GIVE 'EM TO!
THINKING BACK ON IT NOW...
...HE PROBABLY MEANT HE HAD A BOY HE LIKED, HUH?
I HADN'T REALIZED IT YET AT THE TIME.
THUMP
WHUMP
WHOA?! WHAT THE HECK, YURI?!
JUST HOW POPULAR ARE YOU, LI'L BRO?!?!
THAT'S ALL THE CHOCOLATE YOU GOT TODAY?!

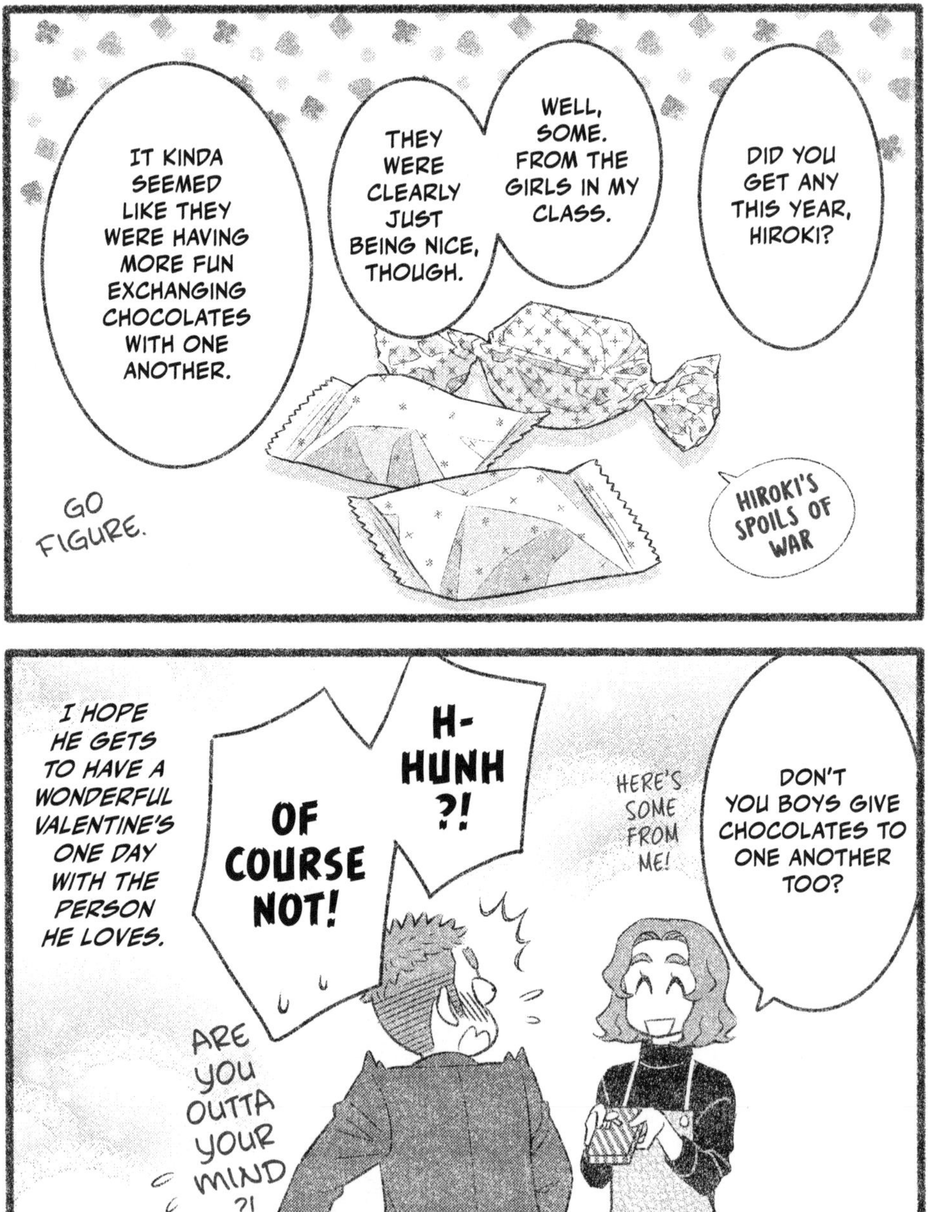
DID YOU GET ANY THIS YEAR, HIROKI?
WELL, SOME. FROM THE GIRLS IN MY CLASS.
THEY WERE CLEARLY JUST BEING NICE, THOUGH.
IT KINDA SEEMED LIKE THEY WERE HAVING MORE FUN EXCHANGING CHOCOLATES WITH ONE ANOTHER.
HIROKI'S SPOILS OF WAR
GO FIGURE.
DON'T YOU BOYS GIVE CHOCOLATES TO ONE ANOTHER TOO?
HERE'S SOME FROM ME!
H-HUNH?!
OF COURSE NOT!
ARE YOU OUTTA YOUR MIND?!
I HOPE HE GETS TO HAVE A WONDERFUL VALENTINE'S ONE DAY WITH THE PERSON HE LOVES.

I Think
Our Son
Is Gay

CHAPTER 32: ASUMI

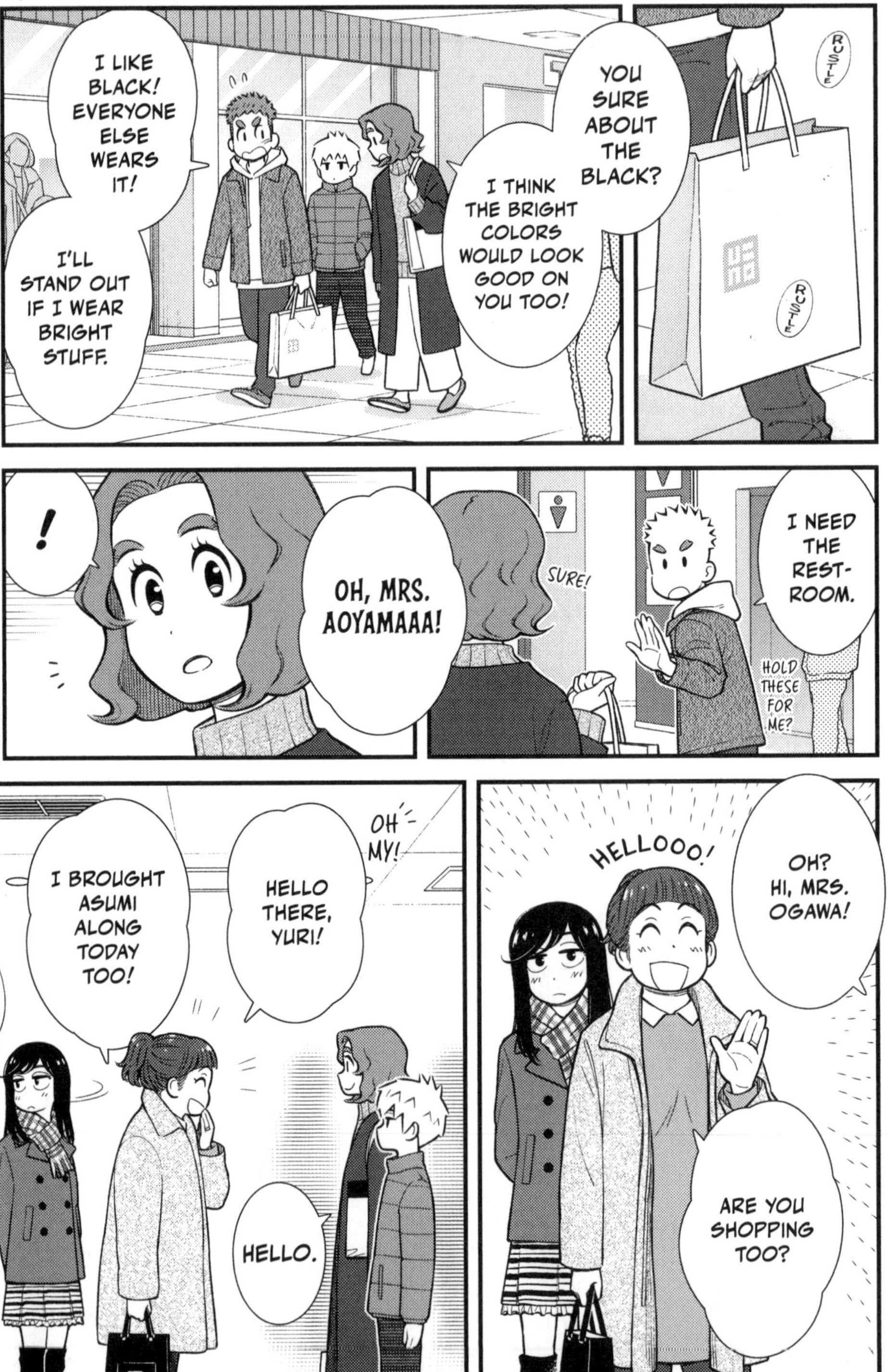
RUSTLE
RUSTLE
YOU SURE ABOUT THE BLACK?
I THINK THE BRIGHT COLORS WOULD LOOK GOOD ON YOU TOO!
I LIKE BLACK! EVERYONE ELSE WEARS IT!
I'LL STAND OUT IF I WEAR BRIGHT STUFF.
I NEED THE REST-ROOM.
HOLD THESE FOR ME?
SURE!
OH, MRS. AOYAMAAAA!
!
HELLOOO!
OH? HI, MRS. OGAWA!
ARE YOU SHOPPING TOO?
OH MY!
HELLO THERE, YURI!
I BROUGHT ASUMI ALONG TODAY TOO!
HELLO.
GLANCE
GLANCE

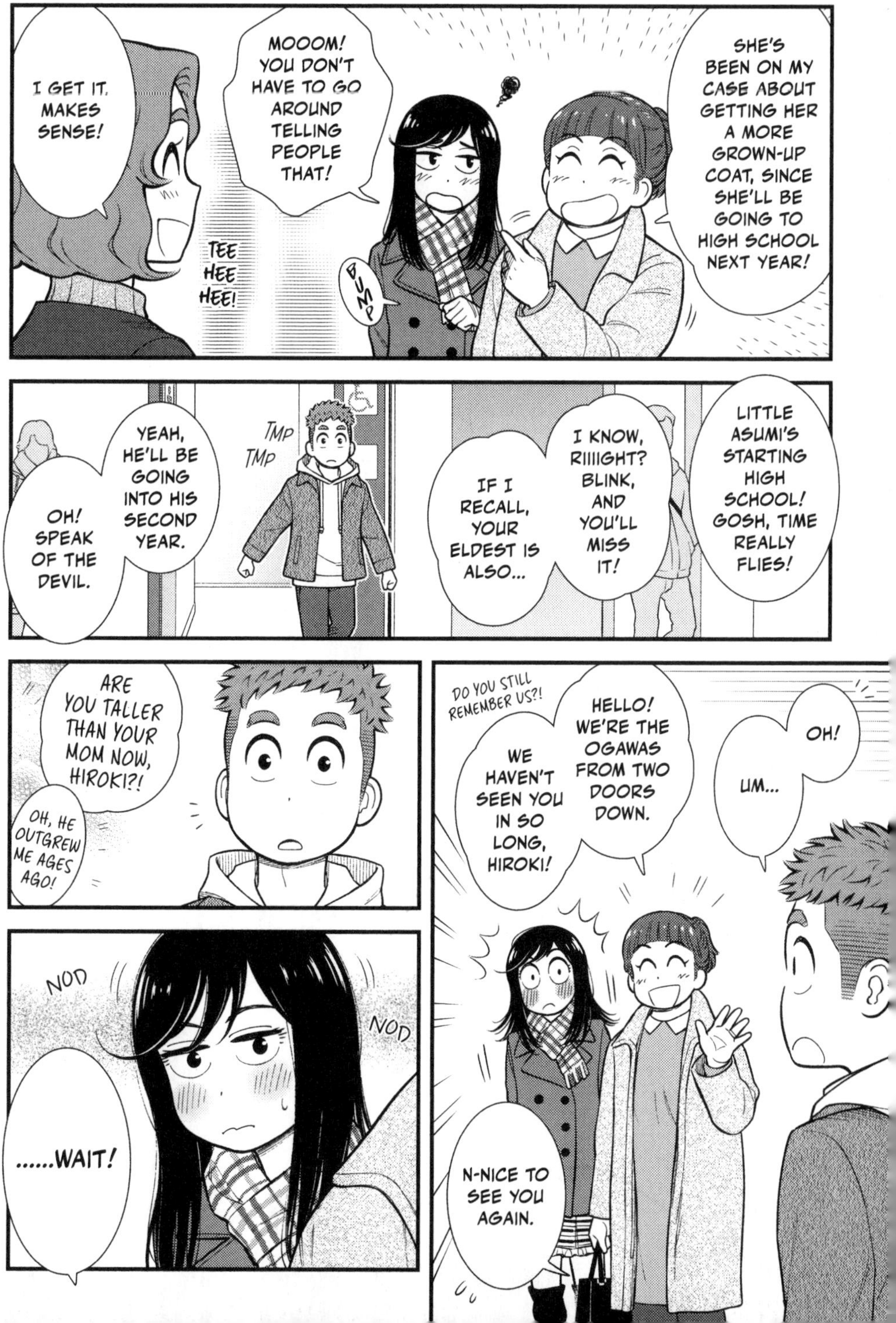

SHE'S BEEN ON MY CASE ABOUT GETTING HER A MORE GROWN-UP COAT, SINCE SHE'LL BE GOING TO HIGH SCHOOL NEXT YEAR!
MOOOM! YOU DON'T HAVE TO GO AROUND TELLING PEOPLE THAT!
BUMP
TEE HEE HEE!
I GET IT. MAKES SENSE!
LITTLE ASUMI'S STARTING HIGH SCHOOL! GOSH, TIME REALLY FLIES!
I KNOW, RIIIIGHT? BLINK, AND YOU'LL MISS IT!
IF I RECALL, YOUR ELDEST IS ALSO...
TMP TMP
YEAH, HE'LL BE GOING INTO HIS SECOND YEAR.
OH! SPEAK OF THE DEVIL.
OH!
UM...
HELLO! WE'RE THE OGAWAS FROM TWO DOORS DOWN.
DO YOU STILL REMEMBER US?!
WE HAVEN'T SEEN YOU IN SO LONG, HIROKI!
N-NICE TO SEE YOU AGAIN.
ARE YOU TALLER THAN YOUR MOM NOW, HIROKI?!
OH, HE OUTGREW ME AGES AGO!
NOD
NOD
......WAIT!

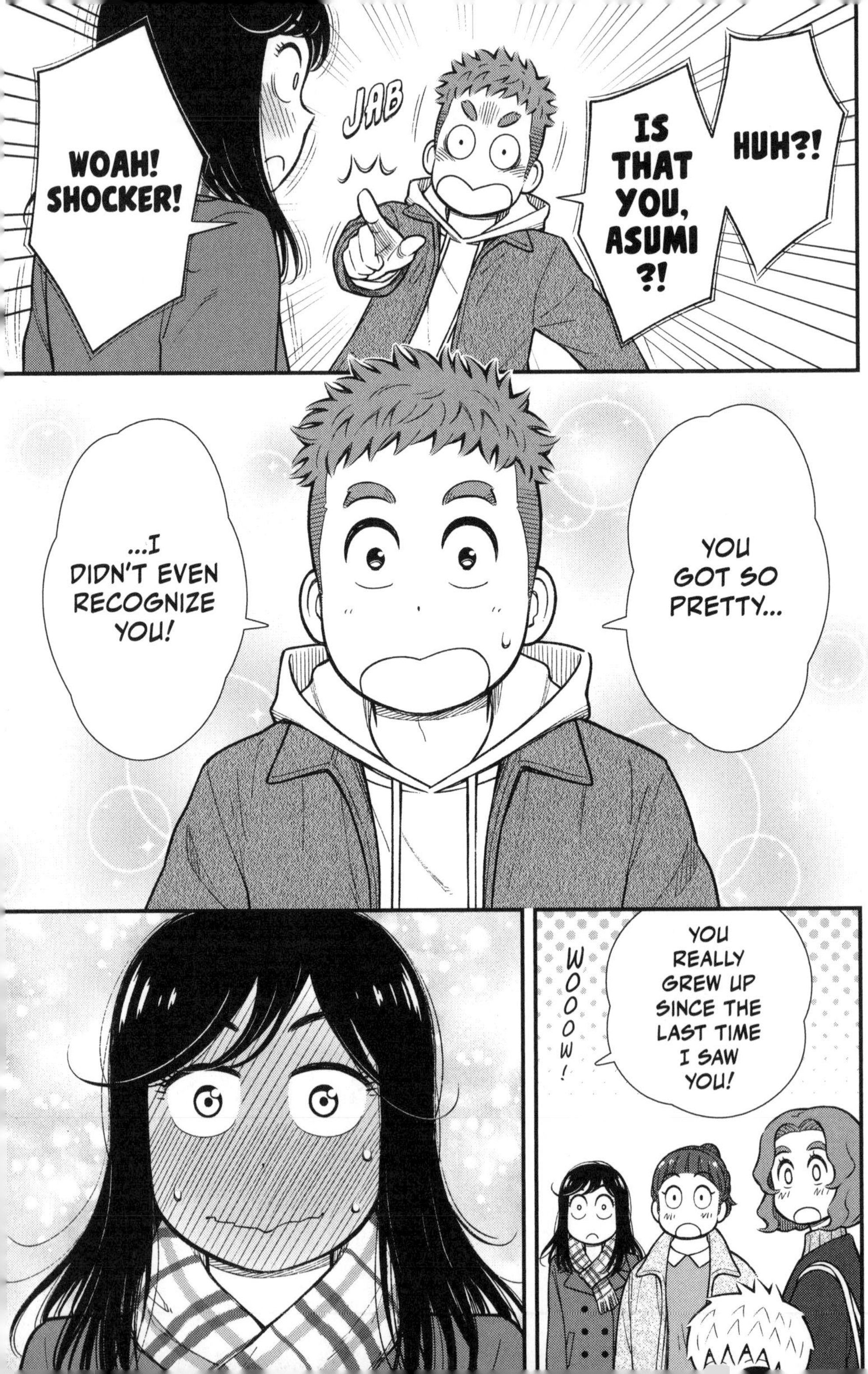
HUH?!
IS THAT YOU, ASUMI?!
JAB
WOAH! SHOCKER!
YOU GOT SO PRETTY...
...I DIDN'T EVEN RECOGNIZE YOU!
YOU REALLY GREW UP SINCE THE LAST TIME I SAW YOU!
WOOOOW!

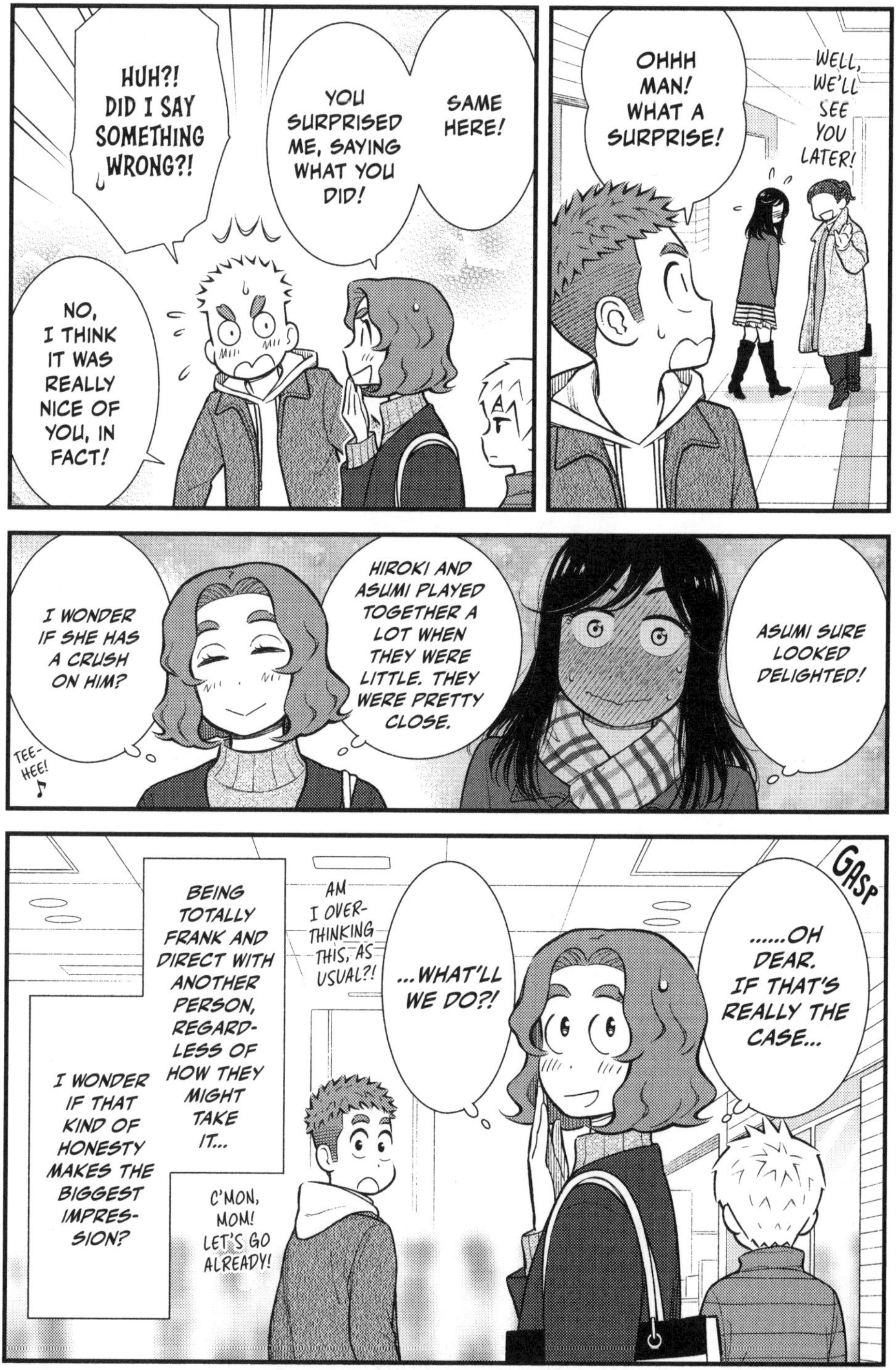
OHHH MAN! WHAT A SURPRISE!
WELL, WE'LL SEE YOU LATER!
SAME HERE!
YOU SURPRISED ME, SAYING WHAT YOU DID!
HUH?! DID I SAY SOMETHING WRONG?!
NO, I THINK IT WAS REALLY NICE OF YOU, IN FACT!
ASUMI SURE LOOKED DELIGHTED!
HIROKI AND ASUMI PLAYED TOGETHER A LOT WHEN THEY WERE LITTLE. THEY WERE PRETTY CLOSE.
I WONDER IF SHE HAS A CRUSH ON HIM?
TEE-HEE! ♪
GASP
......OH DEAR. IF THAT'S REALLY THE CASE...
...WHAT'LL WE DO?!
AM I OVER-THINKING THIS, AS USUAL?!
BEING TOTALLY FRANK AND DIRECT WITH ANOTHER PERSON, REGARD-LESS OF HOW THEY MIGHT TAKE IT...
I WONDER IF THAT KIND OF HONESTY MAKES THE BIGGEST IMPRES-SION?
C'MON, MOM! LET'S GO ALREADY!

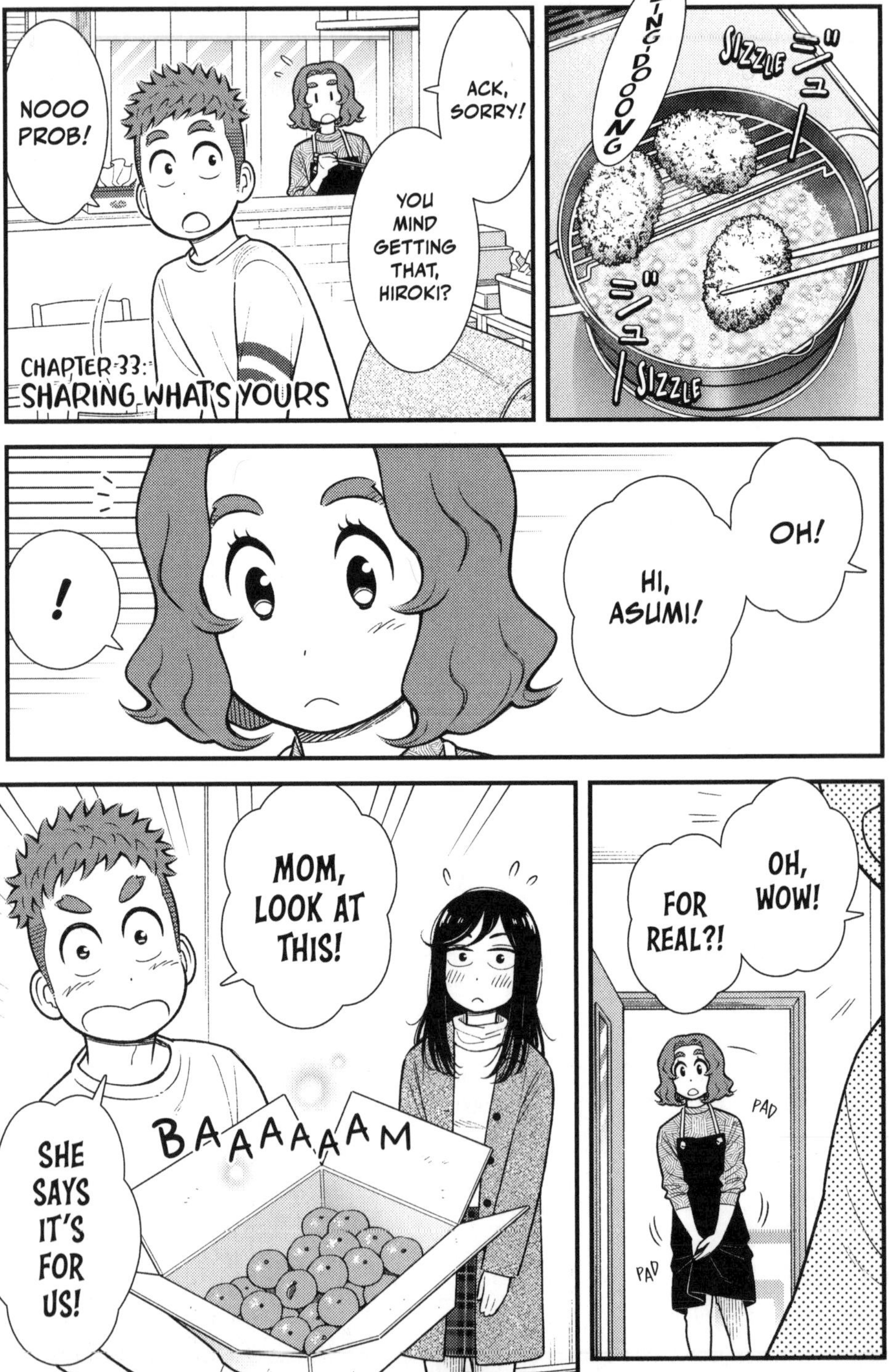
DING-DOOONG
SIZZLE
ジュ
ジュ
SIZZLE
ACK, SORRY!
YOU MIND GETTING THAT, HIROKI?
NOOO PROB!
CHAPTER 33:
SHARING WHAT'S YOURS
OH!
HI, ASUMI!
!
OH, WOW!
FOR REAL?!
PAD
PAD
MOM, LOOK AT THIS!
BAAAAAAM
SHE SAYS IT'S FOR US!

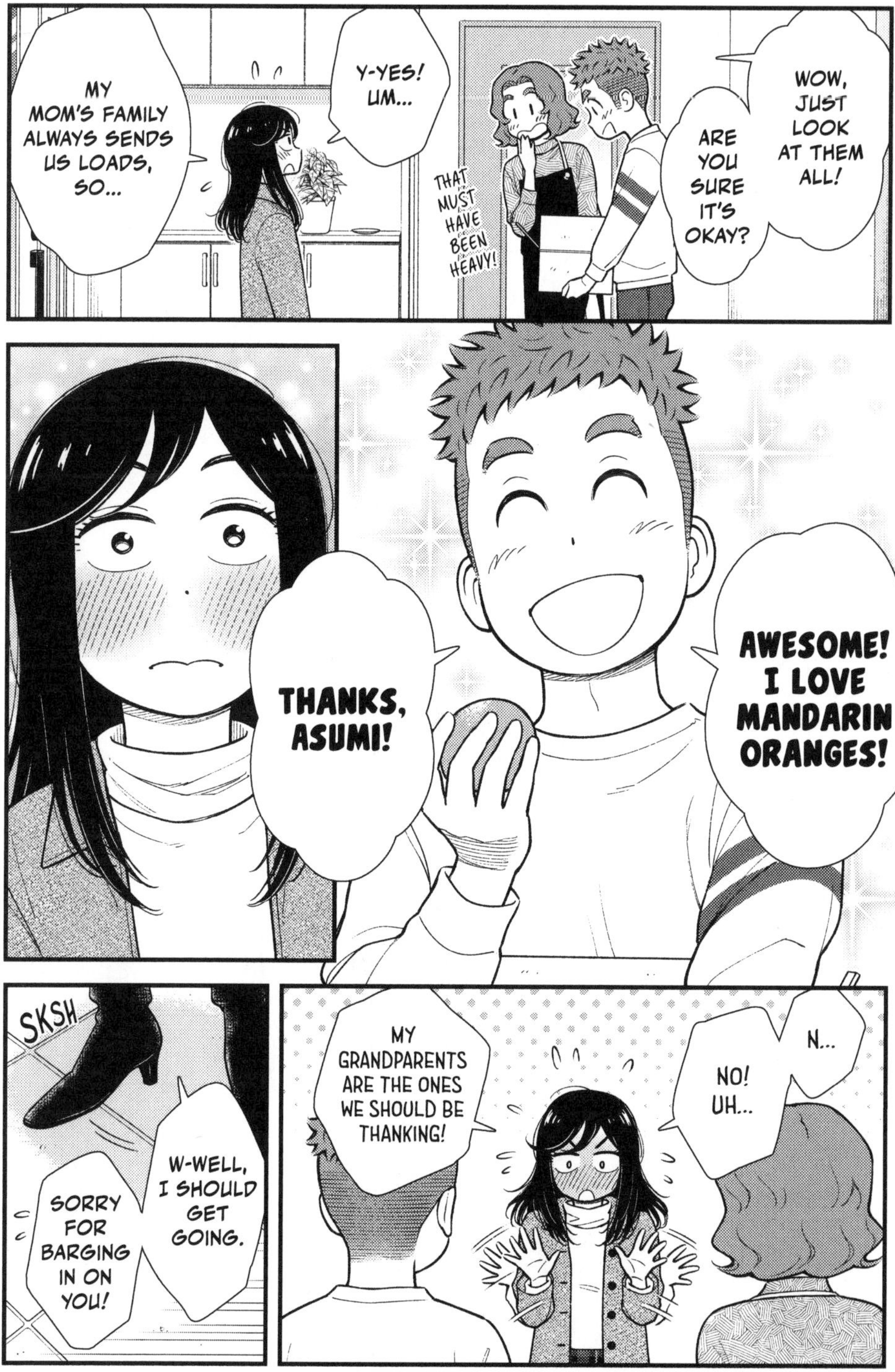
WOW, JUST LOOK AT THEM ALL!
ARE YOU SURE IT'S OKAY?
THAT MUST HAVE BEEN HEAVY!
Y-YES! UM...
MY MOM'S FAMILY ALWAYS SENDS US LOADS, SO...
AWESOME! I LOVE MANDARIN ORANGES!
THANKS, ASUMI!
N...
NO! UH...
MY GRANDPARENTS ARE THE ONES WE SHOULD BE THANKING!
SKSH
W-WELL, I SHOULD GET GOING.
SORRY FOR BARGING IN ON YOU!

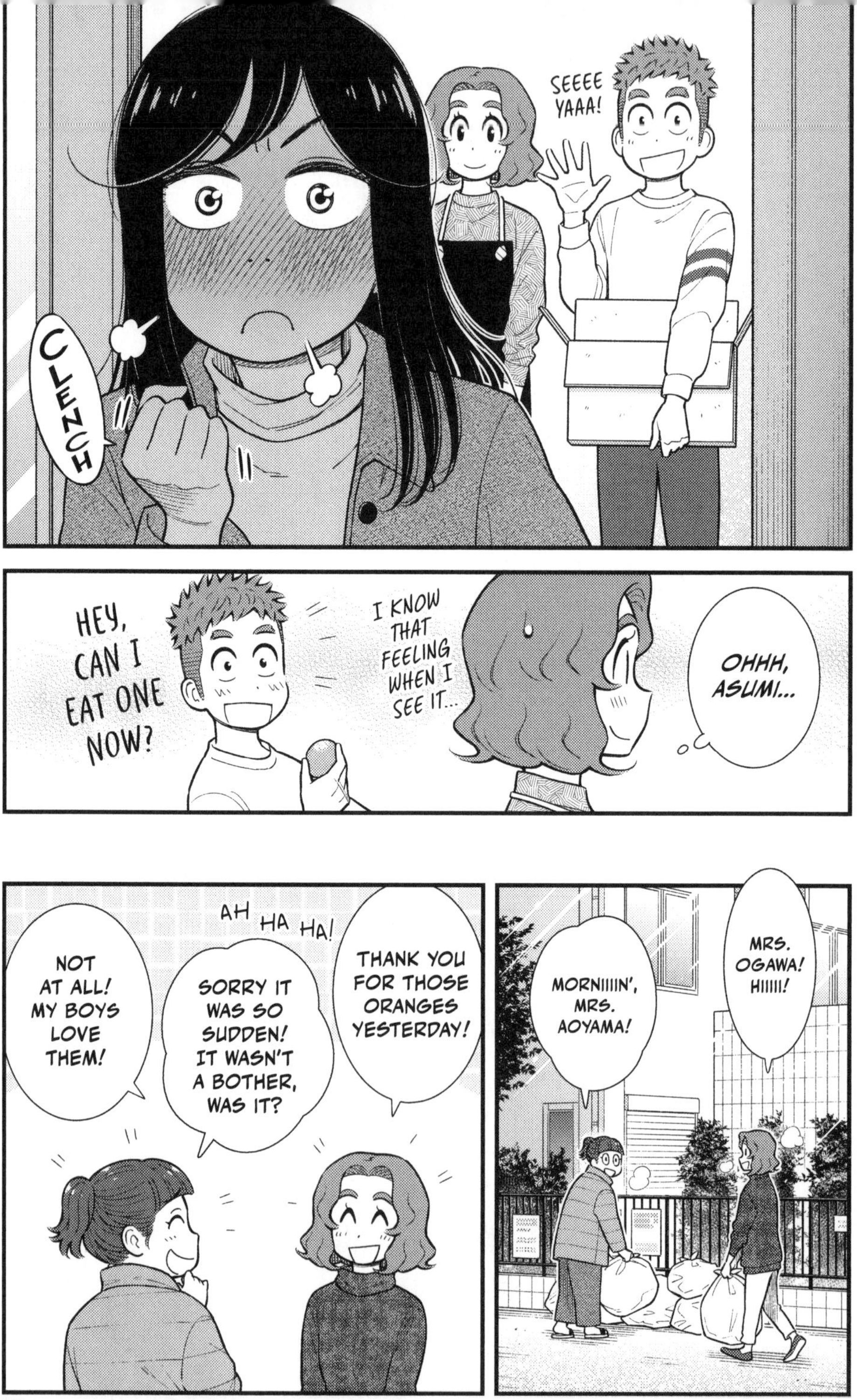
SEEEE YAAA!
CLENCH
OHHH, ASUMI...
I KNOW THAT FEELING WHEN I SEE IT...
HEY, CAN I EAT ONE NOW?
MRS. OGAWA! HIIIII!
MORNIIIIN', MRS. AOYAMA!
THANK YOU FOR THOSE ORANGES YESTERDAY!
AH HA HA!
SORRY IT WAS SO SUDDEN! IT WASN'T A BOTHER, WAS IT?
NOT AT ALL! MY BOYS LOVE THEM!

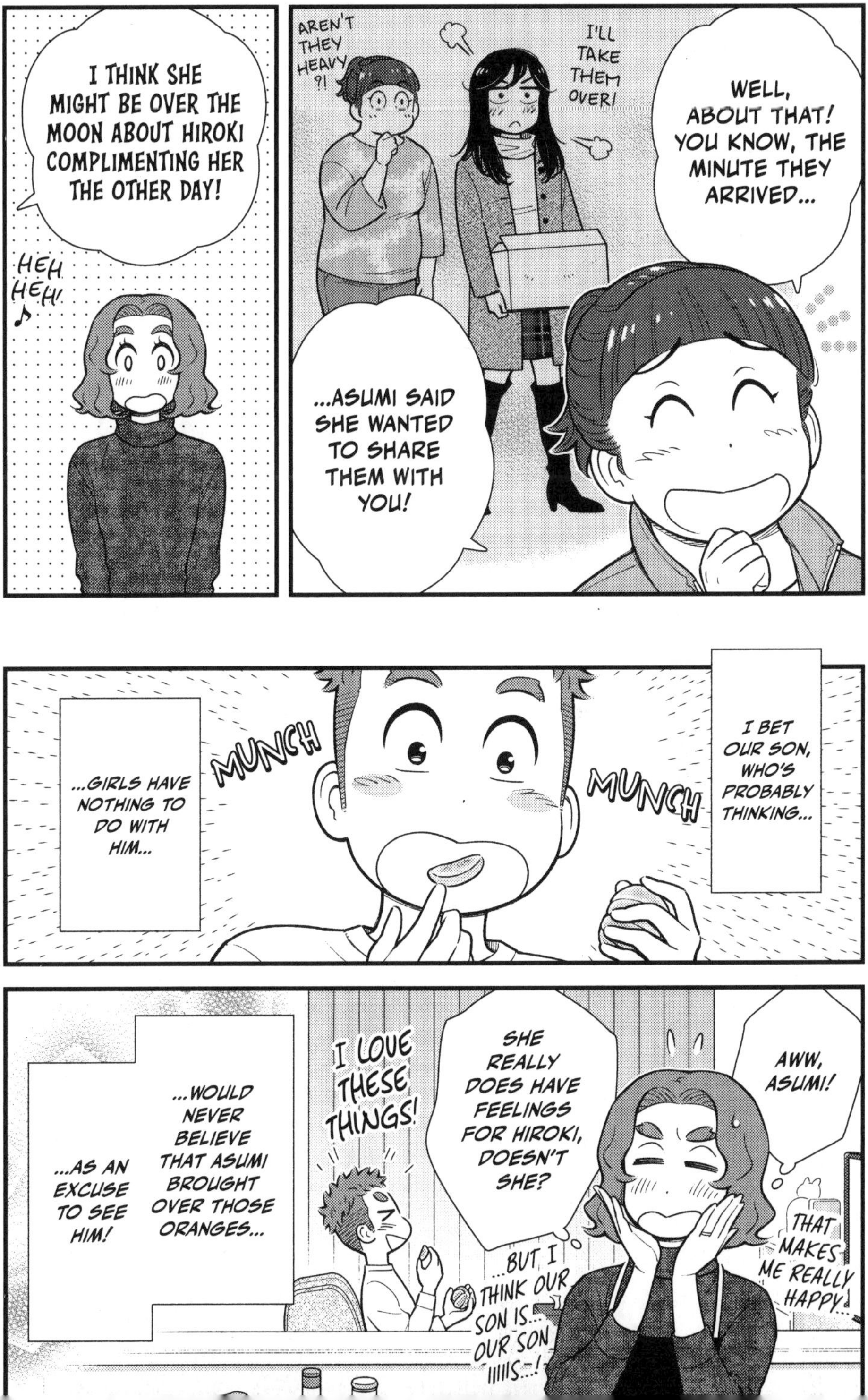
WELL, ABOUT THAT! YOU KNOW, THE MINUTE THEY ARRIVED...
I'LL TAKE THEM OVER!
AREN'T THEY HEAVY?!
...ASUMI SAID SHE WANTED TO SHARE THEM WITH YOU!
I THINK SHE MIGHT BE OVER THE MOON ABOUT HIROKI COMPLIMENTING HER THE OTHER DAY!
HEH HEH♪
I BET OUR SON, WHO'S PROBABLY THINKING...
MUNCH
MUNCH
...GIRLS HAVE NOTHING TO DO WITH HIM...
AWW, ASUMI!
THAT MAKES ME REALLY HAPPY
SHE REALLY DOES HAVE FEELINGS FOR HIROKI, DOESN'T SHE?
...BUT I THINK OUR SON IS... OUR SON IIIIIS...!
I LOVE THESE THINGS!
...WOULD NEVER BELIEVE THAT ASUMI BROUGHT OVER THOSE ORANGES...
...AS AN EXCUSE TO SEE HIM!

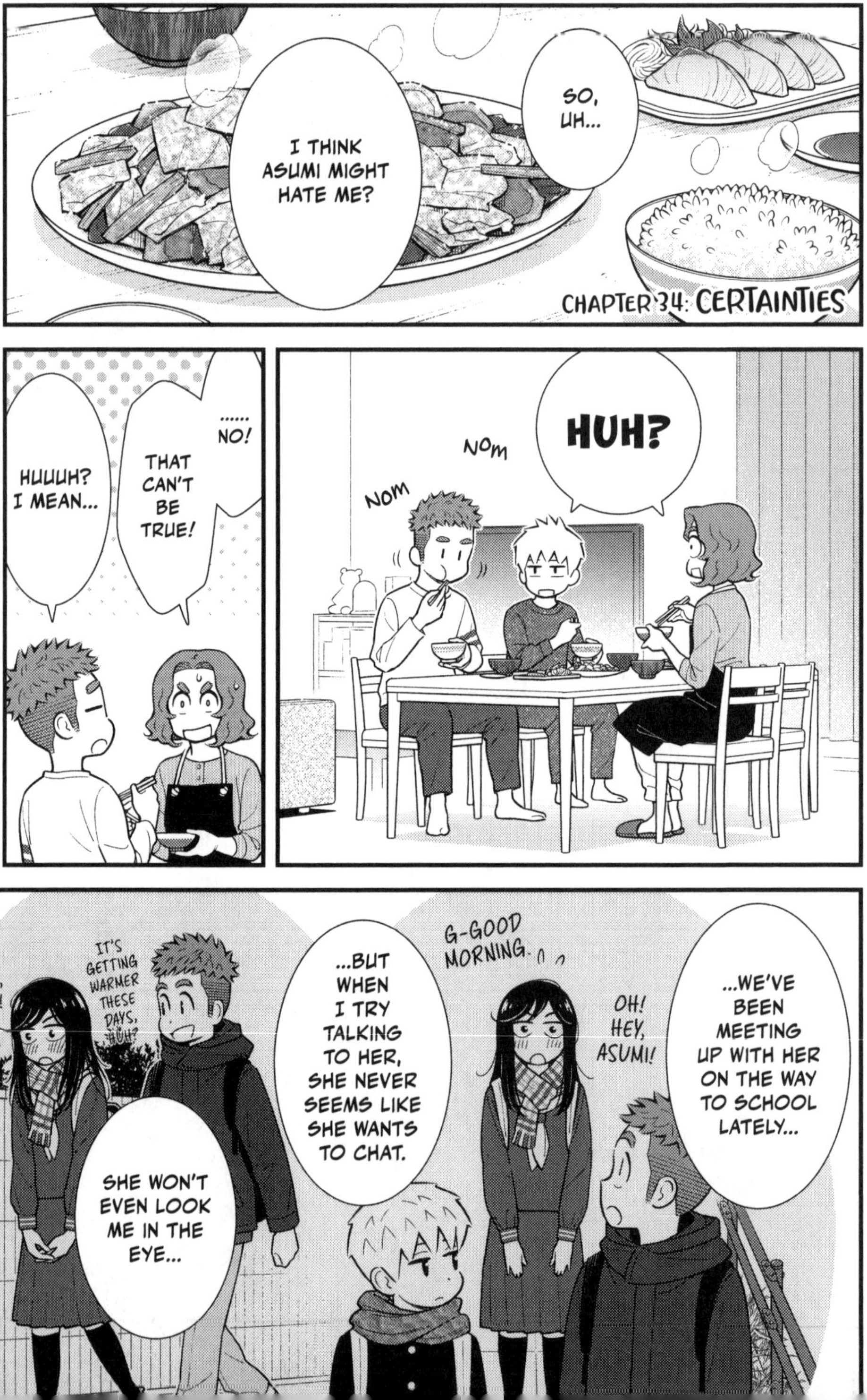
SO, UH...
I THINK ASUMI MIGHT HATE ME?
CHAPTER 34: CERTAINTIES
HUH?
NOM
NOM
......NO!
THAT CAN'T BE TRUE!
HUUUH? I MEAN...
...WE'VE BEEN MEETING UP WITH HER ON THE WAY TO SCHOOL LATELY...
OH! HEY, ASUMI!
G-GOOD MORNING.
...BUT WHEN I TRY TALKING TO HER, SHE NEVER SEEMS LIKE SHE WANTS TO CHAT.
IT'S GETTING WARMER THESE DAYS, HUH?
Y-YES, IT IS!
SHE WON'T EVEN LOOK ME IN THE EYE...

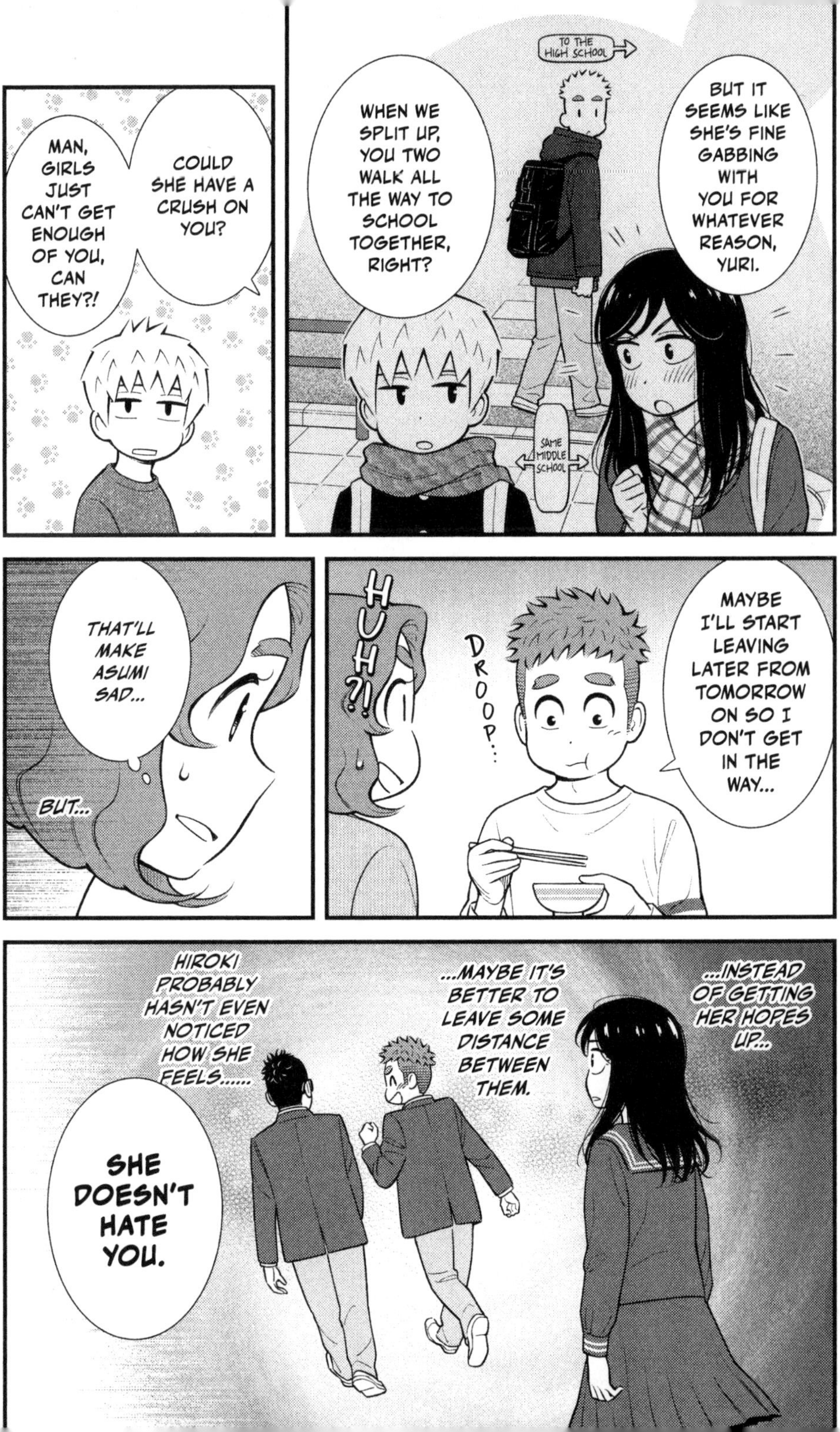
TO THE HIGH SCHOOL
BUT IT SEEMS LIKE SHE'S FINE GABBING WITH YOU FOR WHATEVER REASON, YURI.
WHEN WE SPLIT UP, YOU TWO WALK ALL THE WAY TO SCHOOL TOGETHER, RIGHT?
SAME MIDDLE SCHOOL
COULD SHE HAVE A CRUSH ON YOU?
MAN, GIRLS JUST CAN'T GET ENOUGH OF YOU, CAN THEY?!
MAYBE I'LL START LEAVING LATER FROM TOMORROW ON SO I DON'T GET IN THE WAY...
DROOP...
HUH?!
THAT'LL MAKE ASUMI SAD...
BUT...
...INSTEAD OF GETTING HER HOPES UP...
...MAYBE IT'S BETTER TO LEAVE SOME DISTANCE BETWEEN THEM.
HIROKI PROBABLY HASN'T EVEN NOTICED HOW SHE FEELS......
SHE DOESN'T HATE YOU.

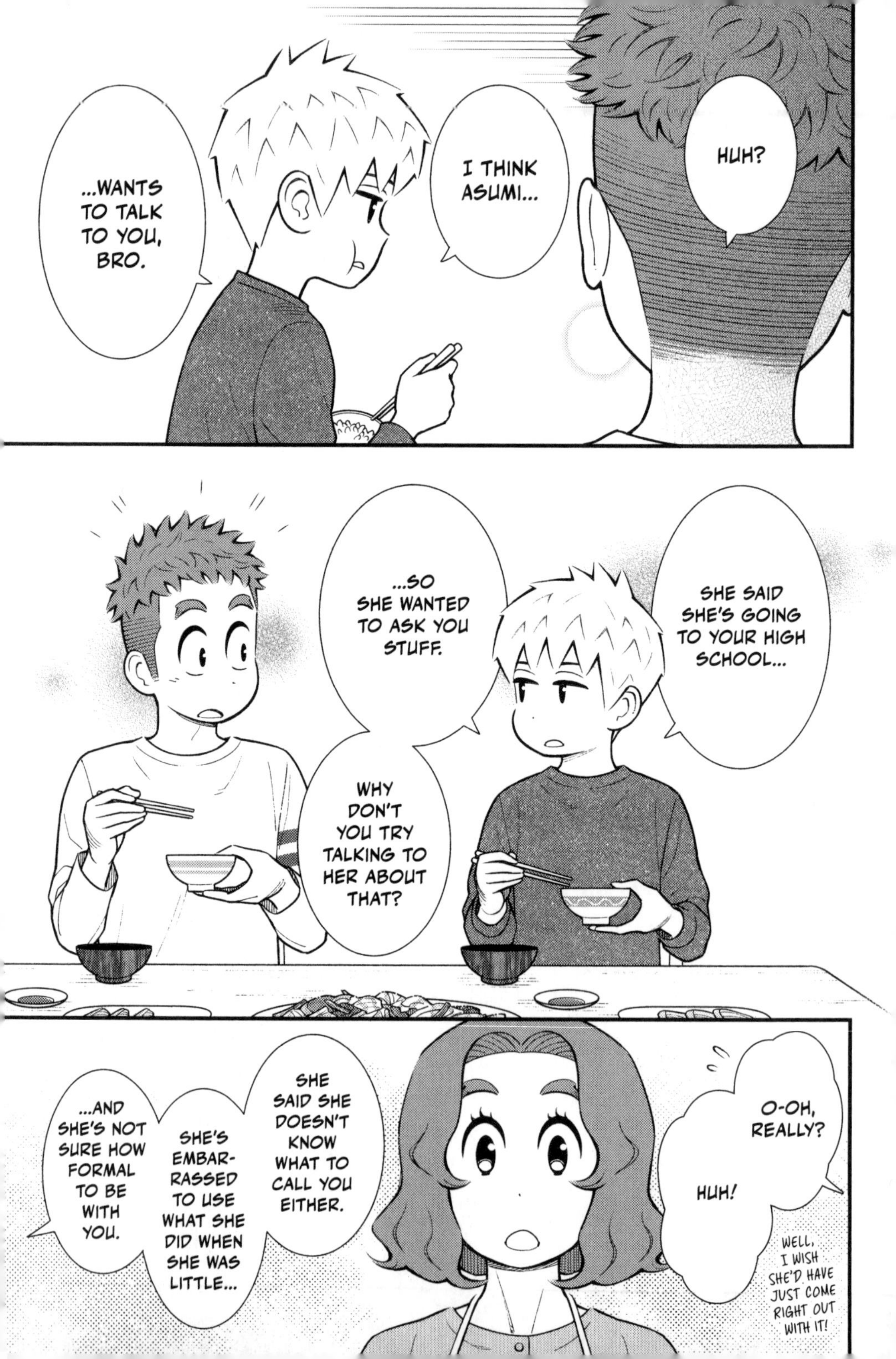
HUH?
I THINK ASUMI...
...WANTS TO TALK TO YOU, BRO.
SHE SAID SHE'S GOING TO YOUR HIGH SCHOOL...
...SO SHE WANTED TO ASK YOU STUFF.
WHY DON'T YOU TRY TALKING TO HER ABOUT THAT?
O-OH, REALLY?
HUH!
WELL, I WISH SHE'D HAVE JUST COME RIGHT OUT WITH IT!
SHE SAID SHE DOESN'T KNOW WHAT TO CALL YOU EITHER.
SHE'S EMBAR-RASSED TO USE WHAT SHE DID WHEN SHE WAS LITTLE...
...AND SHE'S NOT SURE HOW FORMAL TO BE WITH YOU.

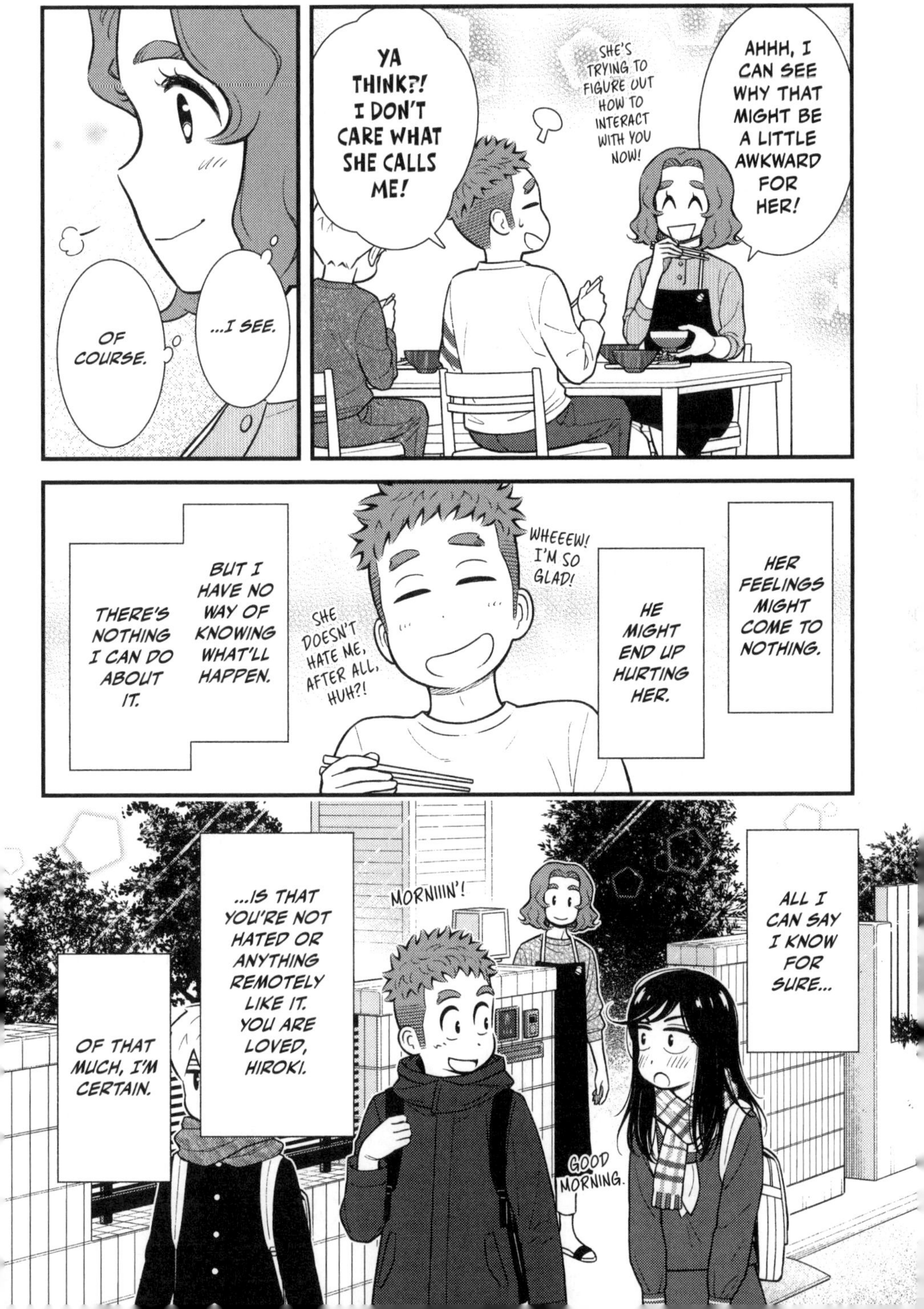
AHHH, I CAN SEE WHY THAT MIGHT BE A LITTLE AWKWARD FOR HER!
SHE'S TRYING TO FIGURE OUT HOW TO INTERACT WITH YOU NOW!
YA THINK?! I DON'T CARE WHAT SHE CALLS ME!
...I SEE.
OF COURSE.
HER FEELINGS MIGHT COME TO NOTHING.
HE MIGHT END UP HURTING HER.
WHEEEW! I'M SO GLAD!
SHE DOESN'T HATE ME, AFTER ALL, HUH?!
BUT I HAVE NO WAY OF KNOWING WHAT'LL HAPPEN.
THERE'S NOTHING I CAN DO ABOUT IT.
ALL I CAN SAY I KNOW FOR SURE...
GOOD MORNING.
MORNIIIN'!
...IS THAT YOU'RE NOT HATED OR ANYTHING REMOTELY LIKE IT. YOU ARE LOVED, HIROKI.
OF THAT MUCH, I'M CERTAIN.

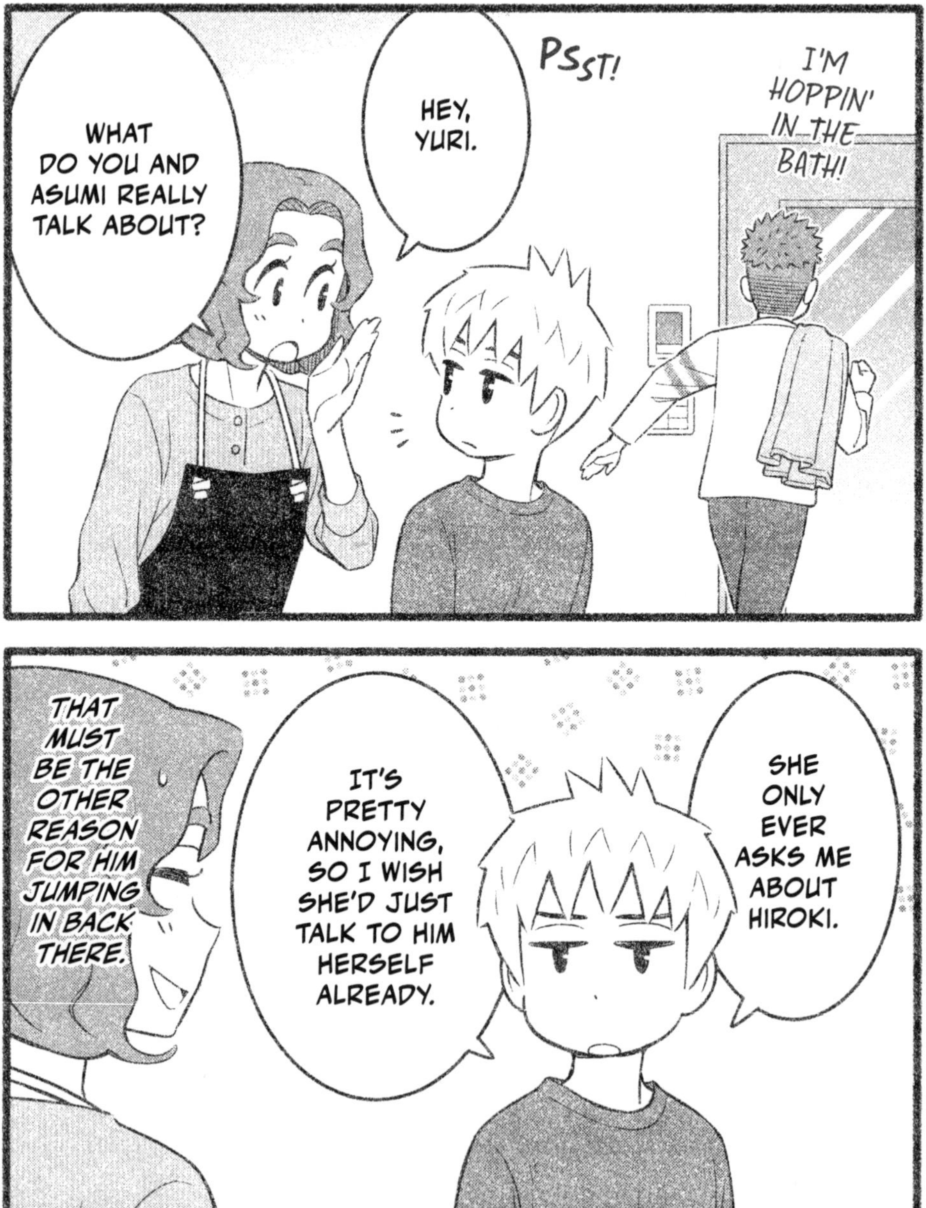
I'M HOPPIN' IN THE BATH!
PSST!
HEY, YURI.
WHAT DO YOU AND ASUMI REALLY TALK ABOUT?
SHE ONLY EVER ASKS ME ABOUT HIROKI.
IT'S PRETTY ANNOYING, SO I WISH SHE'D JUST TALK TO HIM HERSELF ALREADY.
THAT MUST BE THE OTHER REASON FOR HIM JUMPING IN BACK THERE.

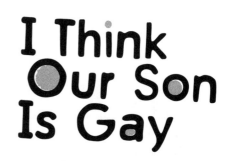

I Think
Our Son
Is Gay

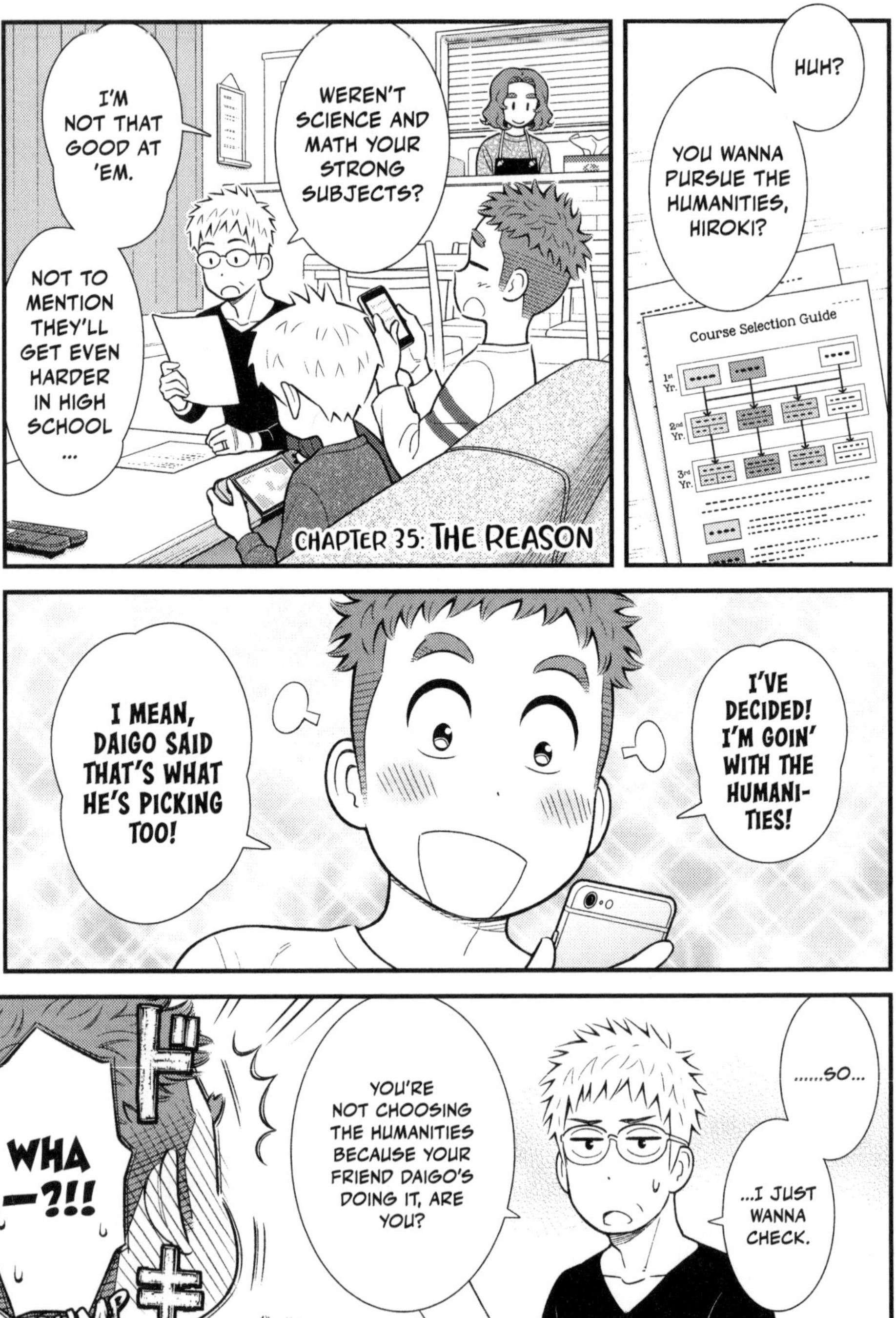
HUH?
YOU WANNA PURSUE THE HUMANITIES, HIROKI?
Course Selection Guide
1st Yr.
2nd Yr.
3rd Yr.
WEREN'T SCIENCE AND MATH YOUR STRONG SUBJECTS?
I'M NOT THAT GOOD AT 'EM.
NOT TO MENTION THEY'LL GET EVEN HARDER IN HIGH SCHOOL ...
CHAPTER 35: THE REASON
I'VE DECIDED! I'M GOIN' WITH THE HUMANI-TIES!
I MEAN, DAIGO SAID THAT'S WHAT HE'S PICKING TOO!
......SO...
...I JUST WANNA CHECK.
YOU'RE NOT CHOOSING THE HUMANITIES BECAUSE YOUR FRIEND DAIGO'S DOING IT, ARE YOU?
ドキ
BADUMP
WHA—?!!

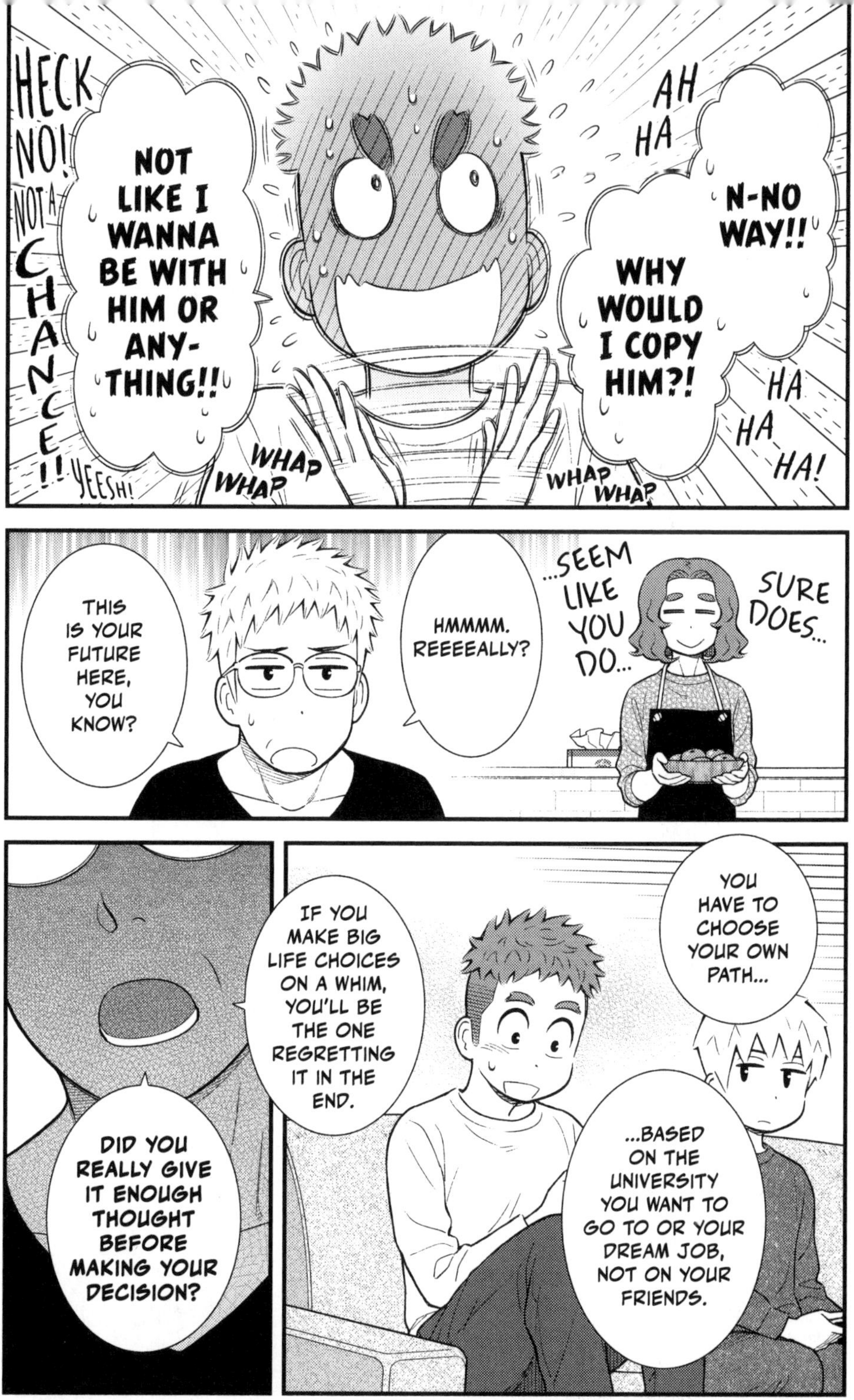
AH HA
N-NO WAY!!
WHY WOULD I COPY HIM?!
HA HA HA!
WHAP WHAP
HECK NO! NOT A CHANCE!!
NOT LIKE I WANNA BE WITH HIM OR ANY-THING!!
YEESH!
WHAP WHAP
SURE DOES...
...SEEM LIKE YOU DO...
HMMMM. REEEEALLY?
THIS IS YOUR FUTURE HERE, YOU KNOW?
YOU HAVE TO CHOOSE YOUR OWN PATH...
...BASED ON THE UNIVERSITY YOU WANT TO GO TO OR YOUR DREAM JOB, NOT ON YOUR FRIENDS.
IF YOU MAKE BIG LIFE CHOICES ON A WHIM, YOU'LL BE THE ONE REGRETTING IT IN THE END.
DID YOU REALLY GIVE IT ENOUGH THOUGHT BEFORE MAKING YOUR DECISION?

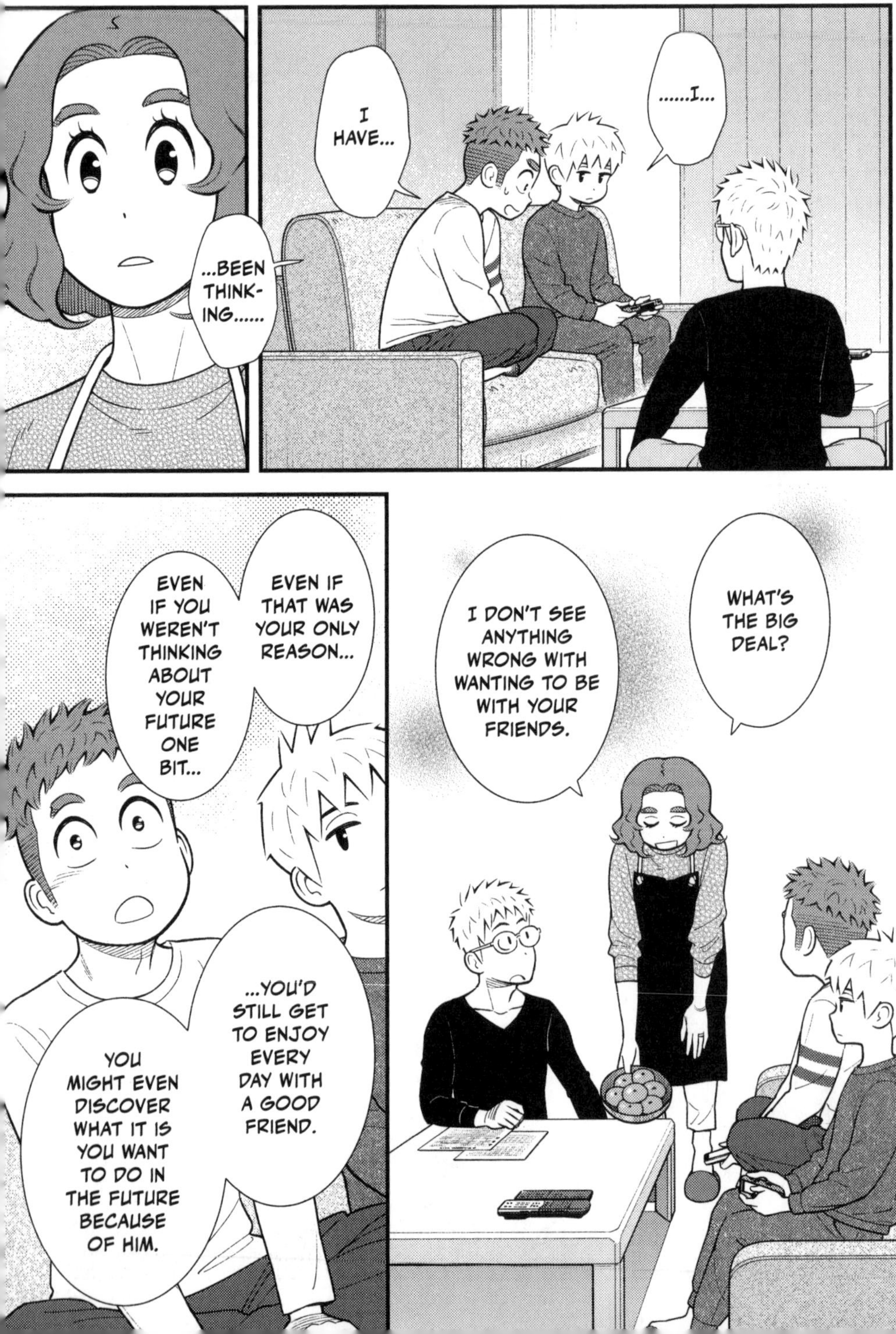
......I...
I HAVE...
...BEEN THINKING......
WHAT'S THE BIG DEAL?
I DON'T SEE ANYTHING WRONG WITH WANTING TO BE WITH YOUR FRIENDS.
EVEN IF THAT WAS YOUR ONLY REASON...
EVEN IF YOU WEREN'T THINKING ABOUT YOUR FUTURE ONE BIT...
...YOU'D STILL GET TO ENJOY EVERY DAY WITH A GOOD FRIEND.
YOU MIGHT EVEN DISCOVER WHAT IT IS YOU WANT TO DO IN THE FUTURE BECAUSE OF HIM.

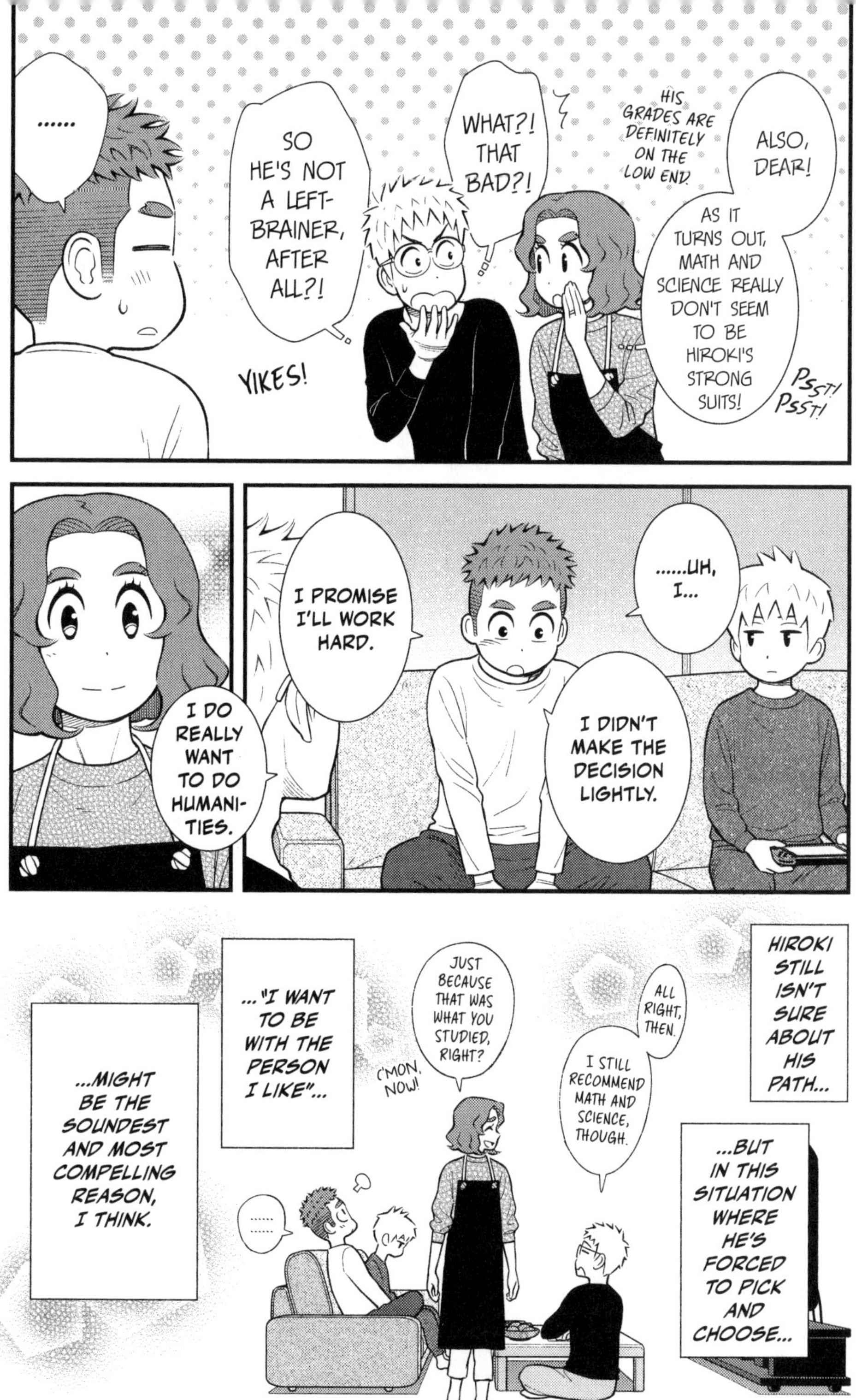
ALSO, DEAR!
HIS GRADES ARE DEFINITELY ON THE LOW END
AS IT TURNS OUT, MATH AND SCIENCE REALLY DON'T SEEM TO BE HIROKI'S STRONG SUITS!
PSST! PSST!
WHAT?! THAT BAD?!
SO HE'S NOT A LEFT-BRAINER, AFTER ALL?!
YIKES!
......
......UH, I...
I DIDN'T MAKE THE DECISION LIGHTLY.
I PROMISE I'LL WORK HARD.
I DO REALLY WANT TO DO HUMANITIES.
HIROKI STILL ISN'T SURE ABOUT HIS PATH...
...BUT IN THIS SITUATION WHERE HE'S FORCED TO PICK AND CHOOSE...
ALL RIGHT, THEN.
I STILL RECOMMEND MATH AND SCIENCE, THOUGH.
JUST BECAUSE THAT WAS WHAT YOU STUDIED, RIGHT?
C'MON, NOW!
..."I WANT TO BE WITH THE PERSON I LIKE"...
...... ......
...MIGHT BE THE SOUNDEST AND MOST COMPELLING REASON, I THINK.

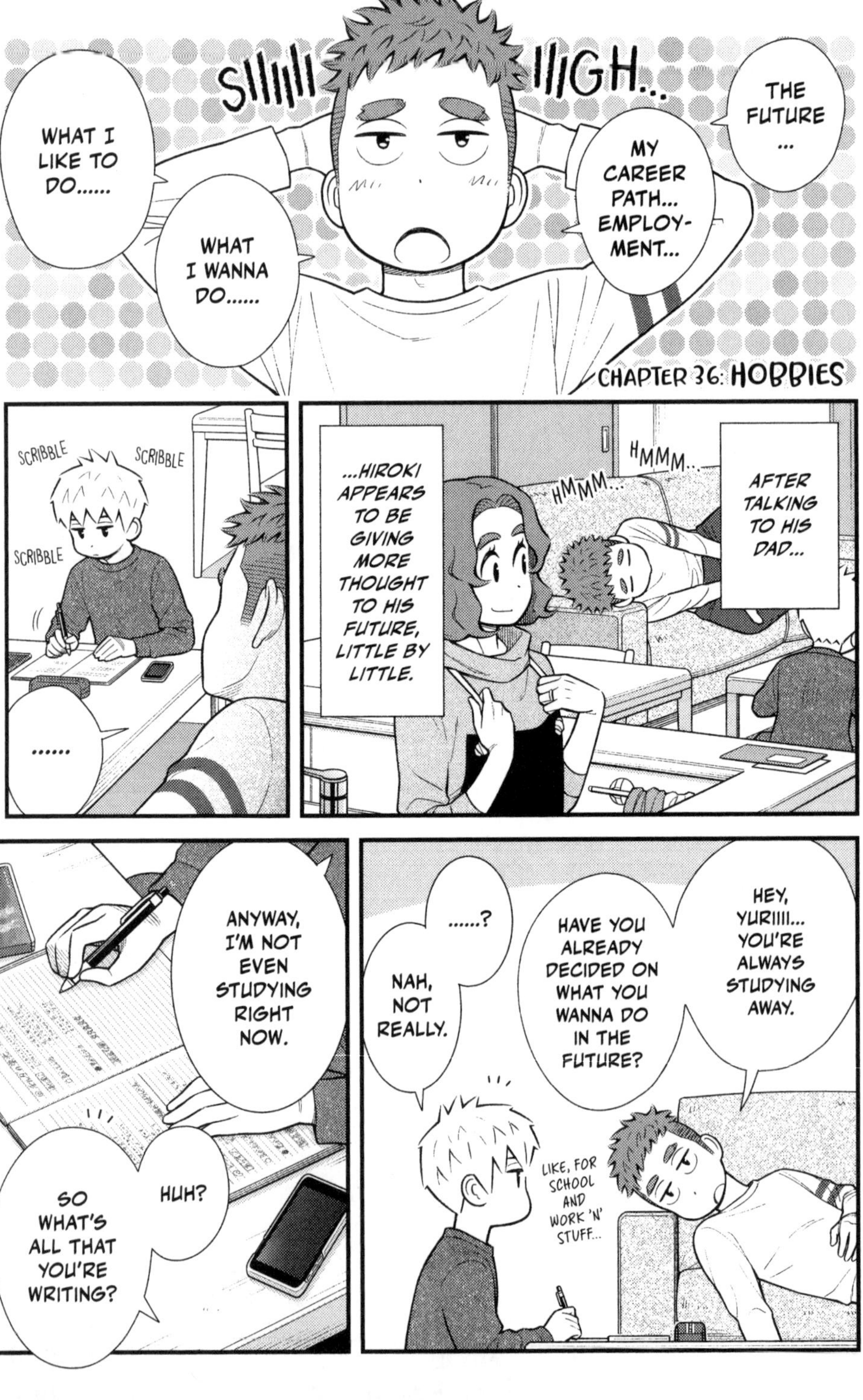
THE FUTURE ...
MY CAREER PATH... EMPLOYMENT...
SIIIIIIIIIGH...
WHAT I LIKE TO DO......
WHAT I WANNA DO......
CHAPTER 36: HOBBIES
AFTER TALKING TO HIS DAD...
HMMM...
HMMM...
...HIROKI APPEARS TO BE GIVING MORE THOUGHT TO HIS FUTURE, LITTLE BY LITTLE.
SCRIBBLE
SCRIBBLE
SCRIBBLE
......
HEY, YURIIII... YOU'RE ALWAYS STUDYING AWAY.
HAVE YOU ALREADY DECIDED ON WHAT YOU WANNA DO IN THE FUTURE?
......?
LIKE, FOR SCHOOL AND WORK 'N' STUFF...
NAH, NOT REALLY.
ANYWAY, I'M NOT EVEN STUDYING RIGHT NOW.
HUH?
SO WHAT'S ALL THAT YOU'RE WRITING?

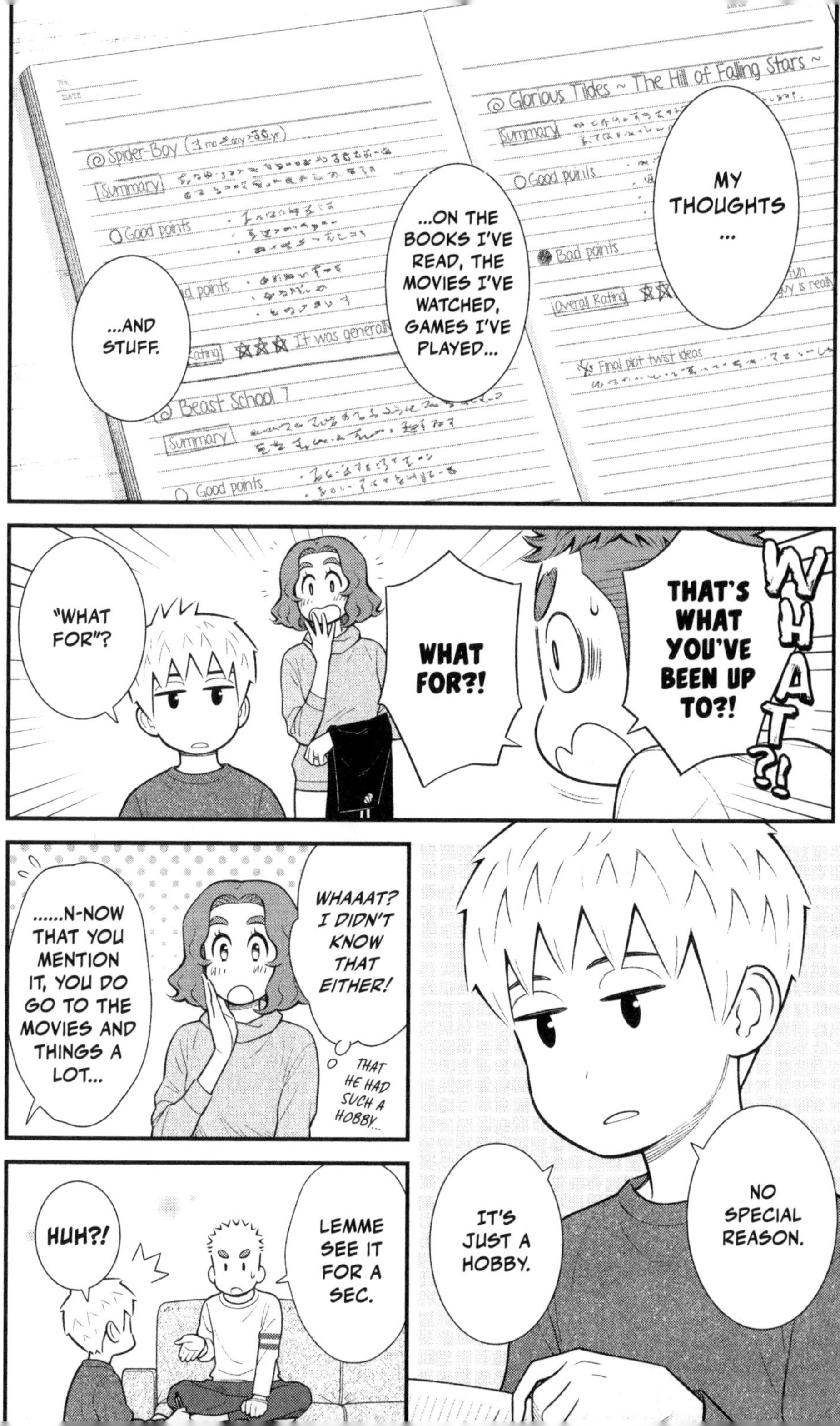
MY THOUGHTS ...
...ON THE BOOKS I'VE READ, THE MOVIES I'VE WATCHED, GAMES I'VE PLAYED...
...AND STUFF.
Glorious Tides ~ The Hill of Falling Stars ~
Summary
Good points
Bad points
Overall Rating
Final plot twist ideas
Spider-Boy
Summary
Good points
Beast School 7
Summary
Good points
WHAT?!
THAT'S WHAT YOU'VE BEEN UP TO?!
WHAT FOR?!
"WHAT FOR"?
NO SPECIAL REASON.
IT'S JUST A HOBBY.
WHAAAT? I DIDN'T KNOW THAT EITHER!
THAT HE HAD SUCH A HOBBY...
......N-NOW THAT YOU MENTION IT, YOU DO GO TO THE MOVIES AND THINGS A LOT...
LEMME SEE IT FOR A SEC.
HUH?!

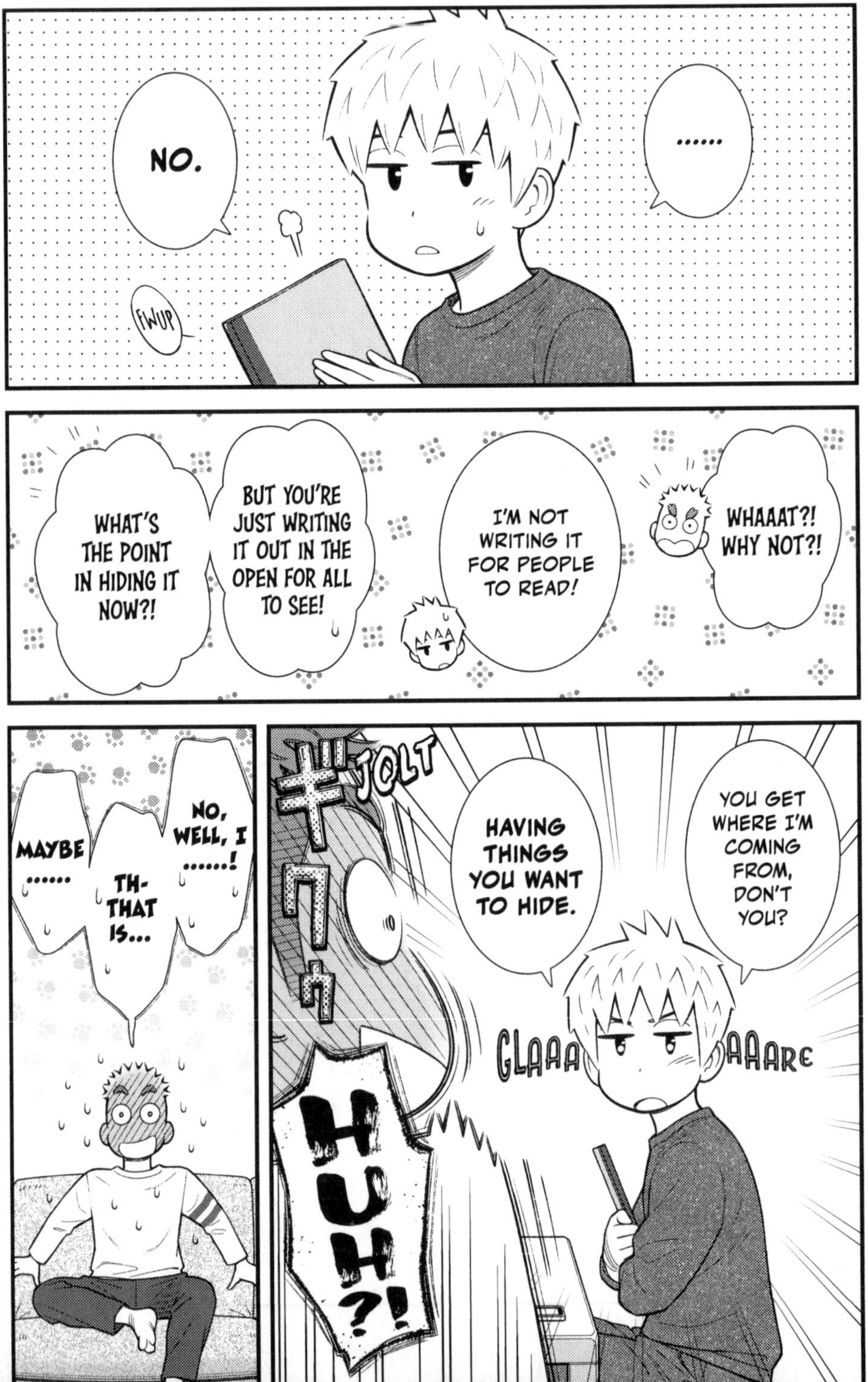
......
NO.
FWUP
WHAAAT?! WHY NOT?!
I'M NOT WRITING IT FOR PEOPLE TO READ!
BUT YOU'RE JUST WRITING IT OUT IN THE OPEN FOR ALL TO SEE!
WHAT'S THE POINT IN HIDING IT NOW?!
YOU GET WHERE I'M COMING FROM, DON'T YOU?
HAVING THINGS YOU WANT TO HIDE.
ギクッ
JOLT
GLAAAAAAARE
HUH?!
NO, WELL, I ......!
TH-THAT IS...
MAYBE ......

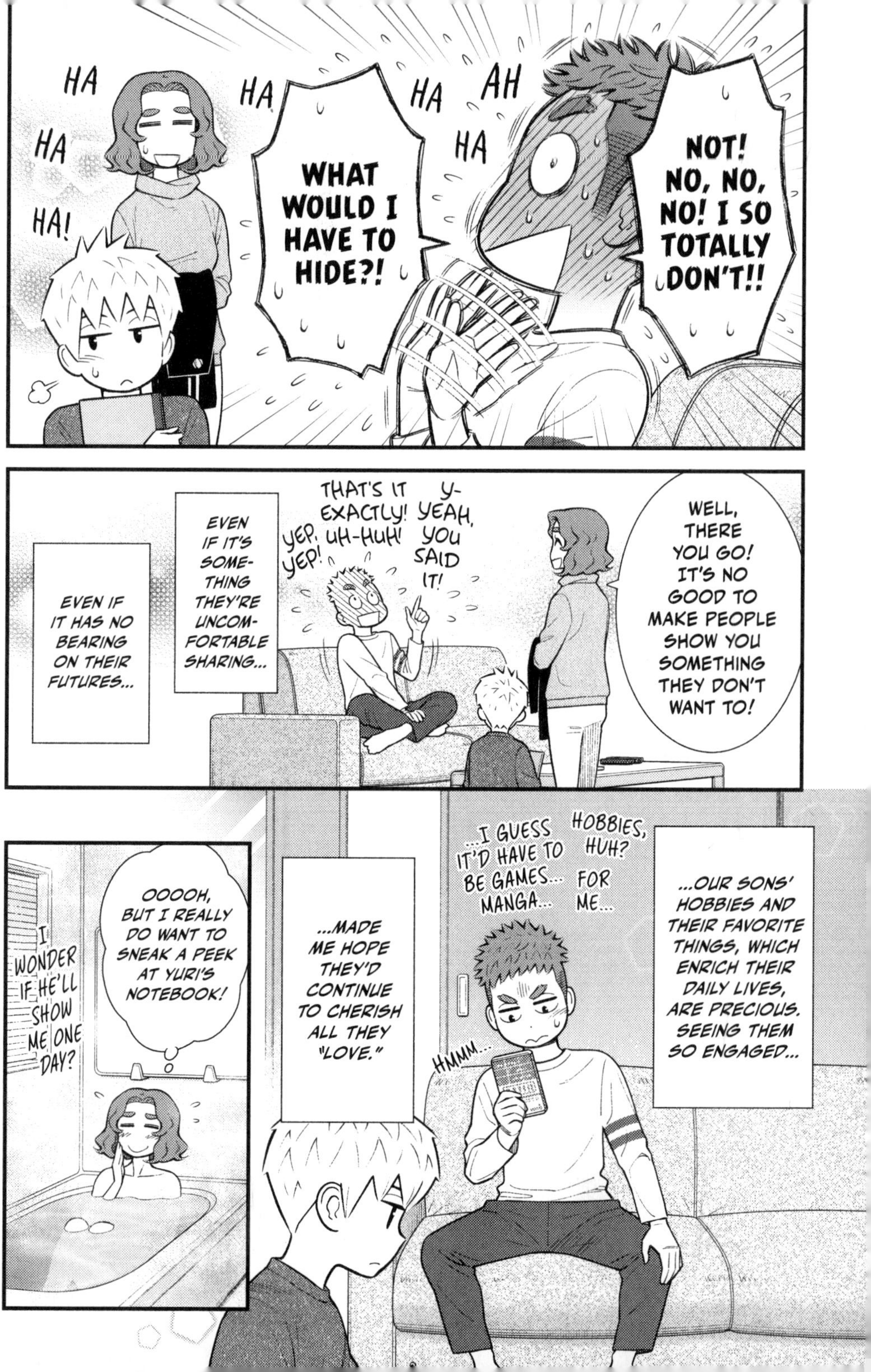
NOT! NO, NO, NO! I SO TOTALLY DON'T!!
AH HA HA HA
WHAT WOULD I HAVE TO HIDE?!
HA HA HA HA!
WELL, THERE YOU GO! IT'S NO GOOD TO MAKE PEOPLE SHOW YOU SOMETHING THEY DON'T WANT TO!
Y-YEAH, YOU SAID IT!
THAT'S IT EXACTLY! UH-HUH!
YEP, YEP!
EVEN IF IT'S SOME-THING THEY'RE UNCOM-FORTABLE SHARING...
EVEN IF IT HAS NO BEARING ON THEIR FUTURES...
...OUR SONS' HOBBIES AND THEIR FAVORITE THINGS, WHICH ENRICH THEIR DAILY LIVES, ARE PRECIOUS. SEEING THEM SO ENGAGED...
HOBBIES, HUH? FOR ME...
...I GUESS IT'D HAVE TO BE GAMES... MANGA...
HMMM...
...MADE ME HOPE THEY'D CONTINUE TO CHERISH ALL THEY "LOVE."
OOOOH, BUT I REALLY DO WANT TO SNEAK A PEEK AT YURI'S NOTEBOOK!
I WONDER IF HE'LL SHOW ME ONE DAY?

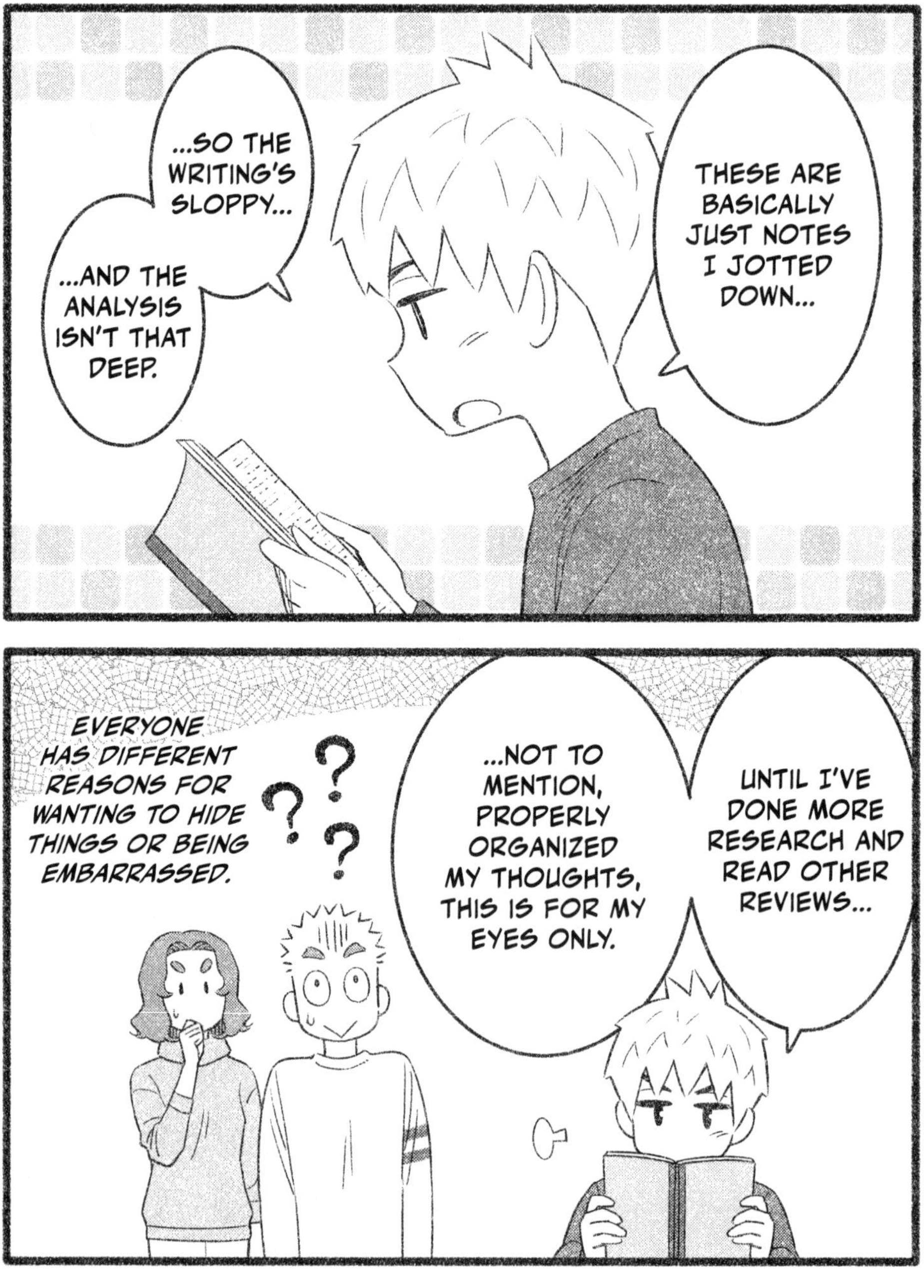
THESE ARE BASICALLY JUST NOTES I JOTTED DOWN...
...SO THE WRITING'S SLOPPY...
...AND THE ANALYSIS ISN'T THAT DEEP.
UNTIL I'VE DONE MORE RESEARCH AND READ OTHER REVIEWS...
...NOT TO MENTION, PROPERLY ORGANIZED MY THOUGHTS, THIS IS FOR MY EYES ONLY.
EVERYONE HAS DIFFERENT REASONS FOR WANTING TO HIDE THINGS OR BEING EMBARRASSED.

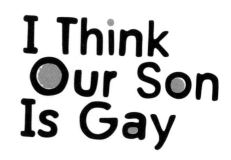

I Think
Our Son
Is Gay

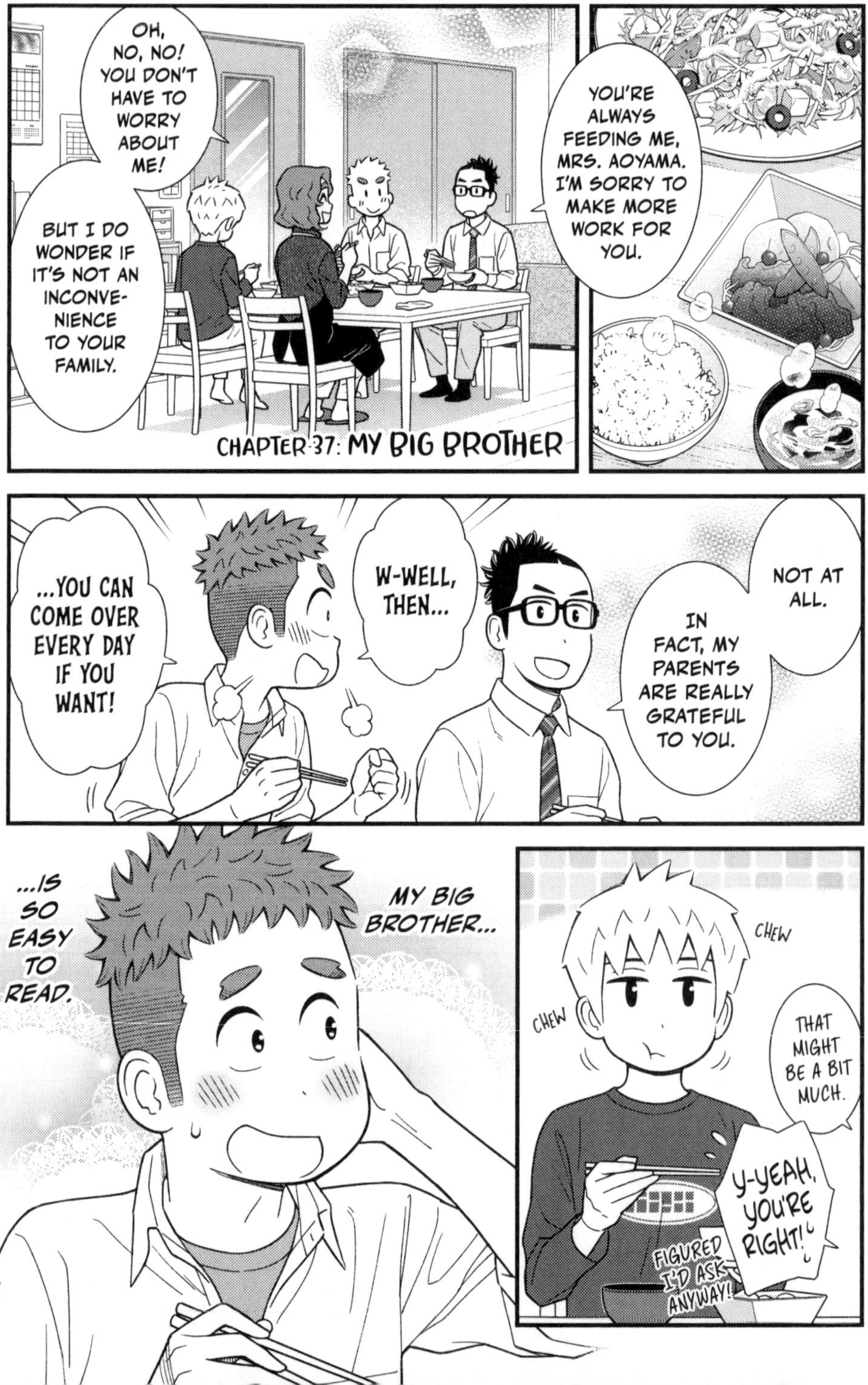
YOU'RE ALWAYS FEEDING ME, MRS. AOYAMA. I'M SORRY TO MAKE MORE WORK FOR YOU.
OH, NO, NO! YOU DON'T HAVE TO WORRY ABOUT ME!
BUT I DO WONDER IF IT'S NOT AN INCONVENIENCE TO YOUR FAMILY.
CHAPTER 37: MY BIG BROTHER
NOT AT ALL.
IN FACT, MY PARENTS ARE REALLY GRATEFUL TO YOU.
W-WELL, THEN...
...YOU CAN COME OVER EVERY DAY IF YOU WANT!
CHEW
CHEW
THAT MIGHT BE A BIT MUCH.
Y-YEAH, YOU'RE RIGHT!
FIGURED I'D ASK ANYWAY!
MY BIG BROTHER...
...IS SO EASY TO READ.

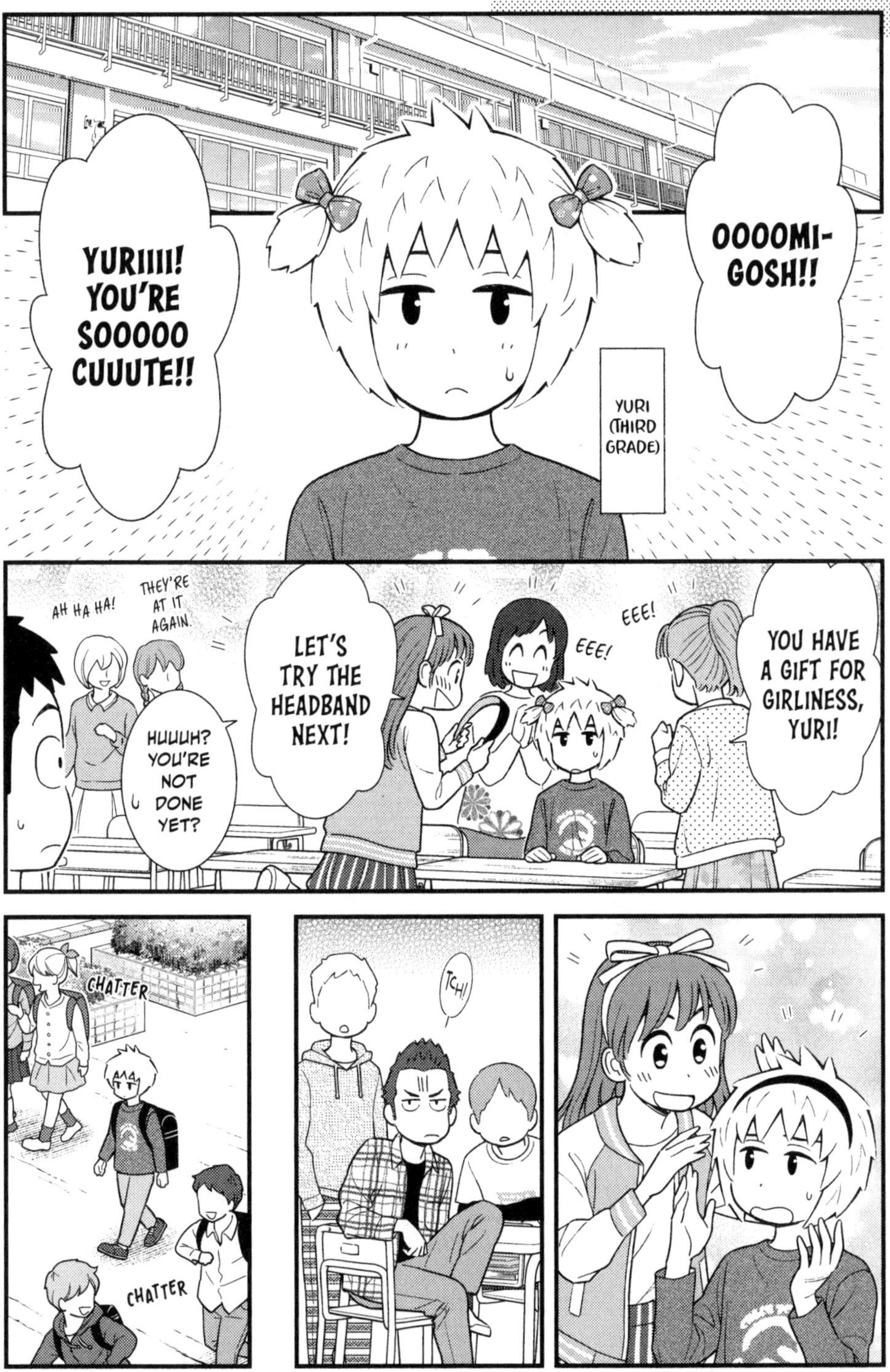
OOOOMI-GOSH!!
YURI (THIRD GRADE)
YURIIII! YOU'RE SOOOOO CUUUTE!!
YOU HAVE A GIFT FOR GIRLINESS, YURI!
EEE!
EEE!
LET'S TRY THE HEADBAND NEXT!
THEY'RE AT IT AGAIN.
AH HA HA!
HUUUH? YOU'RE NOT DONE YET?
TCH!
CHATTER
CHATTER

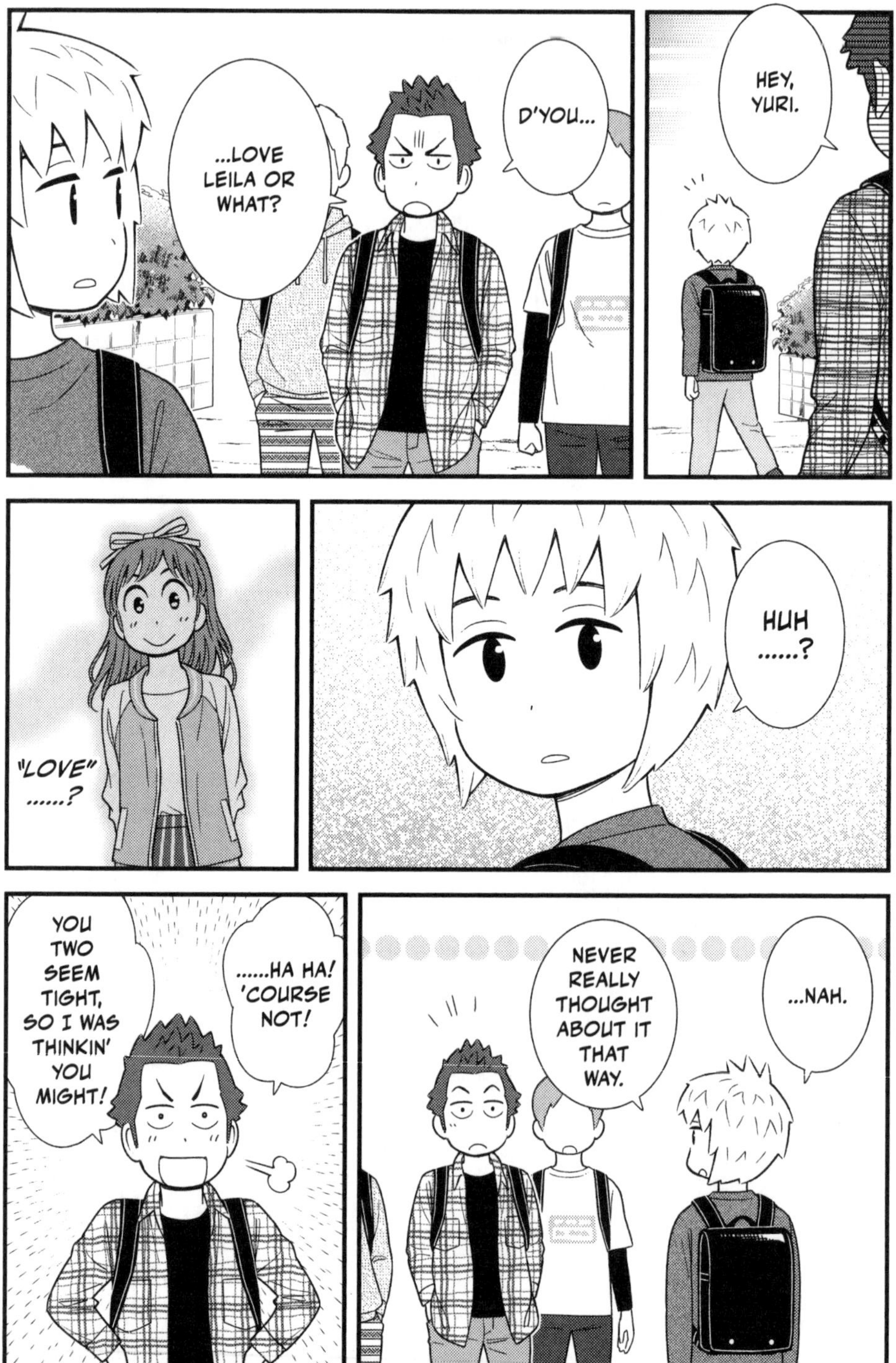
HEY, YURI.
D'YOU...
...LOVE LEILA OR WHAT?
HUH ......?
"LOVE" ......?
...NAH.
NEVER REALLY THOUGHT ABOUT IT THAT WAY.
......HA HA! 'COURSE NOT!
YOU TWO SEEM TIGHT, SO I WAS THINKIN' YOU MIGHT!

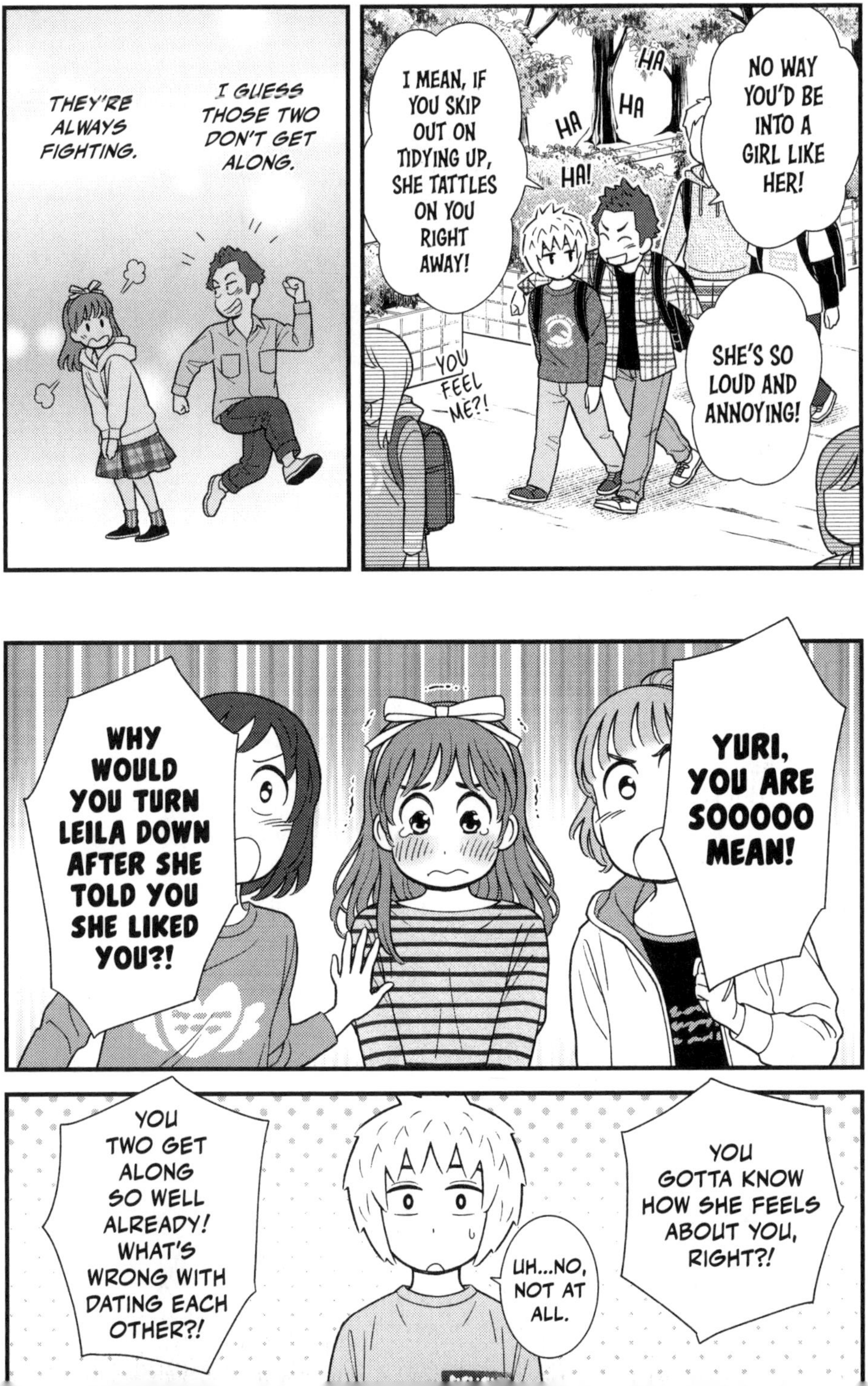
NO WAY YOU'D BE INTO A GIRL LIKE HER!
HA
HA
HA
HA!
I MEAN, IF YOU SKIP OUT ON TIDYING UP, SHE TATTLES ON YOU RIGHT AWAY!
SHE'S SO LOUD AND ANNOYING!
YOU FEEL ME?!
I GUESS THOSE TWO DON'T GET ALONG.
THEY'RE ALWAYS FIGHTING.
YURI, YOU ARE SOOOOO MEAN!
WHY WOULD YOU TURN LEILA DOWN AFTER SHE TOLD YOU SHE LIKED YOU?!
YOU GOTTA KNOW HOW SHE FEELS ABOUT YOU, RIGHT?!
UH...NO, NOT AT ALL.
YOU TWO GET ALONG SO WELL ALREADY! WHAT'S WRONG WITH DATING EACH OTHER?!

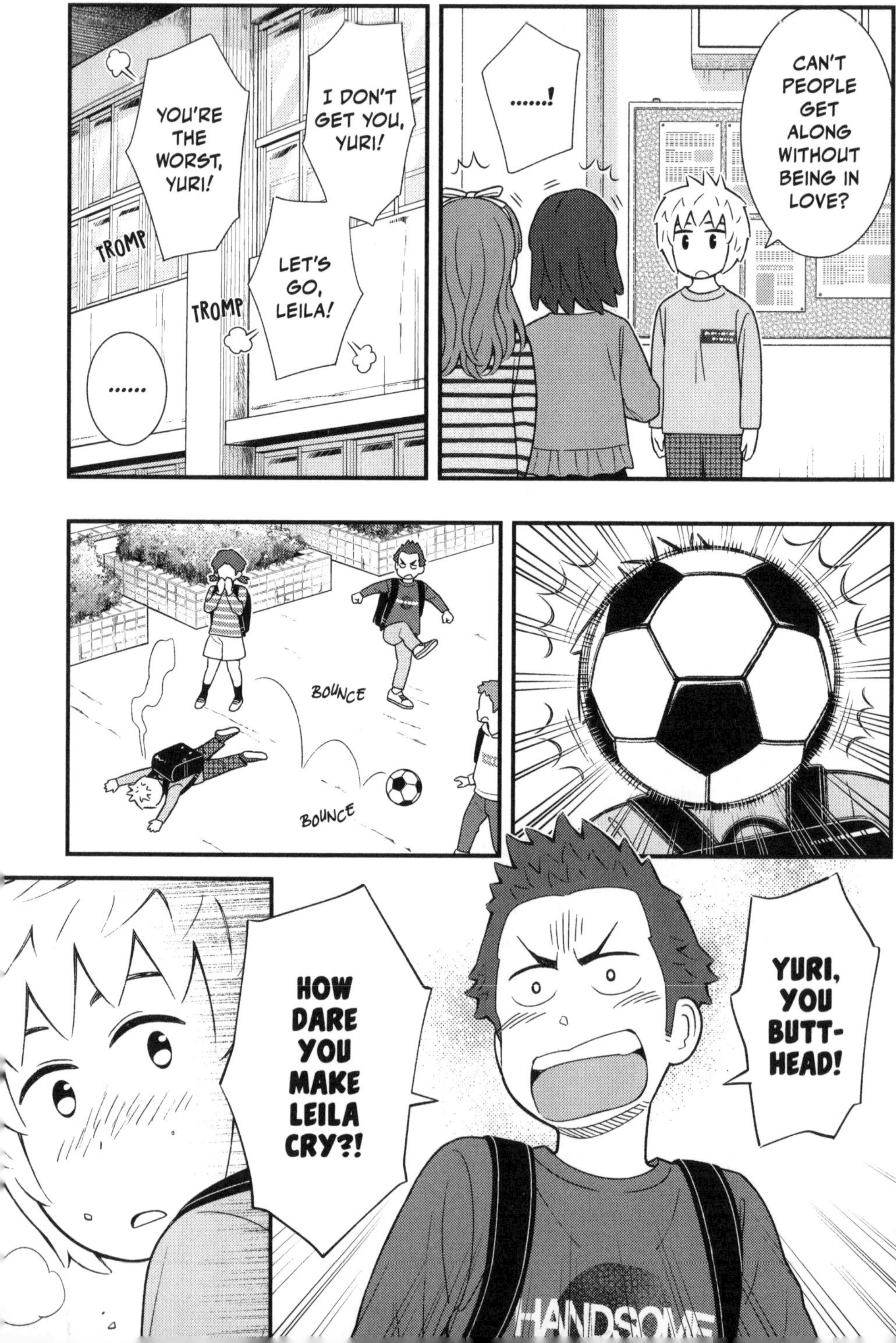
CAN'T PEOPLE GET ALONG WITHOUT BEING IN LOVE?
......!
I DON'T GET YOU, YURI!
YOU'RE THE WORST, YURI!
LET'S GO, LEILA!
TROMP
TROMP
......
BOUNCE
BOUNCE
YURI, YOU BUTT-HEAD!
HOW DARE YOU MAKE LEILA CRY?!
HANDSOME

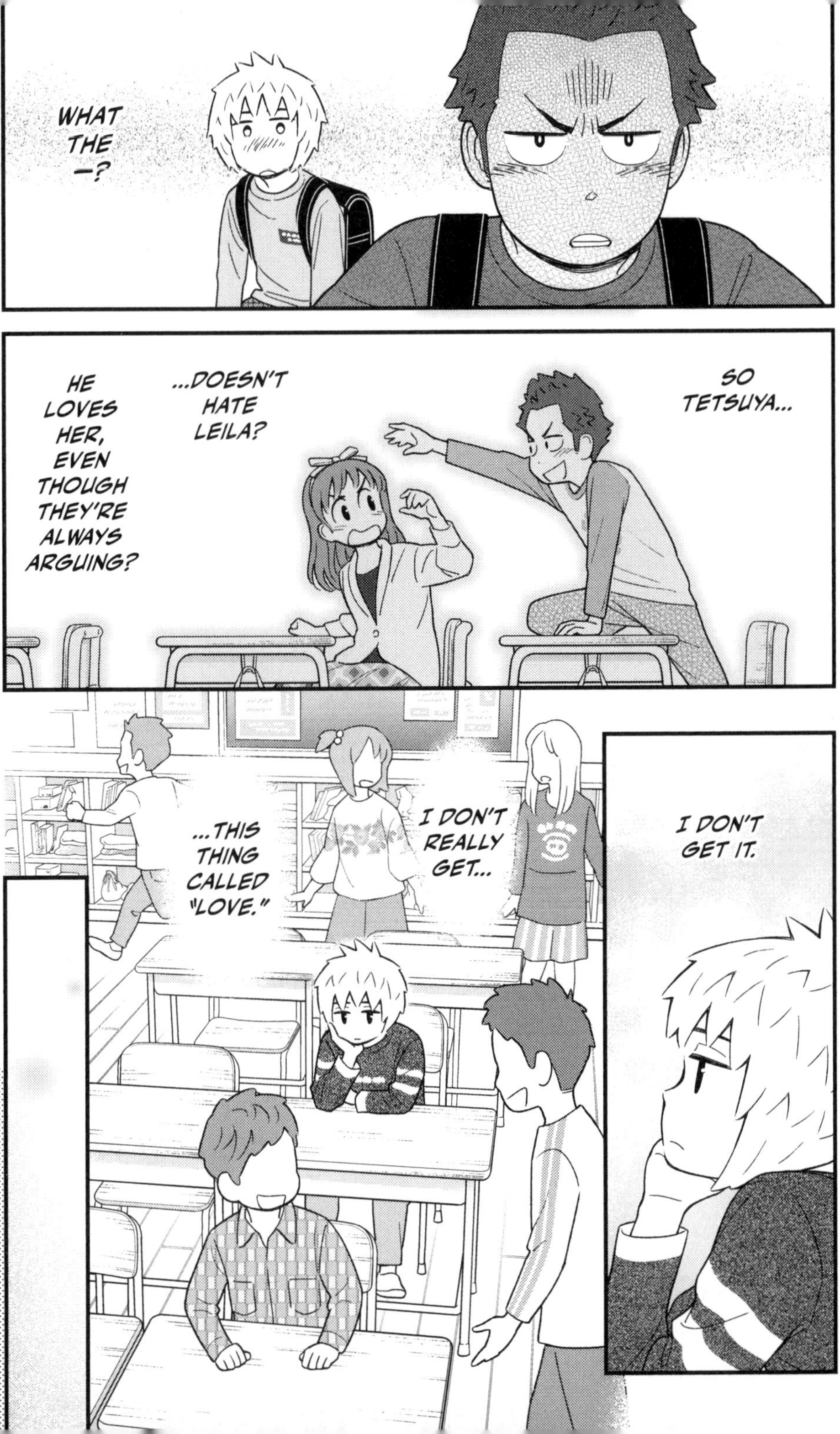
WHAT THE—?
SO TETSUYA...
...DOESN'T HATE LEILA?
HE LOVES HER, EVEN THOUGH THEY'RE ALWAYS ARGUING?
I DON'T GET IT.
I DON'T REALLY GET...
...THIS THING CALLED "LOVE."

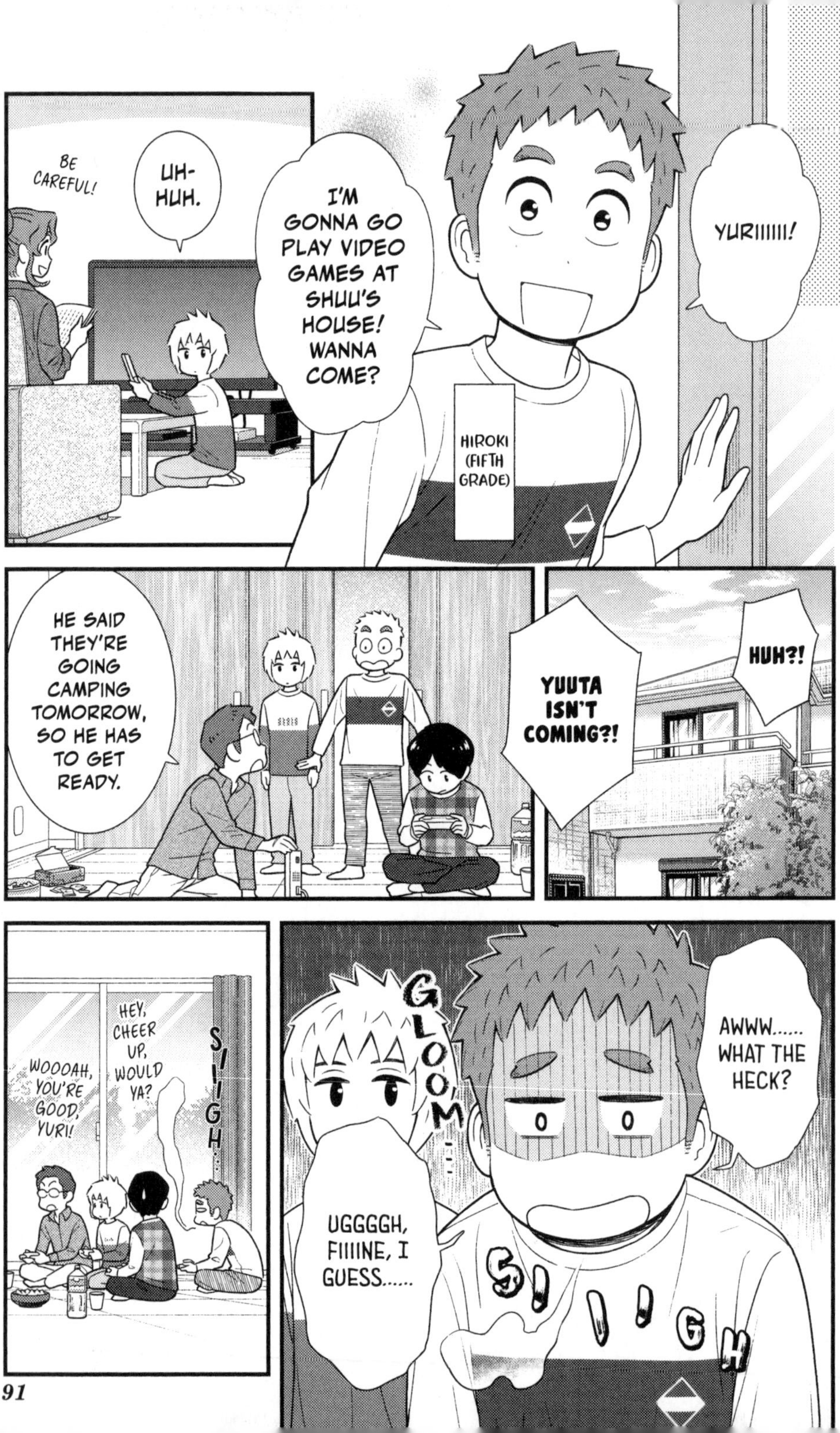
YURIIIIII!
I'M GONNA GO PLAY VIDEO GAMES AT SHUU'S HOUSE! WANNA COME?
HIROKI (FIFTH GRADE)
UH-HUH.
BE CAREFUL!
HUH?!
YUUTA ISN'T COMING?!
HE SAID THEY'RE GOING CAMPING TOMORROW, SO HE HAS TO GET READY.
AWWW...... WHAT THE HECK?
GLOOM...
UGGGGH, FIIIINE, I GUESS......
SIIIGH
HEY, CHEER UP, WOULD YA?
WOOOAH, YOU'RE GOOD, YURI!
SIIIGH...

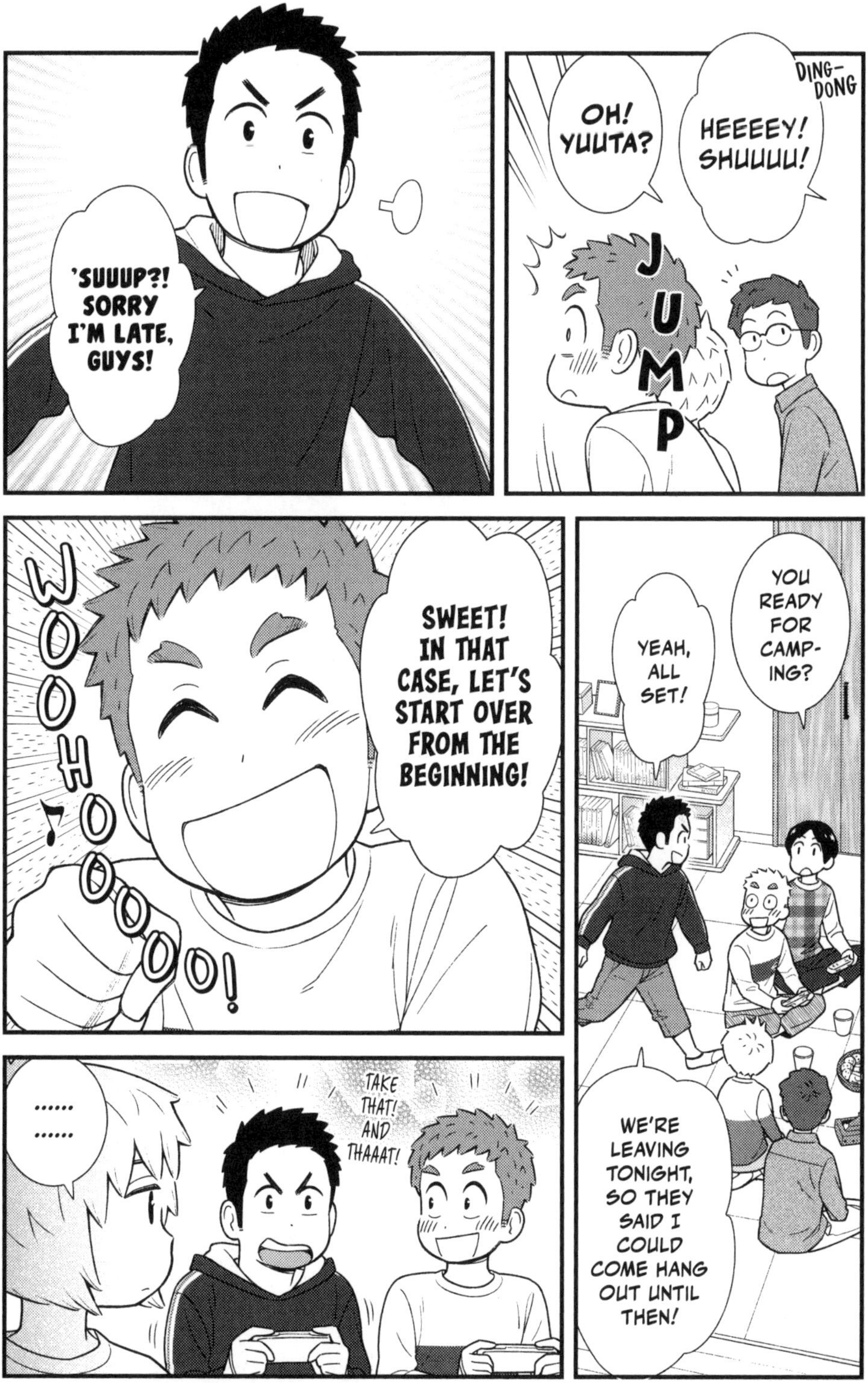
DING-DONG
HEEEEY! SHUUUU!
OH! YUUTA?
JUMP
'SUUUP?! SORRY I'M LATE, GUYS!
YOU READY FOR CAMP-ING?
YEAH, ALL SET!
WE'RE LEAVING TONIGHT, SO THEY SAID I COULD COME HANG OUT UNTIL THEN!
SWEET! IN THAT CASE, LET'S START OVER FROM THE BEGINNING!
WOOHOOOOOO!
TAKE THAT! AND THAAAT!
......
......

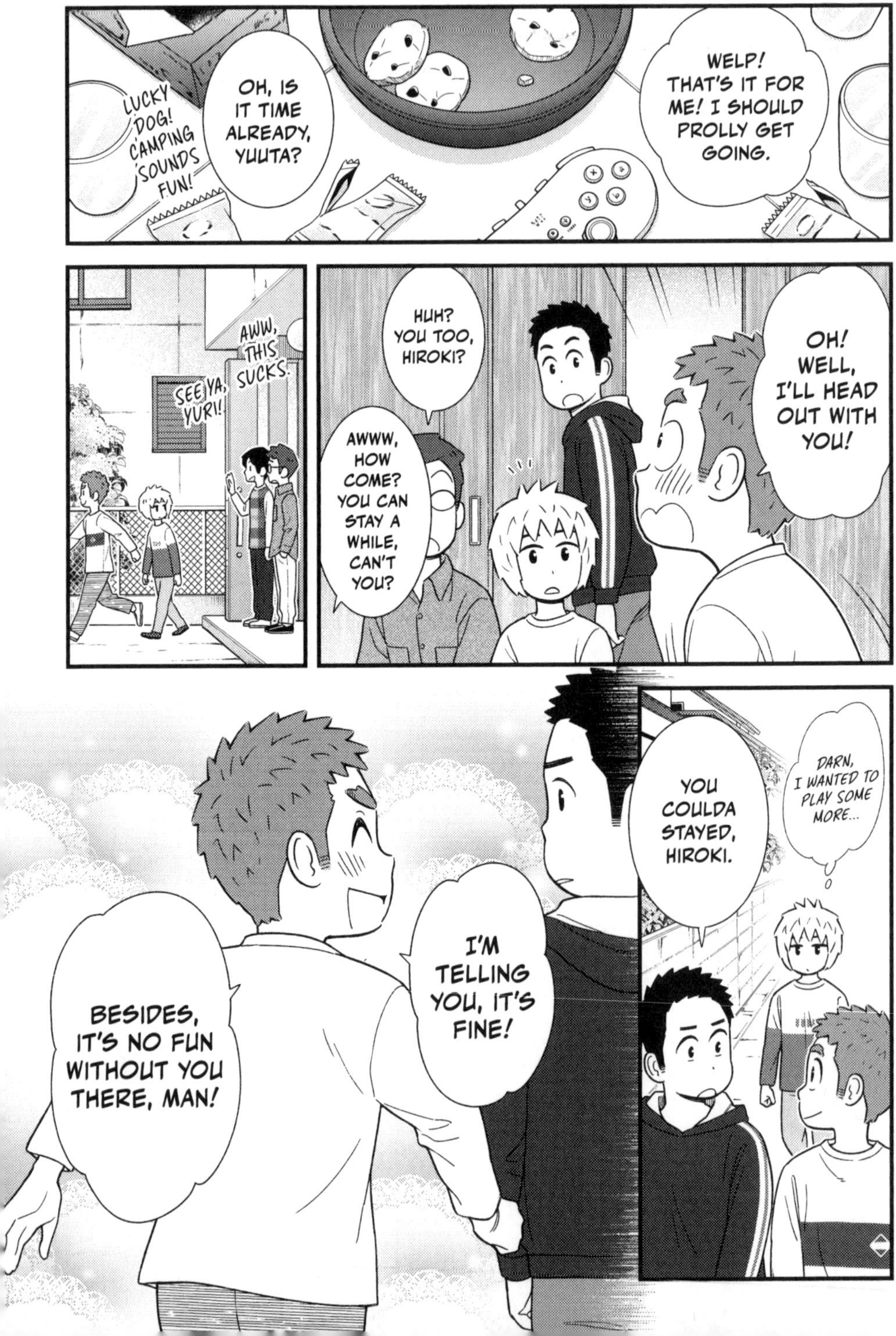
WELP! THAT'S IT FOR ME! I SHOULD PROLLY GET GOING.
OH, IS IT TIME ALREADY, YUUTA?
LUCKY DOG! CAMPING SOUNDS FUN!
OH! WELL, I'LL HEAD OUT WITH YOU!
HUH? YOU TOO, HIROKI?
AWWW, HOW COME? YOU CAN STAY A WHILE, CAN'T YOU?
AWW, THIS SUCKS.
SEE YA, YURI!
DARN, I WANTED TO PLAY SOME MORE...
YOU COULDA STAYED, HIROKI.
I'M TELLING YOU, IT'S FINE!
BESIDES, IT'S NO FUN WITHOUT YOU THERE, MAN!

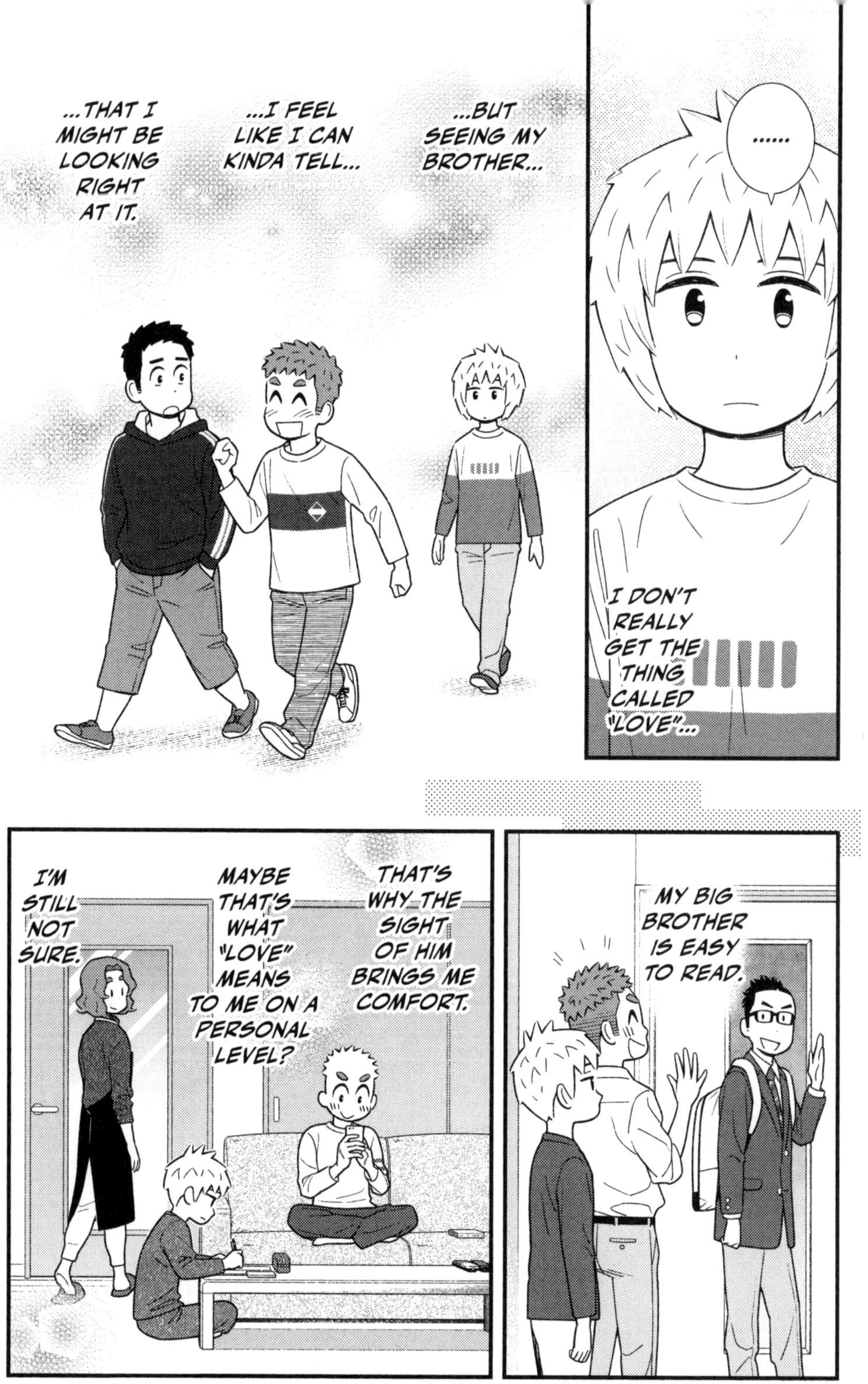
......
I DON'T REALLY GET THE THING CALLED "LOVE"...
...BUT SEEING MY BROTHER...
...I FEEL LIKE I CAN KINDA TELL...
...THAT I MIGHT BE LOOKING RIGHT AT IT.
MY BIG BROTHER IS EASY TO READ.
THAT'S WHY THE SIGHT OF HIM BRINGS ME COMFORT.
MAYBE THAT'S WHAT "LOVE" MEANS TO ME ON A PERSONAL LEVEL?
I'M STILL NOT SURE.

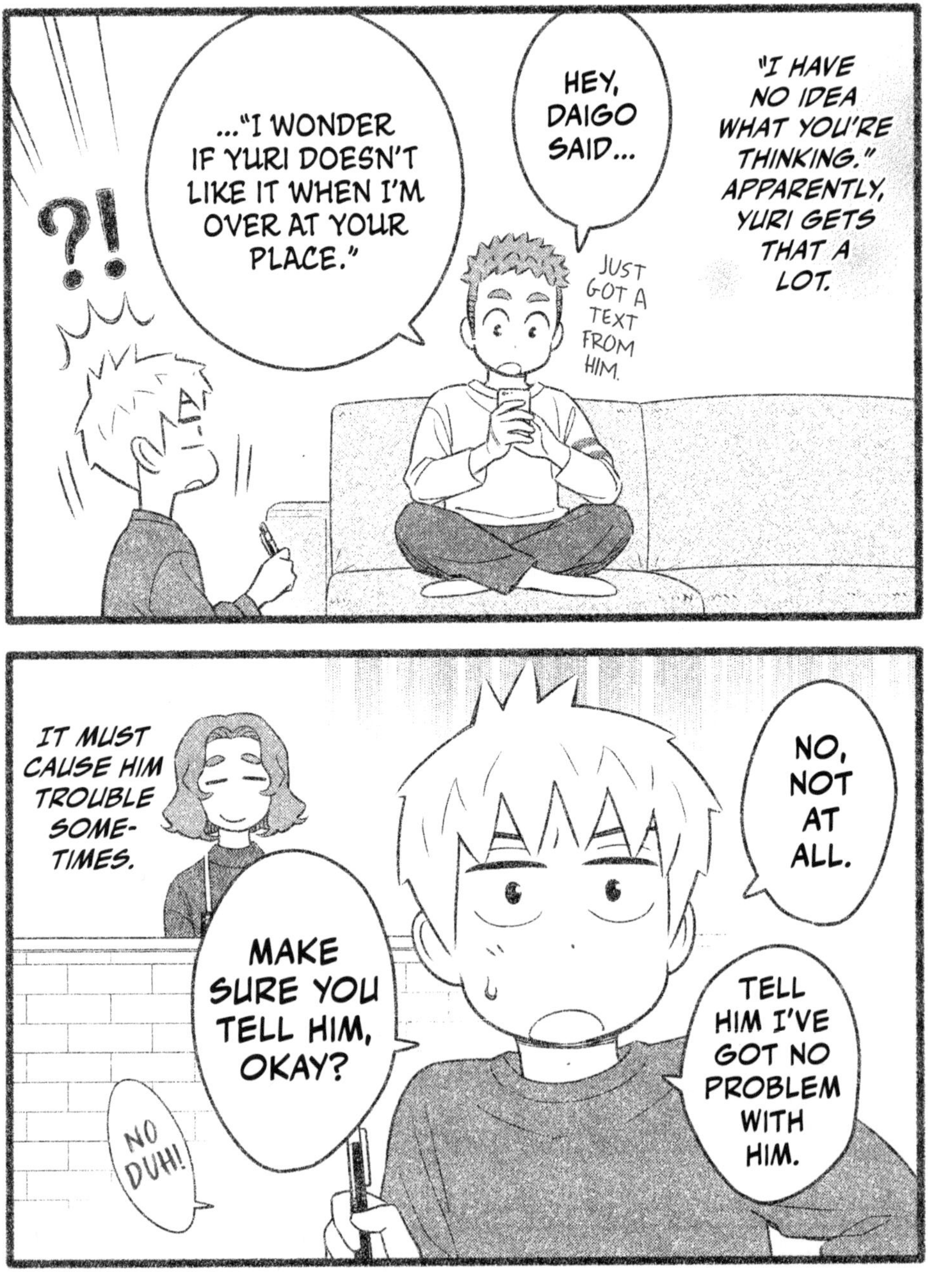
"I HAVE NO IDEA WHAT YOU'RE THINKING." APPARENTLY, YURI GETS THAT A LOT.
HEY, DAIGO SAID...
JUST GOT A TEXT FROM HIM.
..."I WONDER IF YURI DOESN'T LIKE IT WHEN I'M OVER AT YOUR PLACE."
?!
NO, NOT AT ALL.
IT MUST CAUSE HIM TROUBLE SOME-TIMES.
TELL HIM I'VE GOT NO PROBLEM WITH HIM.
MAKE SURE YOU TELL HIM, OKAY?
NO DUH!

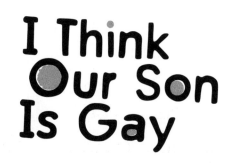

I Think
Our Son
Is Gay

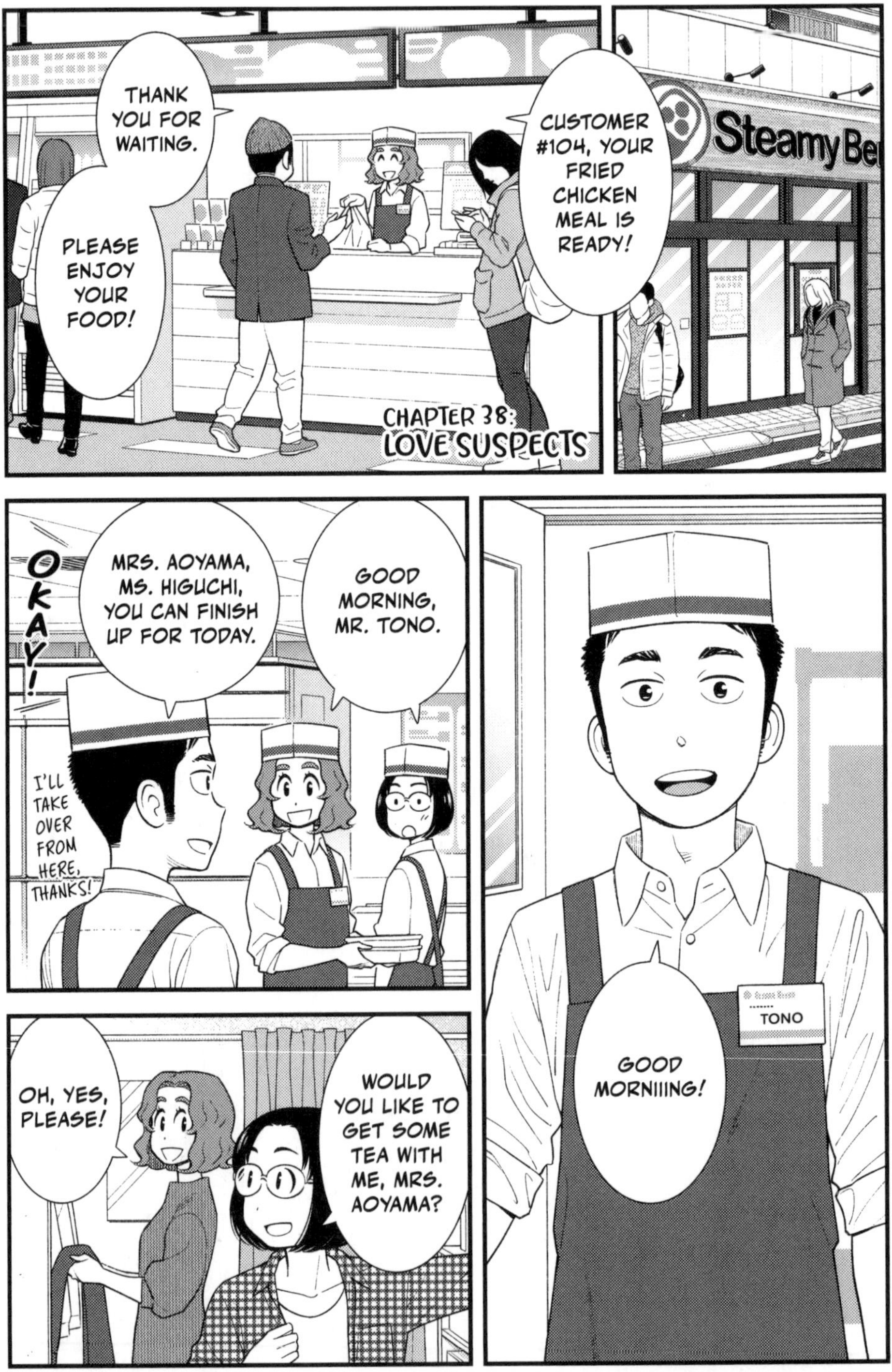
CUSTOMER #104, YOUR FRIED CHICKEN MEAL IS READY!
THANK YOU FOR WAITING.
PLEASE ENJOY YOUR FOOD!
CHAPTER 38: LOVE SUSPECTS
GOOD MORNIIING!
TONO
GOOD MORNING, MR. TONO.
MRS. AOYAMA, MS. HIGUCHI, YOU CAN FINISH UP FOR TODAY.
OKAY!
I'LL TAKE OVER FROM HERE, THANKS!
WOULD YOU LIKE TO GET SOME TEA WITH ME, MRS. AOYAMA?
OH, YES, PLEASE!

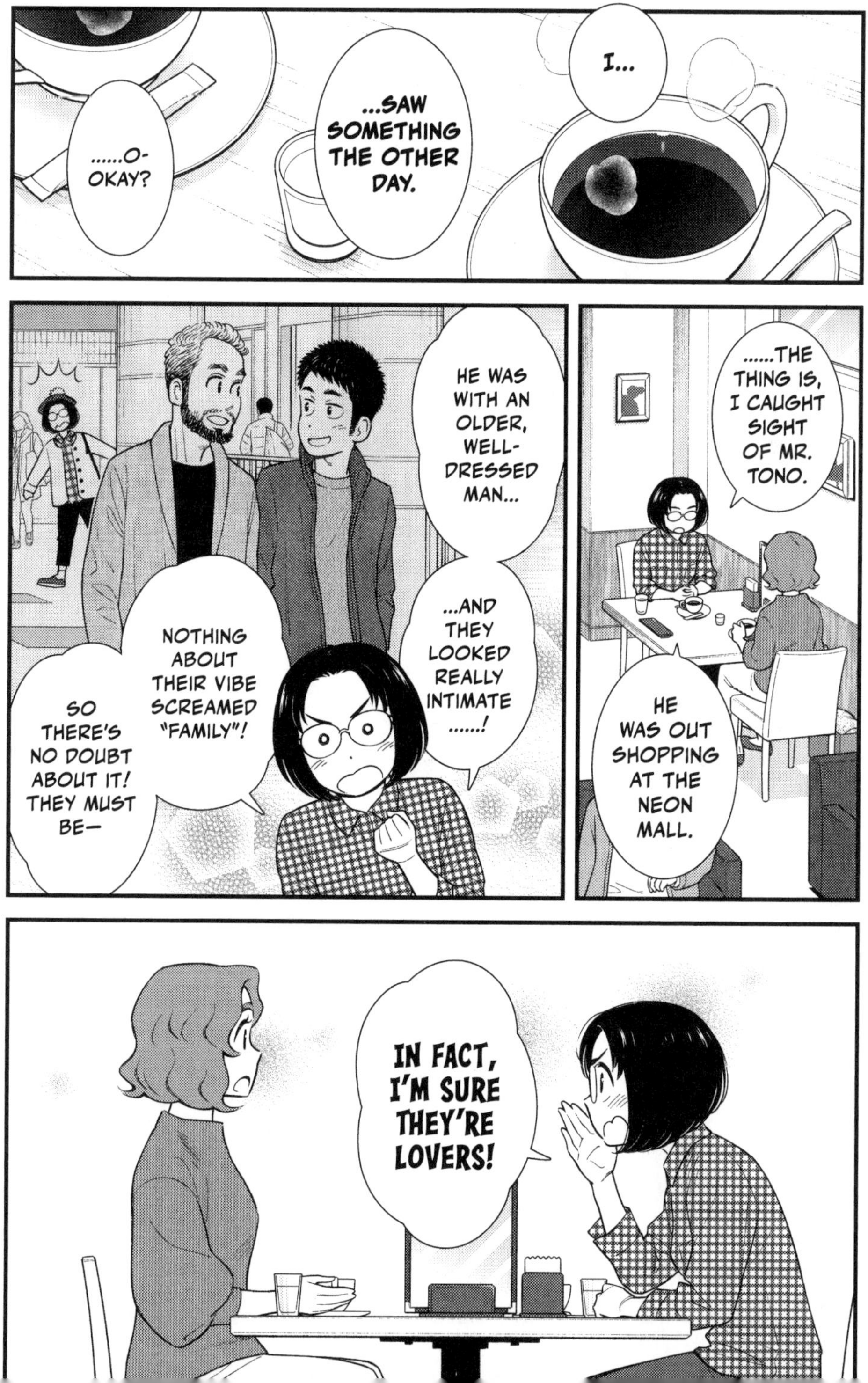
I...
...SAW SOMETHING THE OTHER DAY.
......O-OKAY?
......THE THING IS, I CAUGHT SIGHT OF MR. TONO.
HE WAS OUT SHOPPING AT THE NEON MALL.
HE WAS WITH AN OLDER, WELL-DRESSED MAN...
...AND THEY LOOKED REALLY INTIMATE ......!
NOTHING ABOUT THEIR VIBE SCREAMED "FAMILY"!
SO THERE'S NO DOUBT ABOUT IT! THEY MUST BE—
IN FACT, I'M SURE THEY'RE LOVERS!

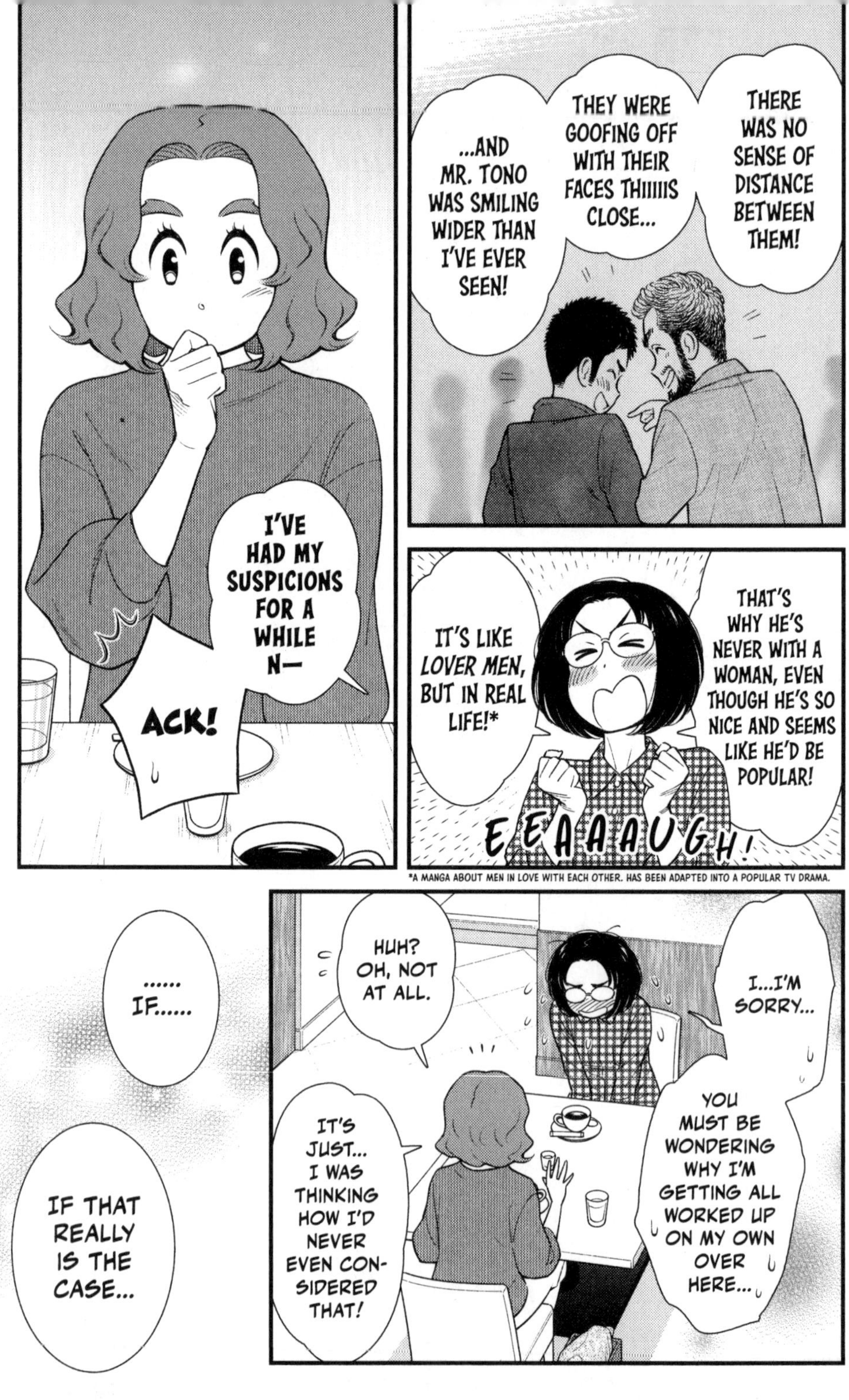
THERE WAS NO SENSE OF DISTANCE BETWEEN THEM!
THEY WERE GOOFING OFF WITH THEIR FACES THIIIIIS CLOSE...
...AND MR. TONO WAS SMILING WIDER THAN I'VE EVER SEEN!
THAT'S WHY HE'S NEVER WITH A WOMAN, EVEN THOUGH HE'S SO NICE AND SEEMS LIKE HE'D BE POPULAR!
IT'S LIKE *LOVER MEN*, BUT IN REAL LIFE!*
EEAAAAUGH!
I'VE HAD MY SUSPICIONS FOR A WHILE N—
ACK!
I...I'M SORRY...
YOU MUST BE WONDERING WHY I'M GETTING ALL WORKED UP ON MY OWN OVER HERE...
HUH? OH, NOT AT ALL.
IT'S JUST... I WAS THINKING HOW I'D NEVER EVEN CON-SIDERED THAT!
......IF......
IF THAT REALLY IS THE CASE...

*A MANGA ABOUT MEN IN LOVE WITH EACH OTHER. HAS BEEN ADAPTED INTO A POPULAR TV DRAMA.

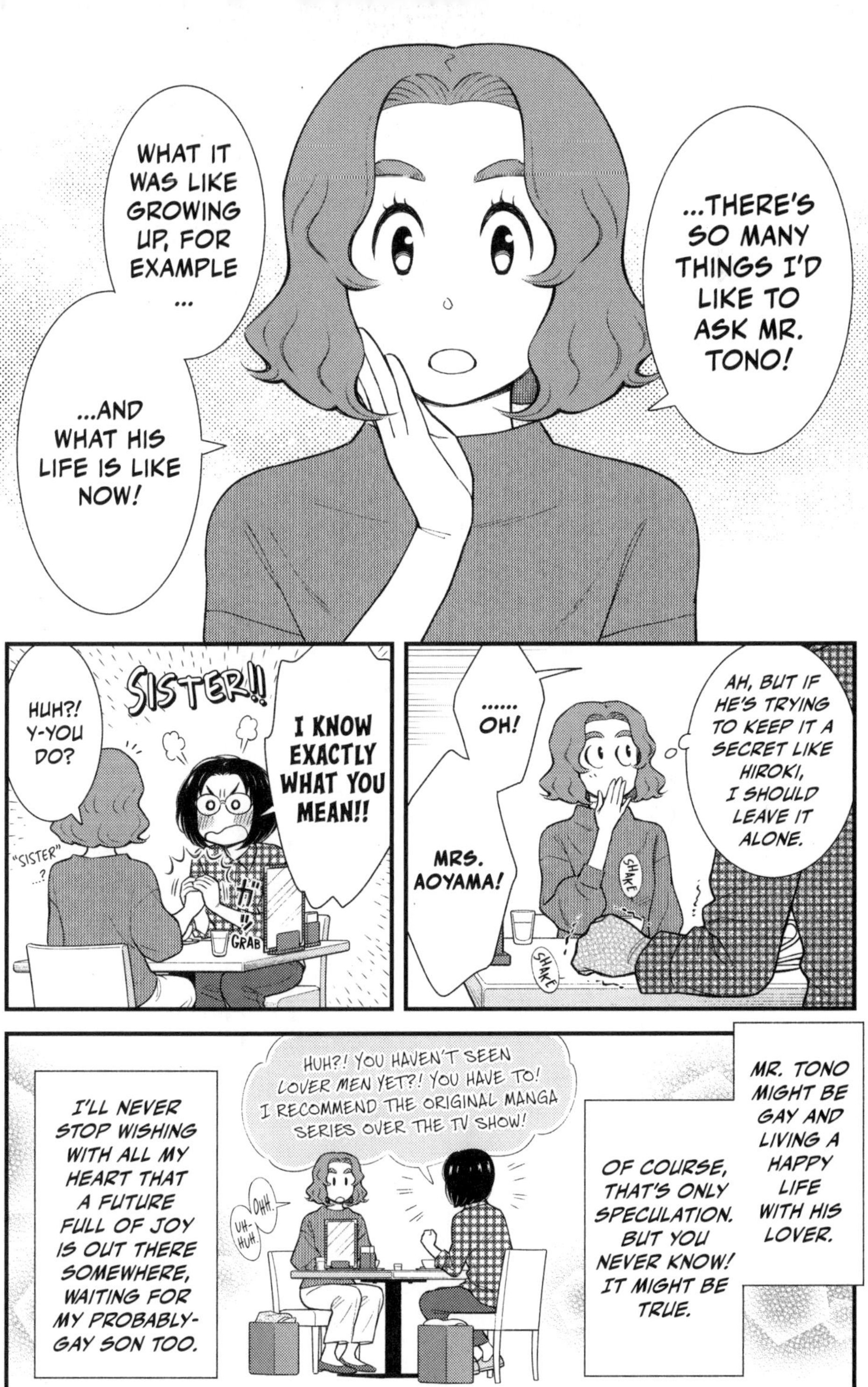
...THERE'S SO MANY THINGS I'D LIKE TO ASK MR. TONO!
WHAT IT WAS LIKE GROWING UP, FOR EXAMPLE ...
...AND WHAT HIS LIFE IS LIKE NOW!
AH, BUT IF HE'S TRYING TO KEEP IT A SECRET LIKE HIROKI, I SHOULD LEAVE IT ALONE.
......OH!
MRS. AOYAMA!
SHAKE
SHAKE
I KNOW EXACTLY WHAT YOU MEAN!!
SISTER!!
HUH?! Y-YOU DO?
GRAB
"SISTER" ...?
MR. TONO MIGHT BE GAY AND LIVING A HAPPY LIFE WITH HIS LOVER.
OF COURSE, THAT'S ONLY SPECULATION. BUT YOU NEVER KNOW! IT MIGHT BE TRUE.
HUH?! YOU HAVEN'T SEEN LOVER MEN YET?! YOU HAVE TO! I RECOMMEND THE ORIGINAL MANGA SERIES OVER THE TV SHOW!
OHH.
UH-HUH.
I'LL NEVER STOP WISHING WITH ALL MY HEART THAT A FUTURE FULL OF JOY IS OUT THERE SOMEWHERE, WAITING FOR MY PROBABLY-GAY SON TOO.

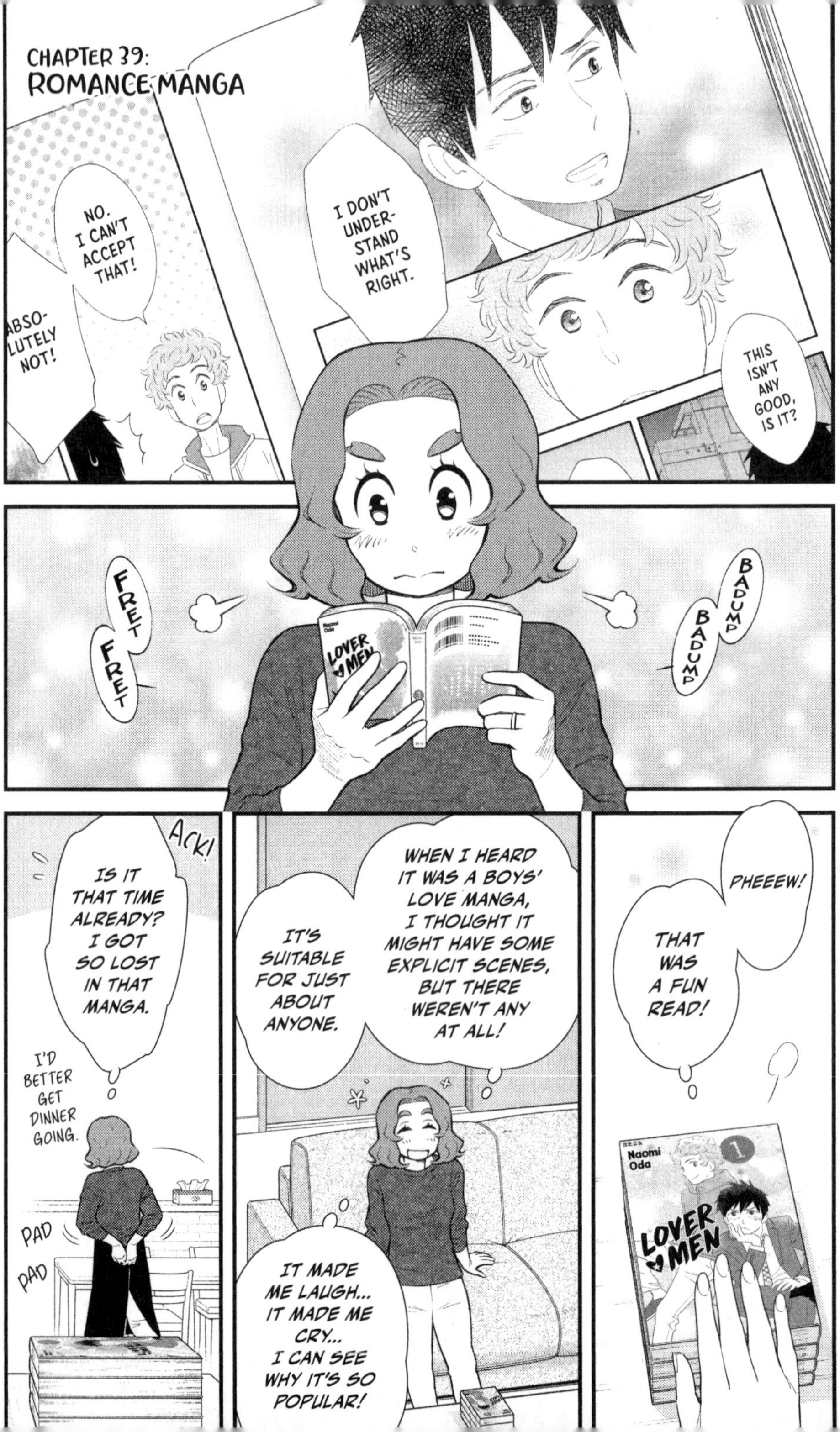
CHAPTER 39: ROMANCE MANGA
I DON'T UNDER-STAND WHAT'S RIGHT.
THIS ISN'T ANY GOOD, IS IT?
NO. I CAN'T ACCEPT THAT!
ABSO-LUTELY NOT!
BADUMP BADUMP
Naomi Oda LOVER MEN
FRET FRET
PHEEEW!
THAT WAS A FUN READ!
Naomi Oda LOVER MEN 1
WHEN I HEARD IT WAS A BOYS' LOVE MANGA, I THOUGHT IT MIGHT HAVE SOME EXPLICIT SCENES, BUT THERE WEREN'T ANY AT ALL!
IT'S SUITABLE FOR JUST ABOUT ANYONE.
IT MADE ME LAUGH... IT MADE ME CRY... I CAN SEE WHY IT'S SO POPULAR!
ACK!
IS IT THAT TIME ALREADY? I GOT SO LOST IN THAT MANGA.
I'D BETTER GET DINNER GOING.
PAD PAD

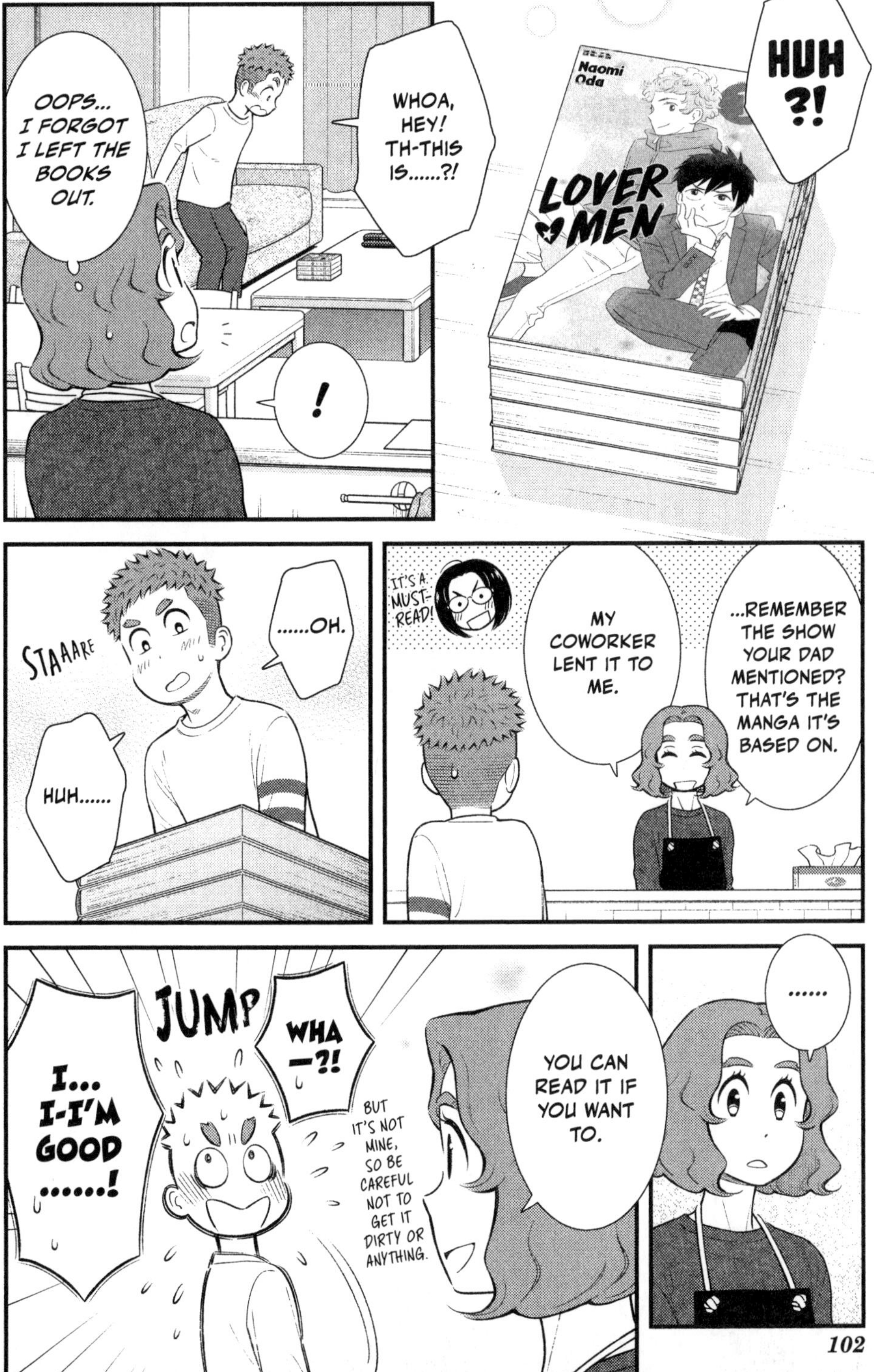
Naomi Oda
LOVER MEN
HUH ?!
WHOA, HEY! TH-THIS IS......?!
OOPS... I FORGOT I LEFT THE BOOKS OUT.
!
...REMEMBER THE SHOW YOUR DAD MENTIONED? THAT'S THE MANGA IT'S BASED ON.
MY COWORKER LENT IT TO ME.
IT'S A MUST-READ!
......OH.
STAAARE
HUH......
......
YOU CAN READ IT IF YOU WANT TO.
BUT IT'S NOT MINE, SO BE CAREFUL NOT TO GET IT DIRTY OR ANYTHING.
WHA—?!
JUMP
I... I-I'M GOOD......!

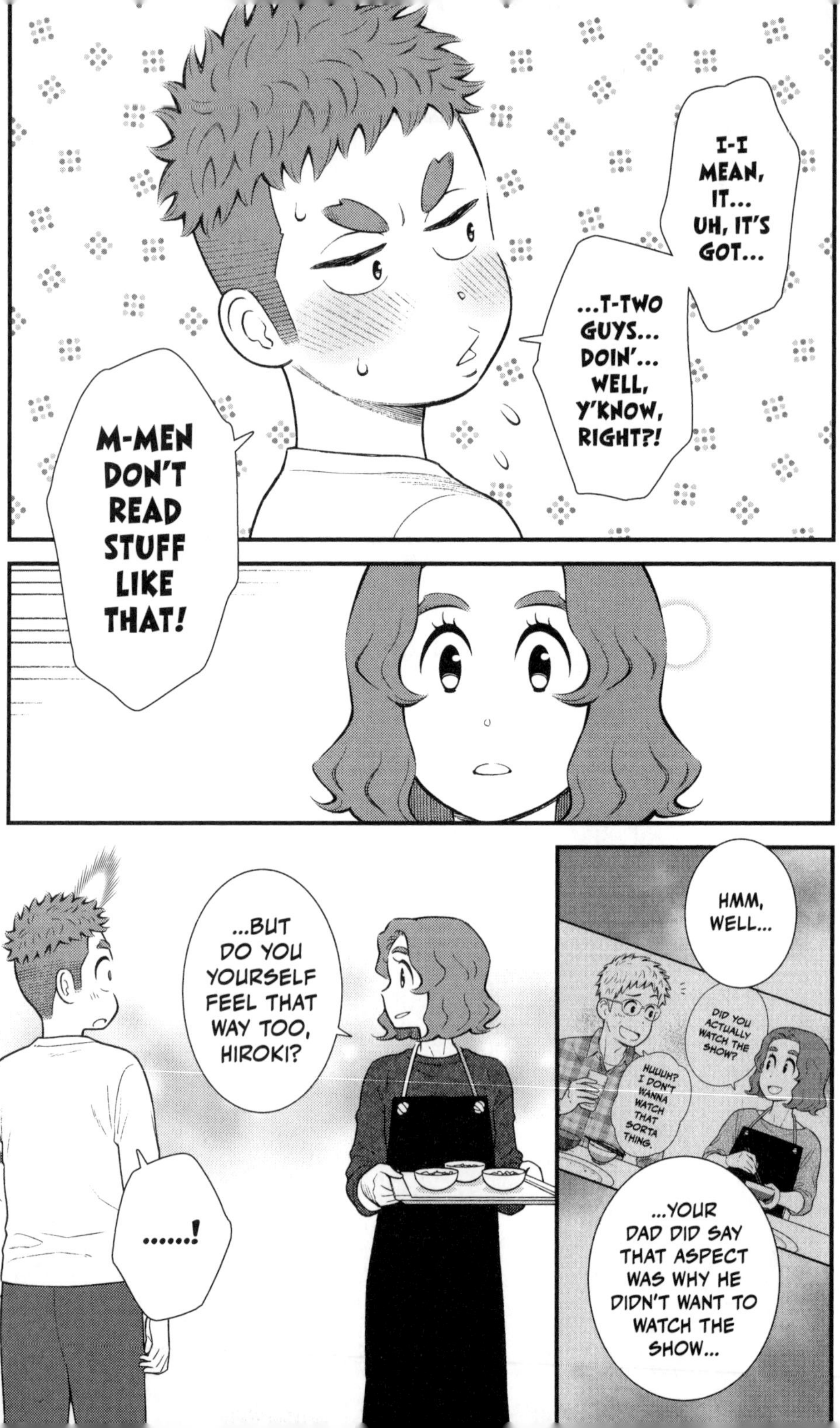
I-I MEAN, IT... UH, IT'S GOT...
...T-TWO GUYS... DOIN'... WELL, Y'KNOW, RIGHT?!
M-MEN DON'T READ STUFF LIKE THAT!
HMM, WELL...
DID YOU ACTUALLY WATCH THE SHOW?
HUUUH? I DON'T WANNA WATCH THAT SORTA THING.
...YOUR DAD DID SAY THAT ASPECT WAS WHY HE DIDN'T WANT TO WATCH THE SHOW...
...BUT DO YOU YOURSELF FEEL THAT WAY TOO, HIROKI?
......!

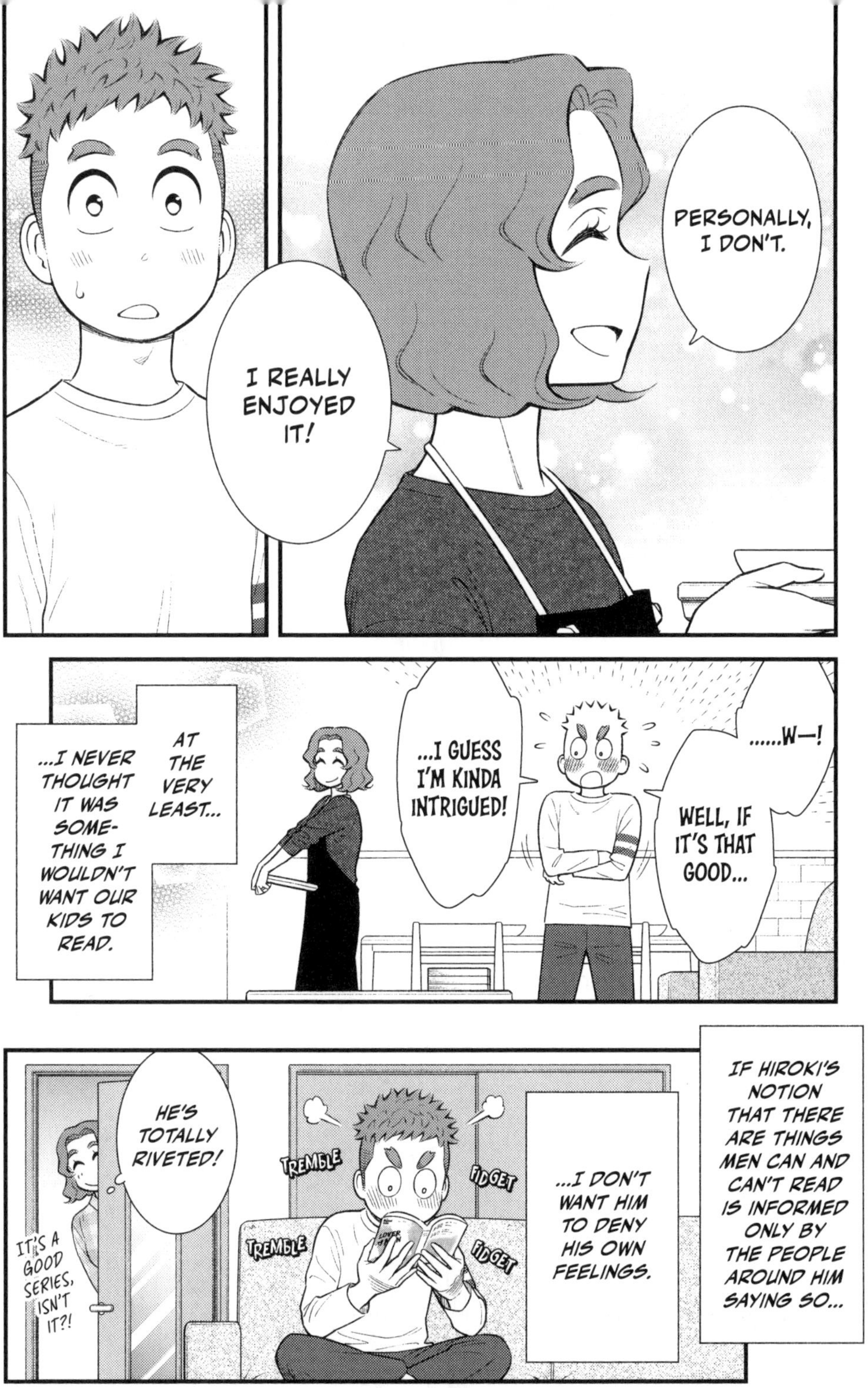
PERSONALLY, I DON'T.
I REALLY ENJOYED IT!
......W—!
WELL, IF IT'S THAT GOOD...
...I GUESS I'M KINDA INTRIGUED!
AT THE VERY LEAST...
...I NEVER THOUGHT IT WAS SOME-THING I WOULDN'T WANT OUR KIDS TO READ.
IF HIROKI'S NOTION THAT THERE ARE THINGS MEN CAN AND CAN'T READ IS INFORMED ONLY BY THE PEOPLE AROUND HIM SAYING SO...
...I DON'T WANT HIM TO DENY HIS OWN FEELINGS.
FIDGET
FIDGET
TREMBLE
TREMBLE
HE'S TOTALLY RIVETED!
IT'S A GOOD SERIES, ISN'T IT?!

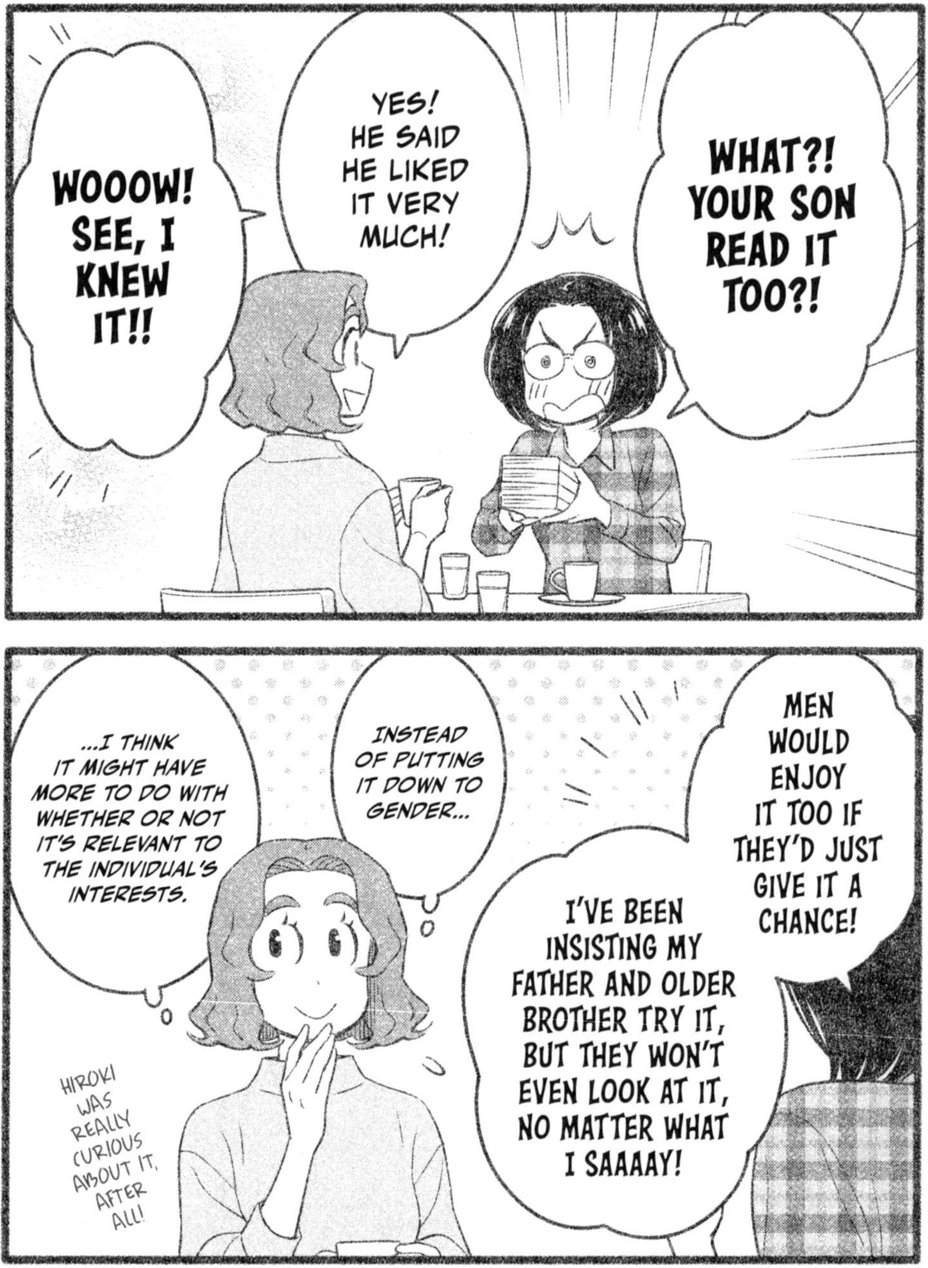
WHAT?! YOUR SON READ IT TOO?!
YES! HE SAID HE LIKED IT VERY MUCH!
WOOOW! SEE, I KNEW IT!!
MEN WOULD ENJOY IT TOO IF THEY'D JUST GIVE IT A CHANCE!
I'VE BEEN INSISTING MY FATHER AND OLDER BROTHER TRY IT, BUT THEY WON'T EVEN LOOK AT IT, NO MATTER WHAT I SAAAAY!
INSTEAD OF PUTTING IT DOWN TO GENDER...
...I THINK IT MIGHT HAVE MORE TO DO WITH WHETHER OR NOT IT'S RELEVANT TO THE INDIVIDUAL'S INTERESTS.
HIROKI WAS REALLY CURIOUS ABOUT IT, AFTER ALL!

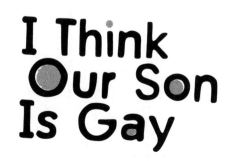

I Think
Our Son
Is Gay

## Chapter 40: What a Waste

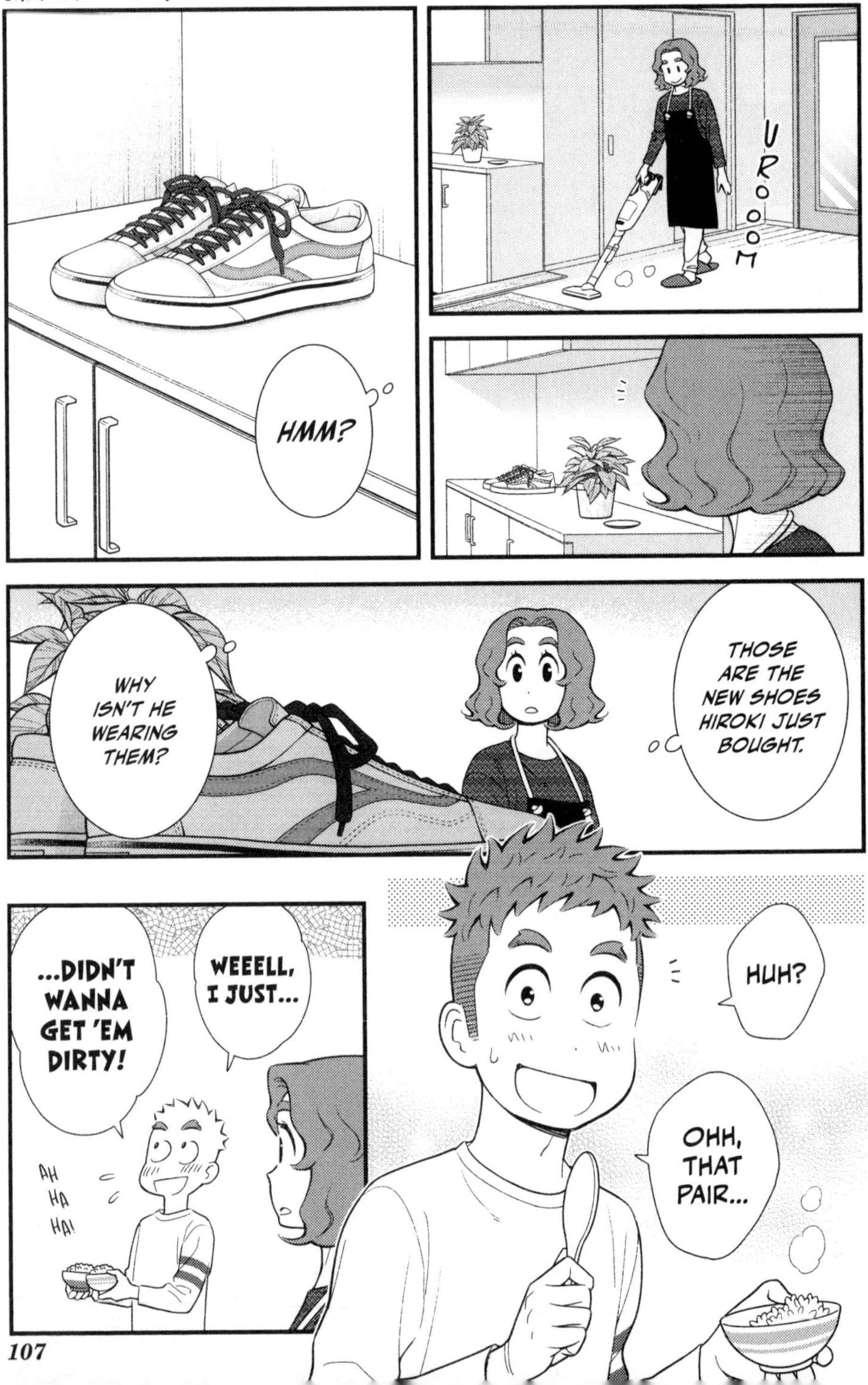

UROOOOM
HMM?
THOSE ARE THE NEW SHOES HIROKI JUST BOUGHT.
WHY ISN'T HE WEARING THEM?
HUH?
OHH, THAT PAIR...
WEEELL, I JUST...
...DIDN'T WANNA GET 'EM DIRTY!
AH HA HA!

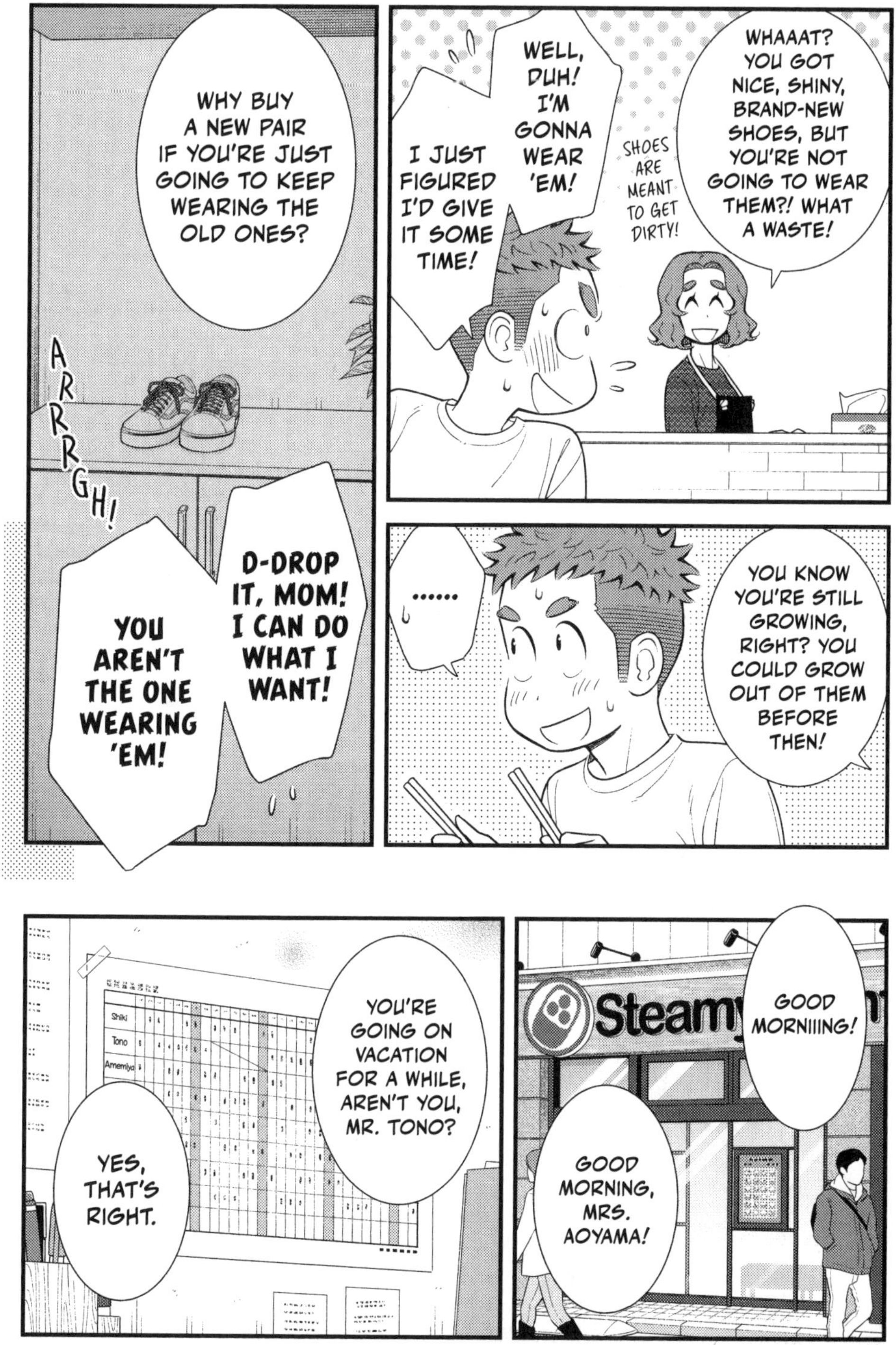
WHAAAT? YOU GOT NICE, SHINY, BRAND-NEW SHOES, BUT YOU'RE NOT GOING TO WEAR THEM?! WHAT A WASTE!
SHOES ARE MEANT TO GET DIRTY!
WELL, DUH! I'M GONNA WEAR 'EM!
I JUST FIGURED I'D GIVE IT SOME TIME!
YOU KNOW YOU'RE STILL GROWING, RIGHT? YOU COULD GROW OUT OF THEM BEFORE THEN!
......
WHY BUY A NEW PAIR IF YOU'RE JUST GOING TO KEEP WEARING THE OLD ONES?
ARRRGH!
D-DROP IT, MOM! I CAN DO WHAT I WANT!
YOU AREN'T THE ONE WEARING 'EM!
Steamy
GOOD MORNIIING!
GOOD MORNING, MRS. AOYAMA!
Shiki
Tono
Amemiya
YOU'RE GOING ON VACATION FOR A WHILE, AREN'T YOU, MR. TONO?
YES, THAT'S RIGHT.

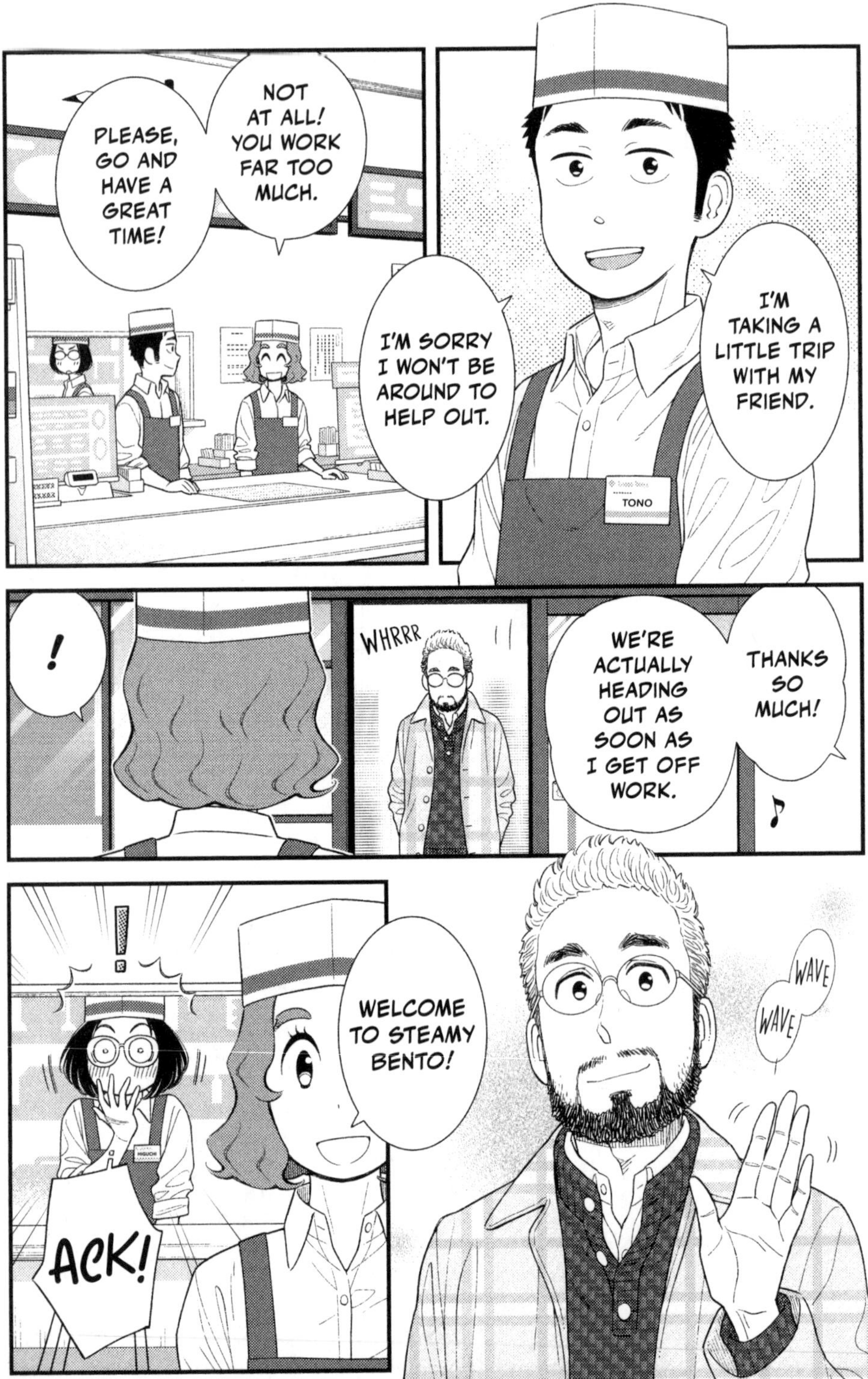
I'M TAKING A LITTLE TRIP WITH MY FRIEND.
I'M SORRY I WON'T BE AROUND TO HELP OUT.
TONO
NOT AT ALL! YOU WORK FAR TOO MUCH.
PLEASE, GO AND HAVE A GREAT TIME!
THANKS SO MUCH!
WE'RE ACTUALLY HEADING OUT AS SOON AS I GET OFF WORK.
WHRRR
!
WAVE
WAVE
WELCOME TO STEAMY BENTO!
!
ACK!

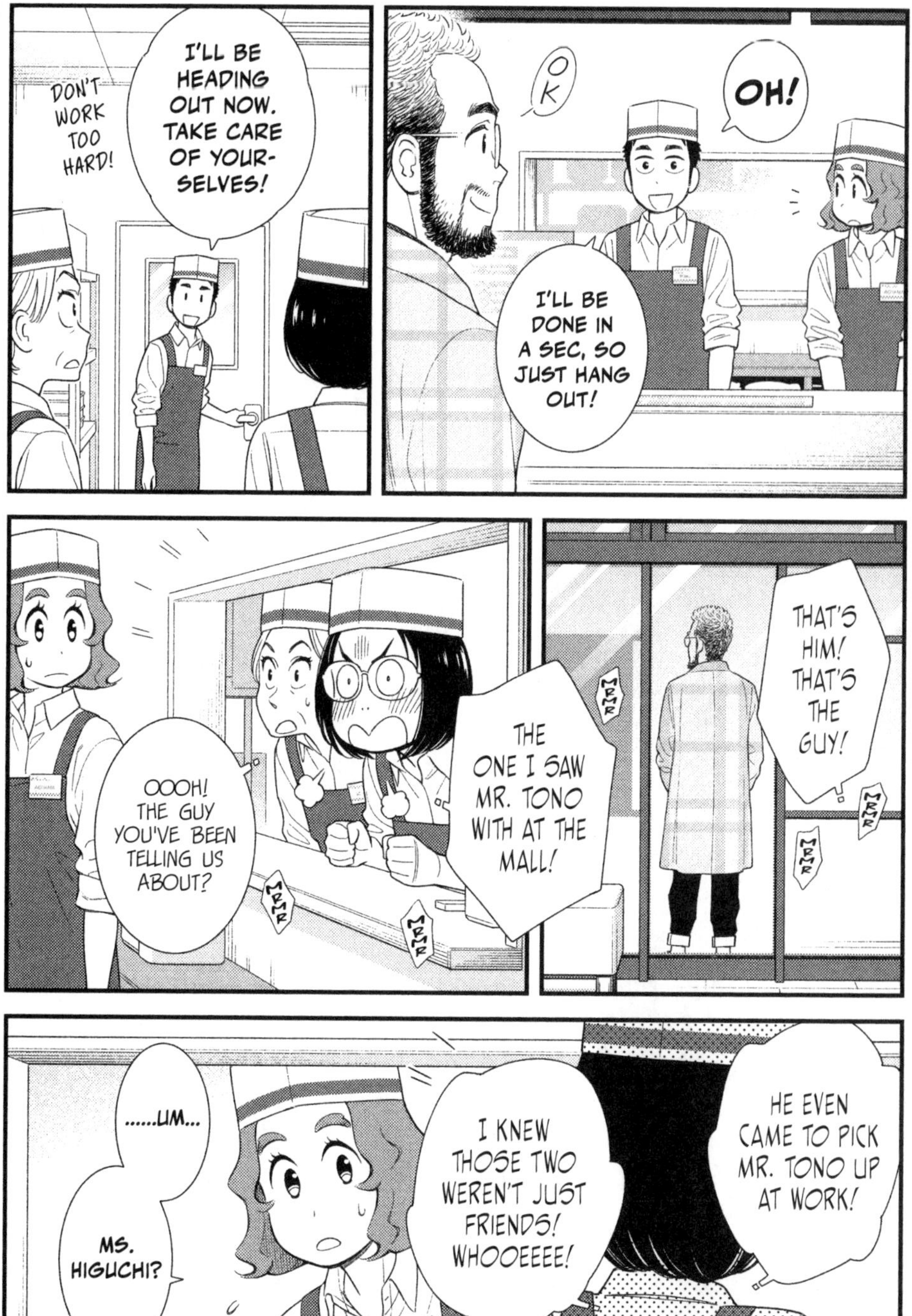
OH!
OK
I'LL BE DONE IN A SEC, SO JUST HANG OUT!
I'LL BE HEADING OUT NOW. TAKE CARE OF YOURSELVES!
DON'T WORK TOO HARD!
THAT'S HIM! THAT'S THE GUY!
MRMR
MRMR
THE ONE I SAW MR. TONO WITH AT THE MALL!
MRMR
OOOH! THE GUY YOU'VE BEEN TELLING US ABOUT?
MRMR
MRMR
HE EVEN CAME TO PICK MR. TONO UP AT WORK!
I KNEW THOSE TWO WEREN'T JUST FRIENDS! WHOOEEEE!
......UM...
MS. HIGUCHI?

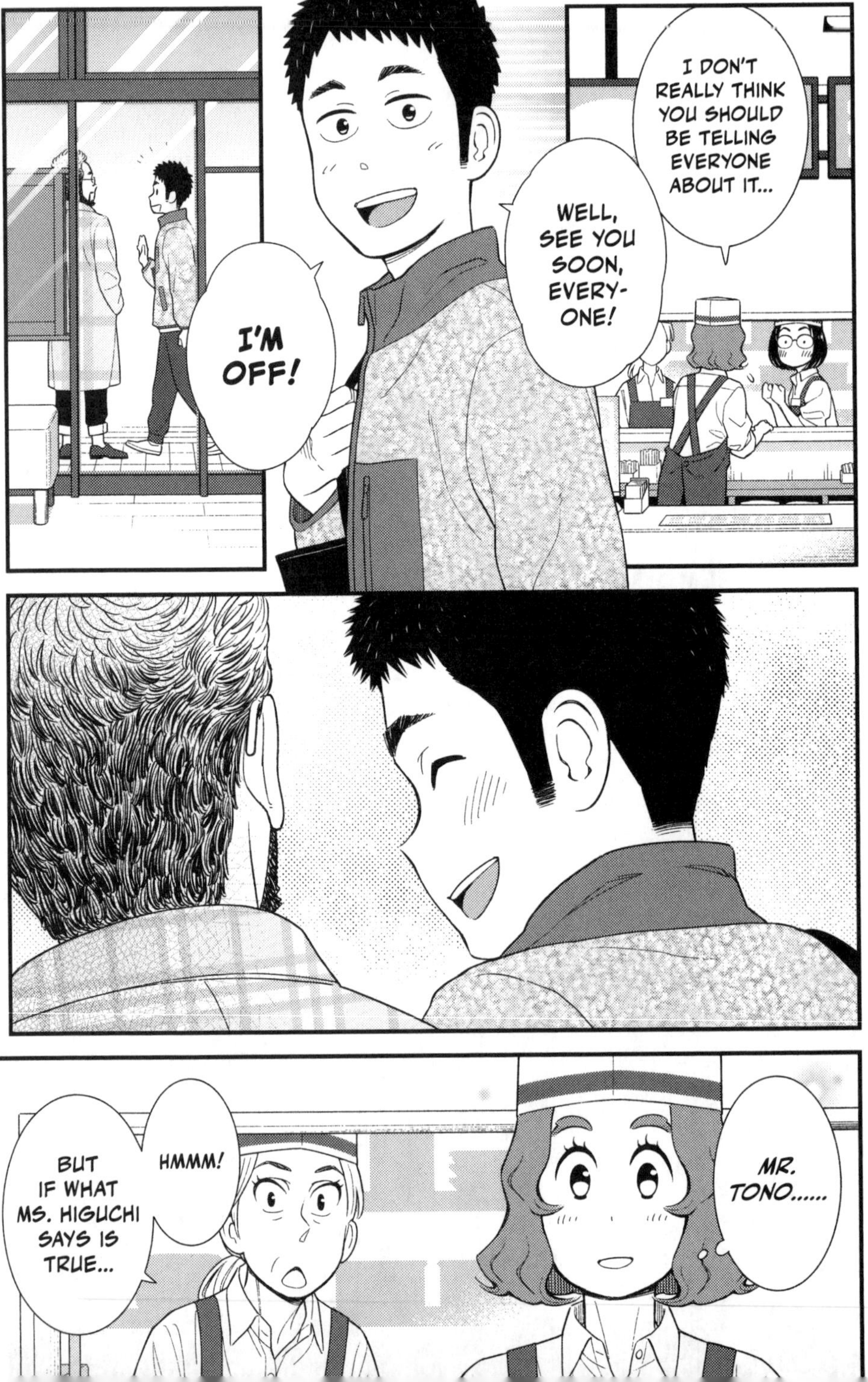
I DON'T REALLY THINK YOU SHOULD BE TELLING EVERYONE ABOUT IT...
WELL, SEE YOU SOON, EVERY-ONE!
I'M OFF!
MR. TONO......
HMMM!
BUT IF WHAT MS. HIGUCHI SAYS IS TRUE...

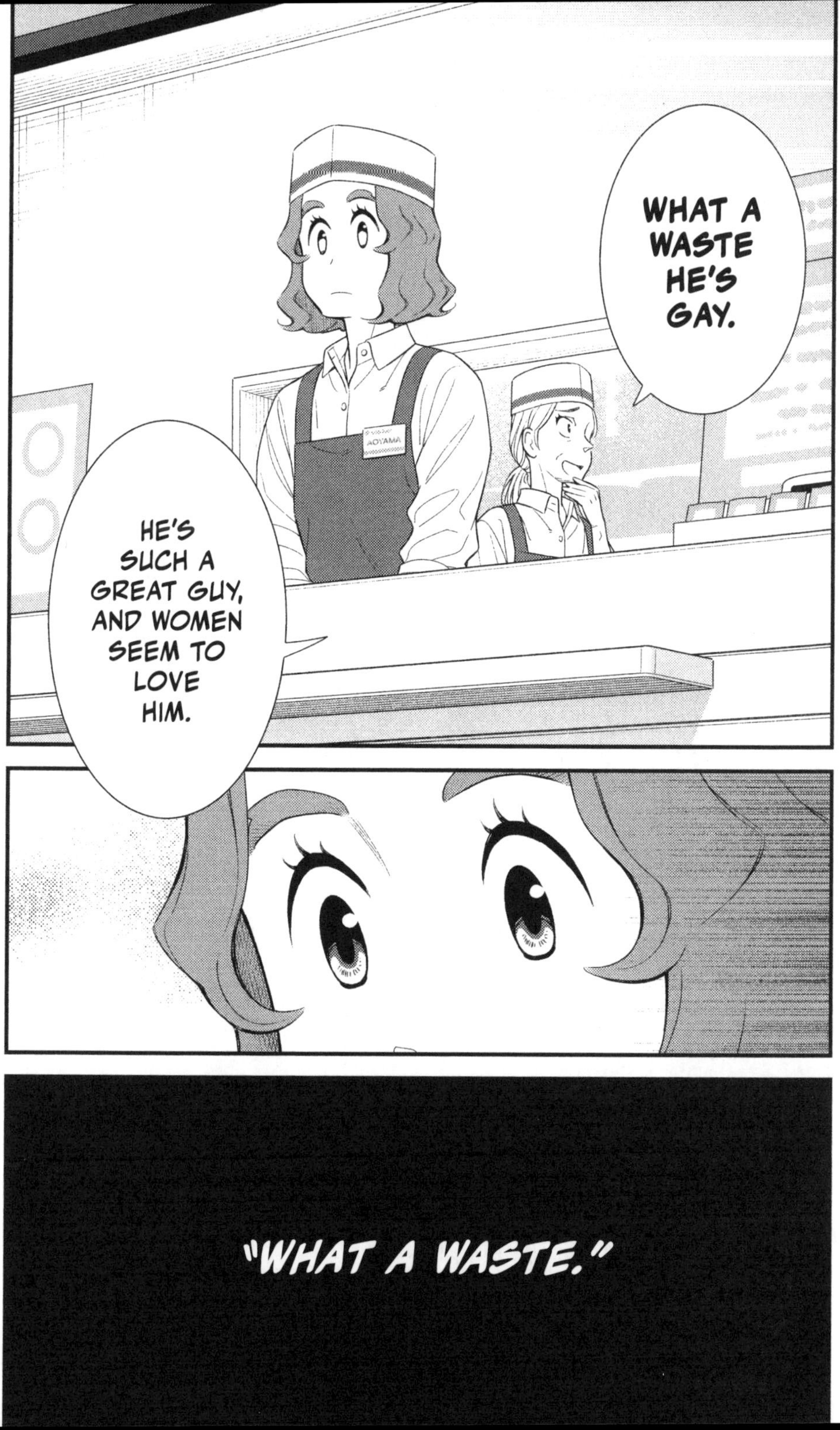
WHAT A WASTE HE'S GAY.
HE'S SUCH A GREAT GUY, AND WOMEN SEEM TO LOVE HIM.
AOYAMA
"WHAT A WASTE."

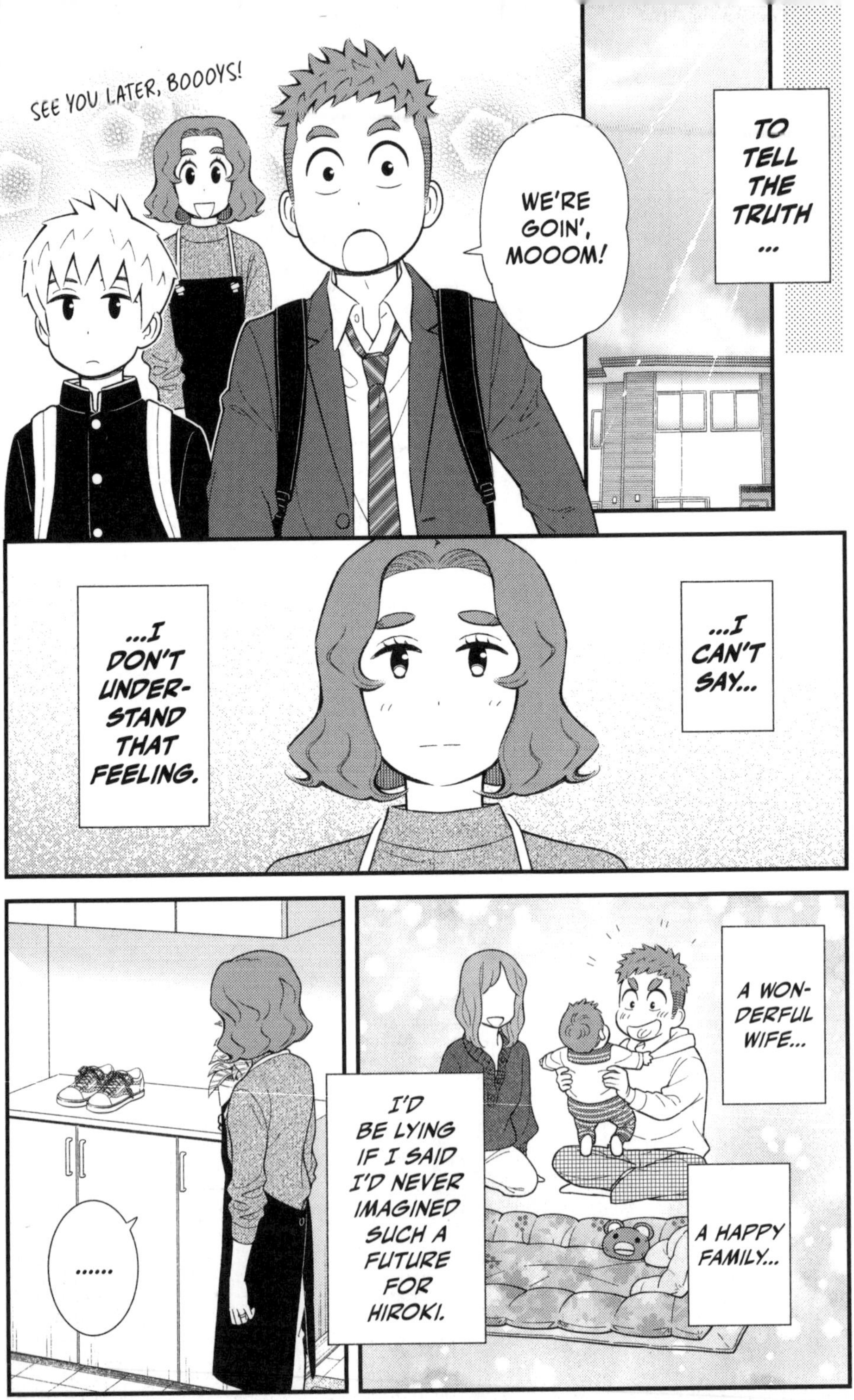
TO TELL THE TRUTH...
WE'RE GOIN', MOOOM!
SEE YOU LATER, BOOOYS!
...I CAN'T SAY...
...I DON'T UNDER-STAND THAT FEELING.
A WON-DERFUL WIFE...
A HAPPY FAMILY...
I'D BE LYING IF I SAID I'D NEVER IMAGINED SUCH A FUTURE FOR HIROKI.
......

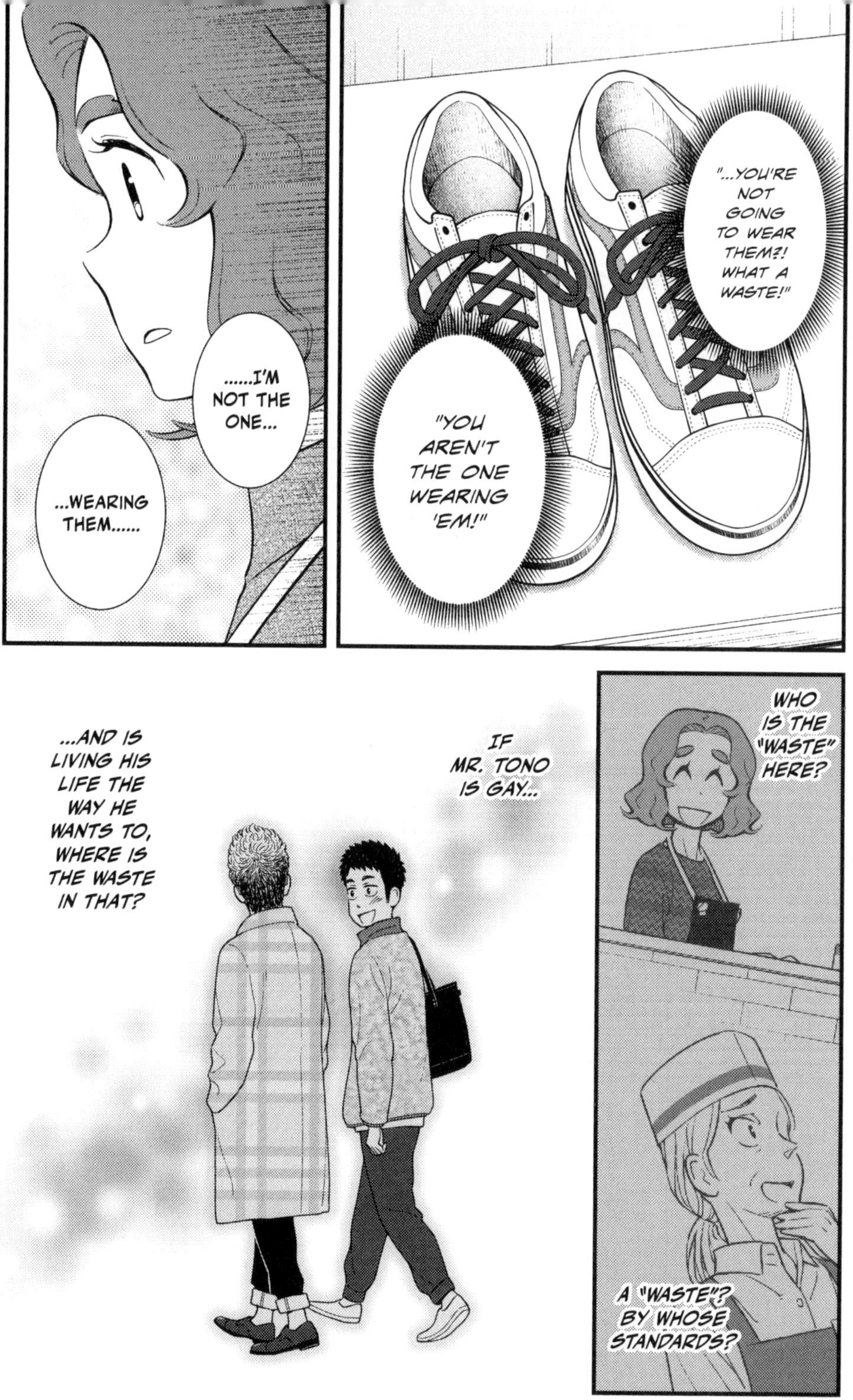
"...YOU'RE NOT GOING TO WEAR THEM?! WHAT A WASTE!"
"YOU AREN'T THE ONE WEARING 'EM!"
......I'M NOT THE ONE...
...WEARING THEM......
WHO IS THE "WASTE" HERE?
A "WASTE"? BY WHOSE STANDARDS?
IF MR. TONO IS GAY...
...AND IS LIVING HIS LIFE THE WAY HE WANTS TO, WHERE IS THE WASTE IN THAT?

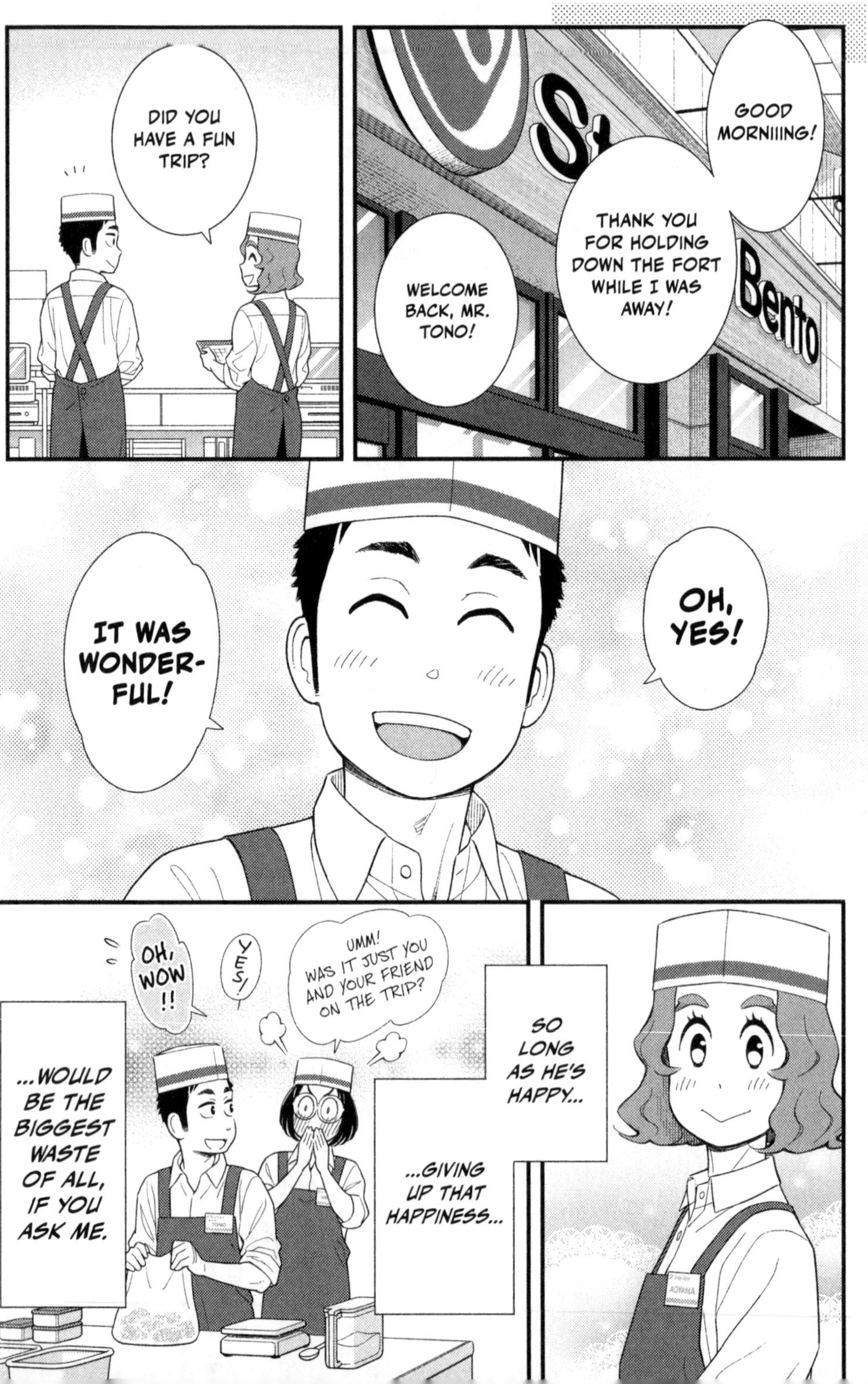
Bento
GOOD MORNIIING!
THANK YOU FOR HOLDING DOWN THE FORT WHILE I WAS AWAY!
WELCOME BACK, MR. TONO!
DID YOU HAVE A FUN TRIP?
OH, YES!
IT WAS WONDERFUL!
SO LONG AS HE'S HAPPY...
...GIVING UP THAT HAPPINESS...
UMM! WAS IT JUST YOU AND YOUR FRIEND ON THE TRIP?
YES!
OH, WOW!!
...WOULD BE THE BIGGEST WASTE OF ALL, IF YOU ASK ME.

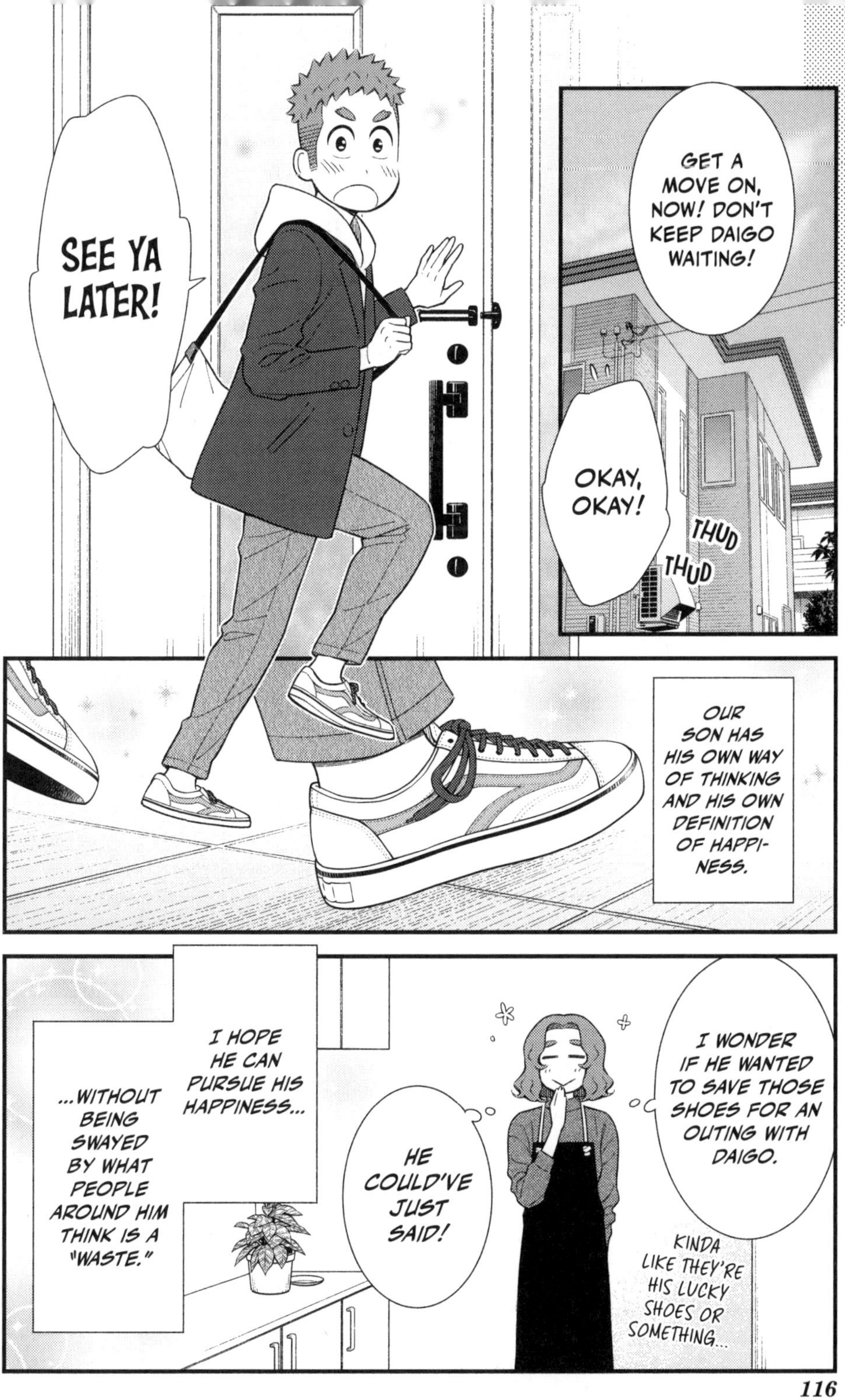
GET A MOVE ON, NOW! DON'T KEEP DAIGO WAITING!
OKAY, OKAY!
THUD THUD
SEE YA LATER!
OUR SON HAS HIS OWN WAY OF THINKING AND HIS OWN DEFINITION OF HAPPI-NESS.
I WONDER IF HE WANTED TO SAVE THOSE SHOES FOR AN OUTING WITH DAIGO.
KINDA LIKE THEY'RE HIS LUCKY SHOES OR SOMETHING...
HE COULD'VE JUST SAID!
I HOPE HE CAN PURSUE HIS HAPPINESS...
...WITHOUT BEING SWAYED BY WHAT PEOPLE AROUND HIM THINK IS A "WASTE."

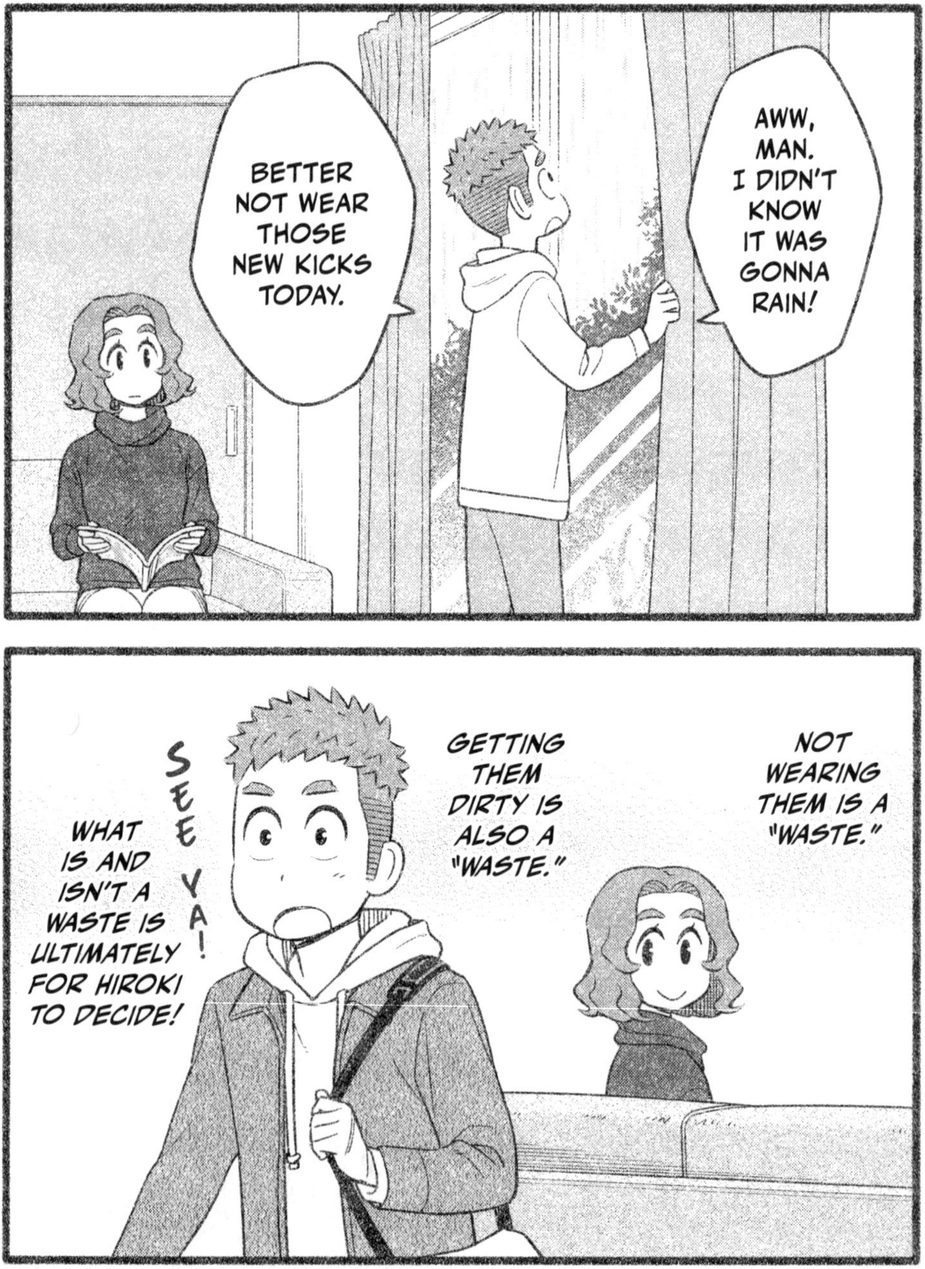
AWW, MAN. I DIDN'T KNOW IT WAS GONNA RAIN!
BETTER NOT WEAR THOSE NEW KICKS TODAY.
NOT WEARING THEM IS A "WASTE."
GETTING THEM DIRTY IS ALSO A "WASTE."
SEE YA!
WHAT IS AND ISN'T A WASTE IS ULTIMATELY FOR HIROKI TO DECIDE!

# I Think
## Our Son
# Is Gay

CHAPTER 41: WITH HIM

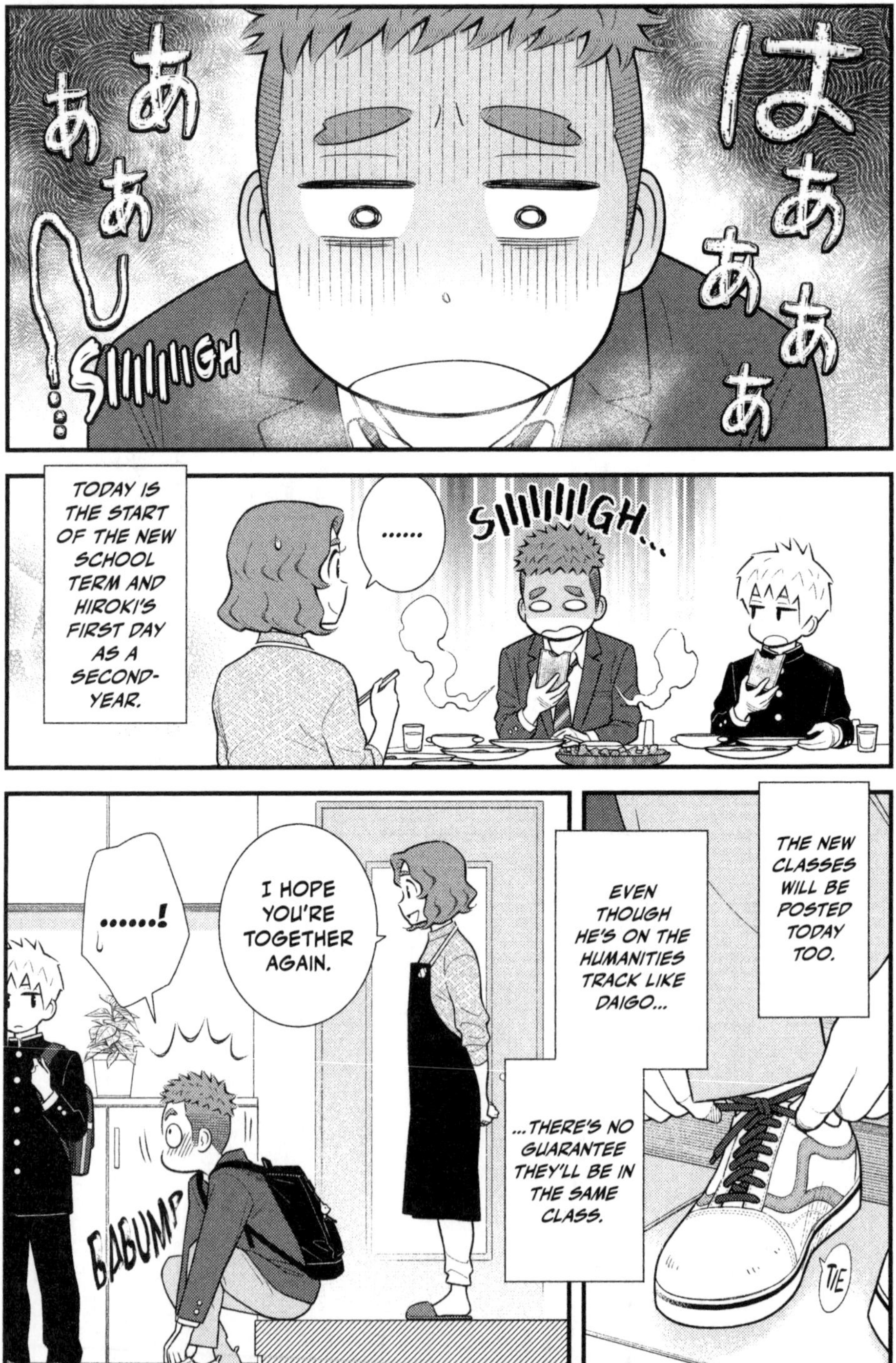
はあああああ
あああ～…
SIIIIIIGH
TODAY IS THE START OF THE NEW SCHOOL TERM AND HIROKI'S FIRST DAY AS A SECOND-YEAR.
......
SIIIIIIGH...
THE NEW CLASSES WILL BE POSTED TODAY TOO.
EVEN THOUGH HE'S ON THE HUMANITIES TRACK LIKE DAIGO...
...THERE'S NO GUARANTEE THEY'LL BE IN THE SAME CLASS.
TIE
I HOPE YOU'RE TOGETHER AGAIN.
......!
BABUMP

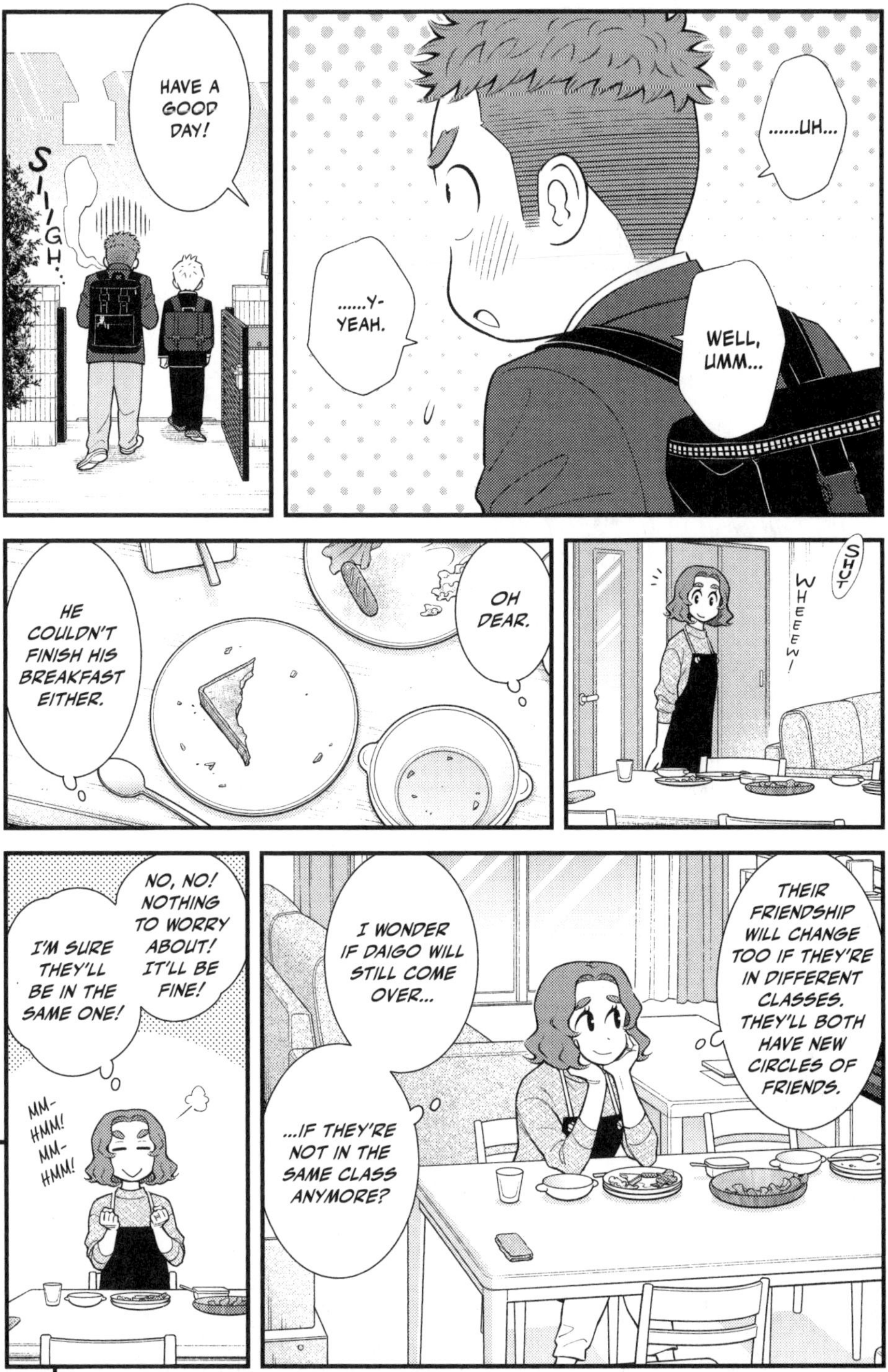

......UH...
WELL, UMM...
......Y-YEAH.
HAVE A GOOD DAY!
SIIIGH...
SHUT
WHEEEEW!
OH DEAR.
HE COULDN'T FINISH HIS BREAKFAST EITHER.
THEIR FRIENDSHIP WILL CHANGE TOO IF THEY'RE IN DIFFERENT CLASSES. THEY'LL BOTH HAVE NEW CIRCLES OF FRIENDS.
I WONDER IF DAIGO WILL STILL COME OVER...
...IF THEY'RE NOT IN THE SAME CLASS ANYMORE?
NO, NO! NOTHING TO WORRY ABOUT! IT'LL BE FINE!
I'M SURE THEY'LL BE IN THE SAME ONE!
MM-HMM! MM-HMM!

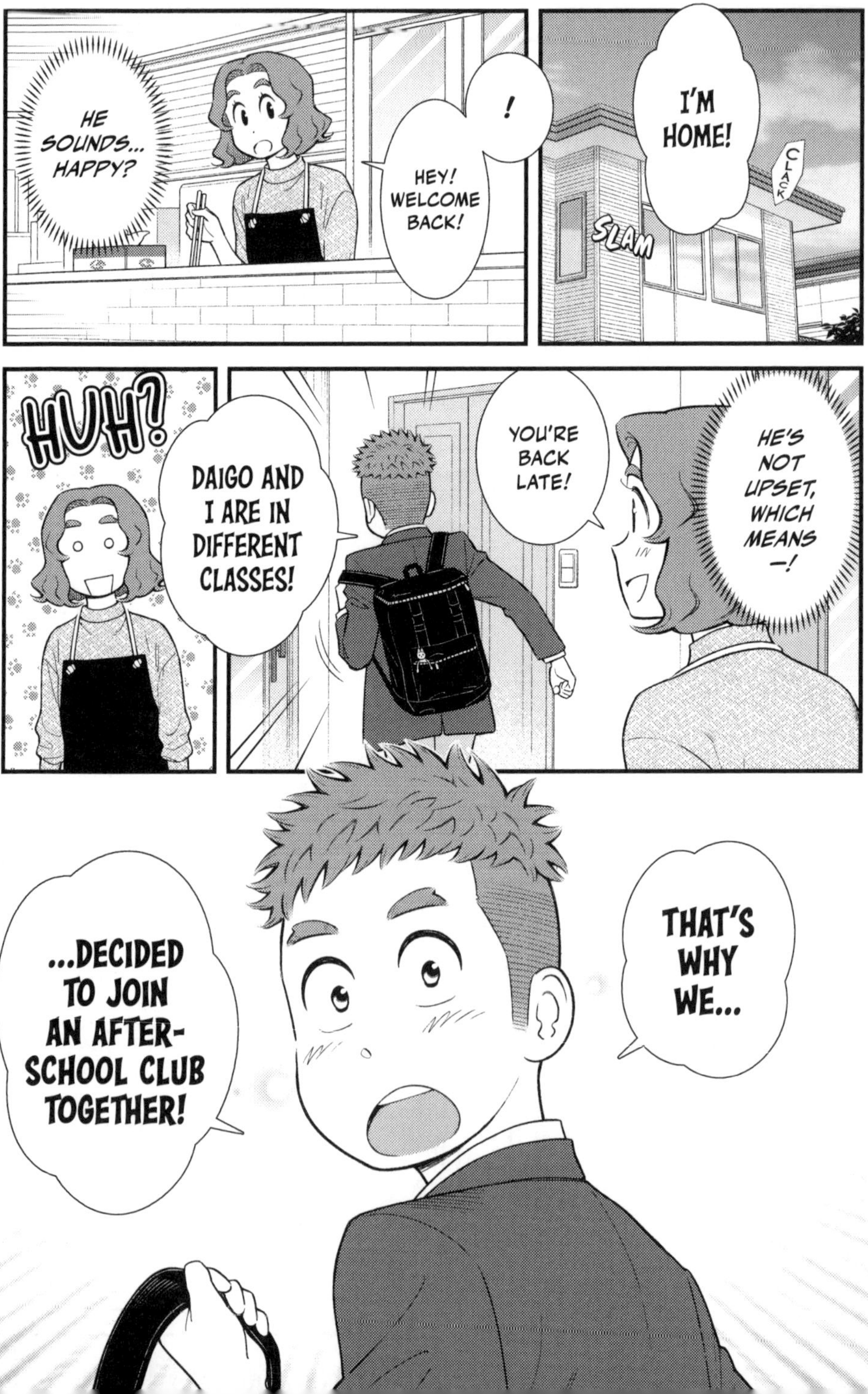
I'M HOME!
CLACK
SLAM
!
HEY! WELCOME BACK!
HE SOUNDS... HAPPY?
HE'S NOT UPSET, WHICH MEANS—!
YOU'RE BACK LATE!
DAIGO AND I ARE IN DIFFERENT CLASSES!
HUH?
THAT'S WHY WE...
...DECIDED TO JOIN AN AFTER-SCHOOL CLUB TOGETHER!

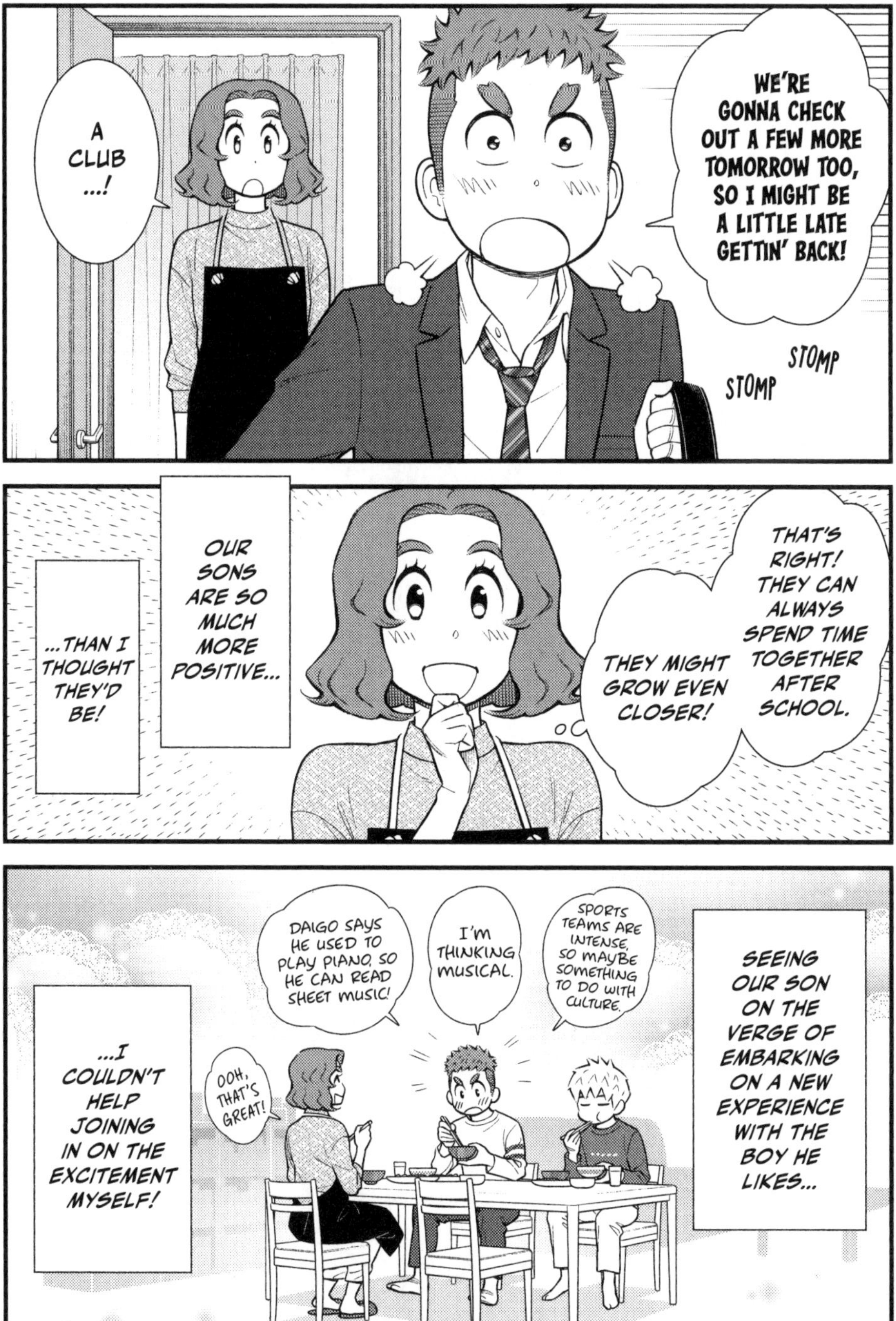
WE'RE GONNA CHECK OUT A FEW MORE TOMORROW TOO, SO I MIGHT BE A LITTLE LATE GETTIN' BACK!
STOMP
STOMP
A CLUB ...!
THAT'S RIGHT! THEY CAN ALWAYS SPEND TIME TOGETHER AFTER SCHOOL.
THEY MIGHT GROW EVEN CLOSER!
OUR SONS ARE SO MUCH MORE POSITIVE...
...THAN I THOUGHT THEY'D BE!
SEEING OUR SON ON THE VERGE OF EMBARKING ON A NEW EXPERIENCE WITH THE BOY HE LIKES...
SPORTS TEAMS ARE INTENSE, SO MAYBE SOMETHING TO DO WITH CULTURE.
I'M THINKING MUSICAL.
DAIGO SAYS HE USED TO PLAY PIANO, SO HE CAN READ SHEET MUSIC!
OOH, THAT'S GREAT!
...I COULDN'T HELP JOINING IN ON THE EXCITEMENT MYSELF!

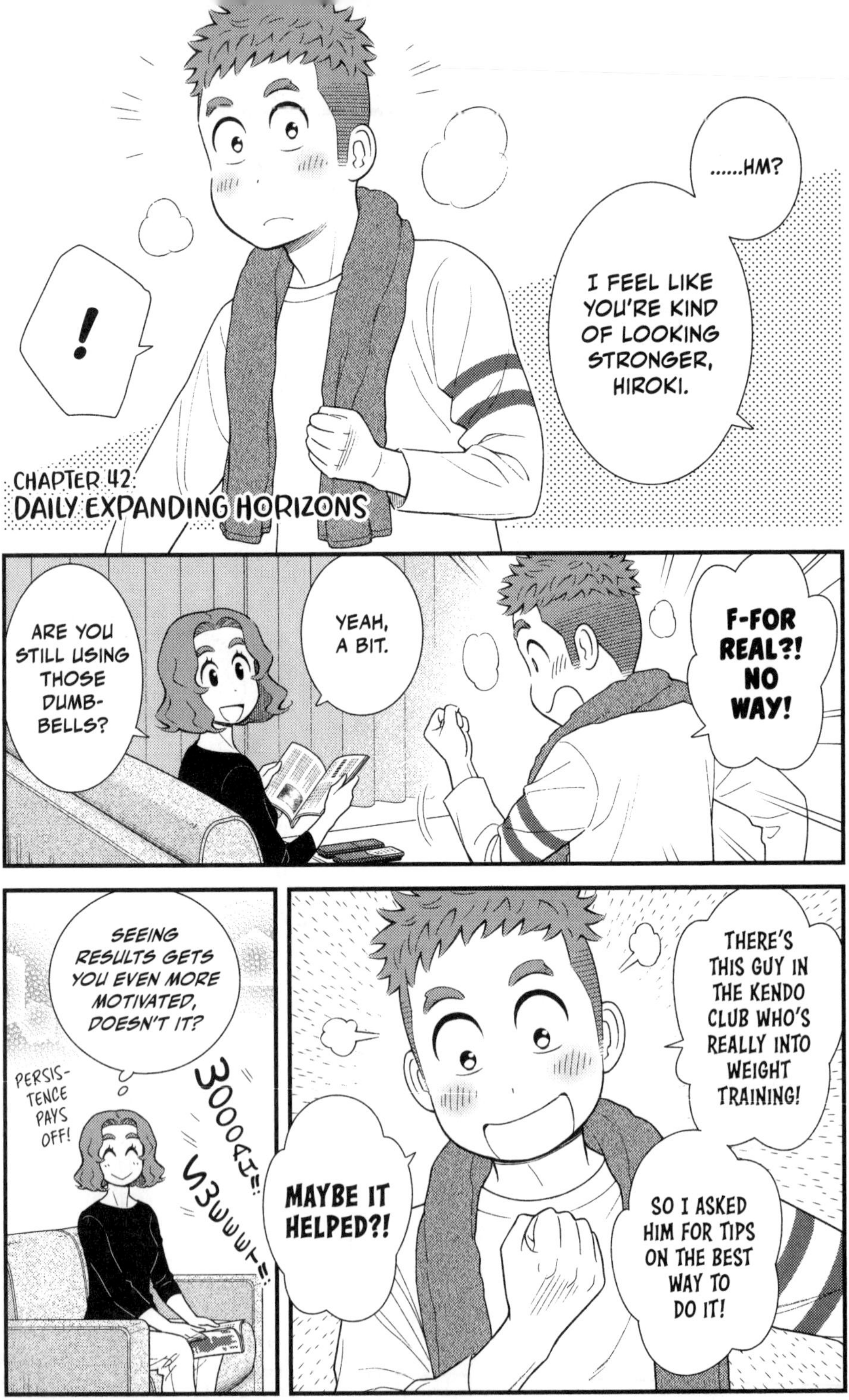
......HM?
I FEEL LIKE YOU'RE KIND OF LOOKING STRONGER, HIROKI.
!
CHAPTER 42: DAILY EXPANDING HORIZONS
F-FOR REAL?! NO WAY!
YEAH, A BIT.
ARE YOU STILL USING THOSE DUMB-BELLS?
THERE'S THIS GUY IN THE KENDO CLUB WHO'S REALLY INTO WEIGHT TRAINING!
SO I ASKED HIM FOR TIPS ON THE BEST WAY TO DO IT!
MAYBE IT HELPED?!
SEEING RESULTS GETS YOU EVEN MORE MOTIVATED, DOESN'T IT?
PERSIS-TENCE PAYS OFF!

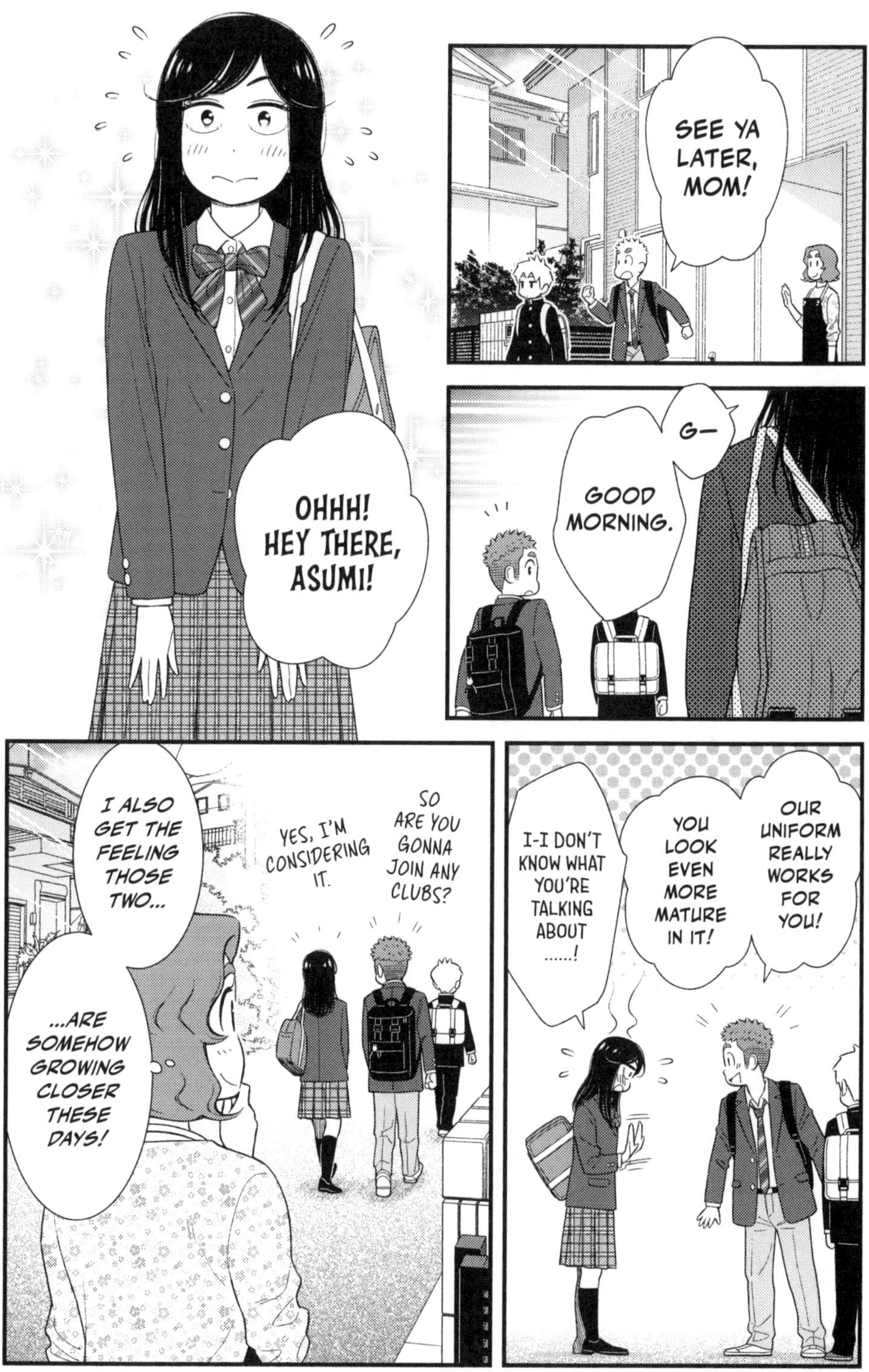
SEE YA LATER, MOM!
G—
GOOD MORNING.
OHHH! HEY THERE, ASUMI!
OUR UNIFORM REALLY WORKS FOR YOU!
YOU LOOK EVEN MORE MATURE IN IT!
I-I DON'T KNOW WHAT YOU'RE TALKING ABOUT ......!
SO ARE YOU GONNA JOIN ANY CLUBS?
YES, I'M CONSIDERING IT.
I ALSO GET THE FEELING THOSE TWO...
...ARE SOMEHOW GROWING CLOSER THESE DAYS!

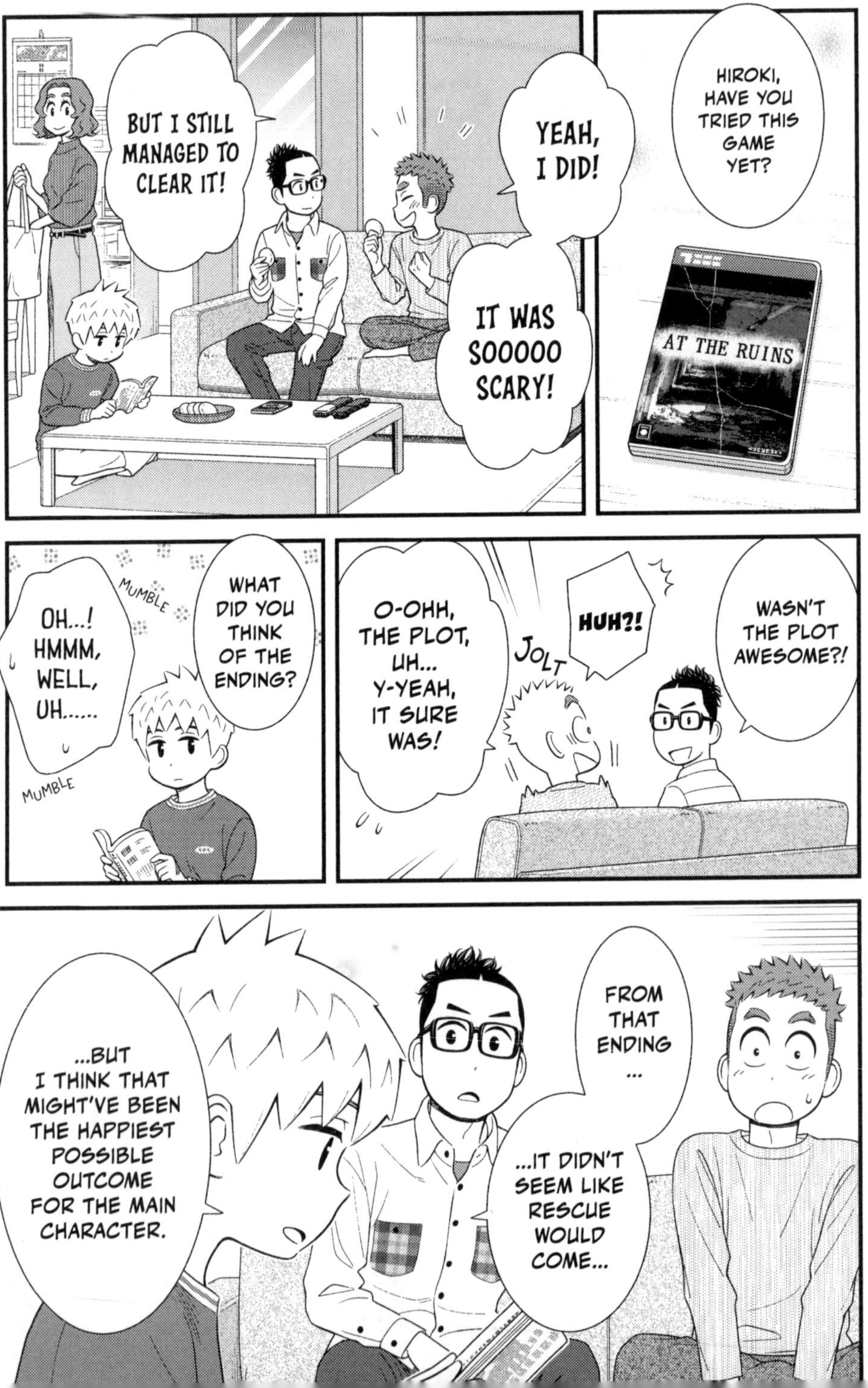
HIROKI, HAVE YOU TRIED THIS GAME YET?
AT THE RUINS
YEAH, I DID!
IT WAS SOOOOO SCARY!
BUT I STILL MANAGED TO CLEAR IT!
WASN'T THE PLOT AWESOME?!
HUH?!
JOLT
O-OHH, THE PLOT, UH... Y-YEAH, IT SURE WAS!
WHAT DID YOU THINK OF THE ENDING?
MUMBLE
OH...! HMMM, WELL, UH......
MUMBLE
FROM THAT ENDING ...
...IT DIDN'T SEEM LIKE RESCUE WOULD COME...
...BUT I THINK THAT MIGHT'VE BEEN THE HAPPIEST POSSIBLE OUTCOME FOR THE MAIN CHARACTER.

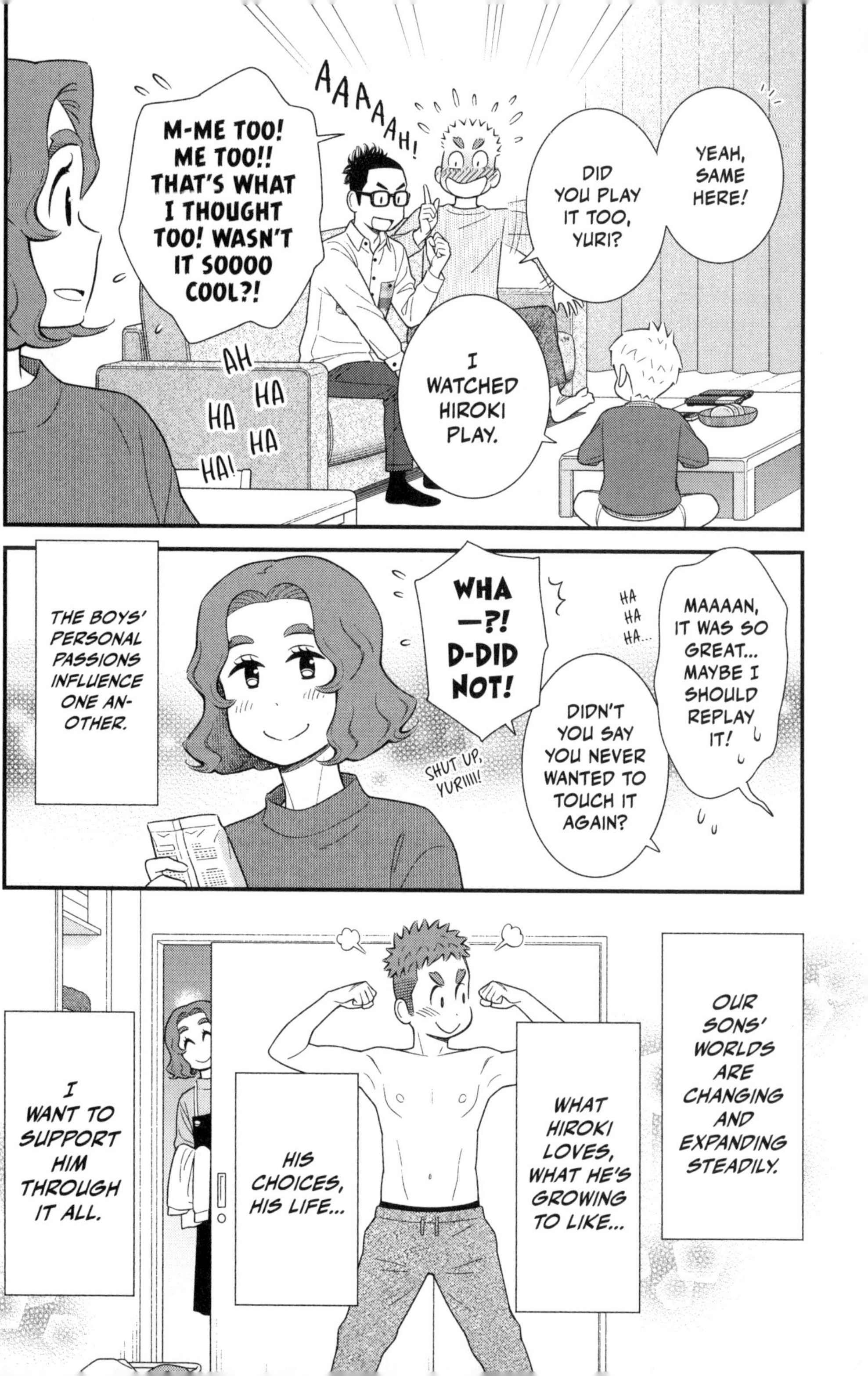
YEAH, SAME HERE!
DID YOU PLAY IT TOO, YURI?
I WATCHED HIROKI PLAY.
AAAAAAH!
M-ME TOO! ME TOO!! THAT'S WHAT I THOUGHT TOO! WASN'T IT SOOOO COOL?!
AH HA HA HA HA!
MAAAAN, IT WAS SO GREAT... MAYBE I SHOULD REPLAY IT!
HA HA HA...
DIDN'T YOU SAY YOU NEVER WANTED TO TOUCH IT AGAIN?
WHA—?! D-DID NOT!
SHUT UP, YURIIII!
THE BOYS' PERSONAL PASSIONS INFLUENCE ONE AN-OTHER.
OUR SONS' WORLDS ARE CHANGING AND EXPANDING STEADILY.
WHAT HIROKI LOVES, WHAT HE'S GROWING TO LIKE...
HIS CHOICES, HIS LIFE...
I WANT TO SUPPORT HIM THROUGH IT ALL.

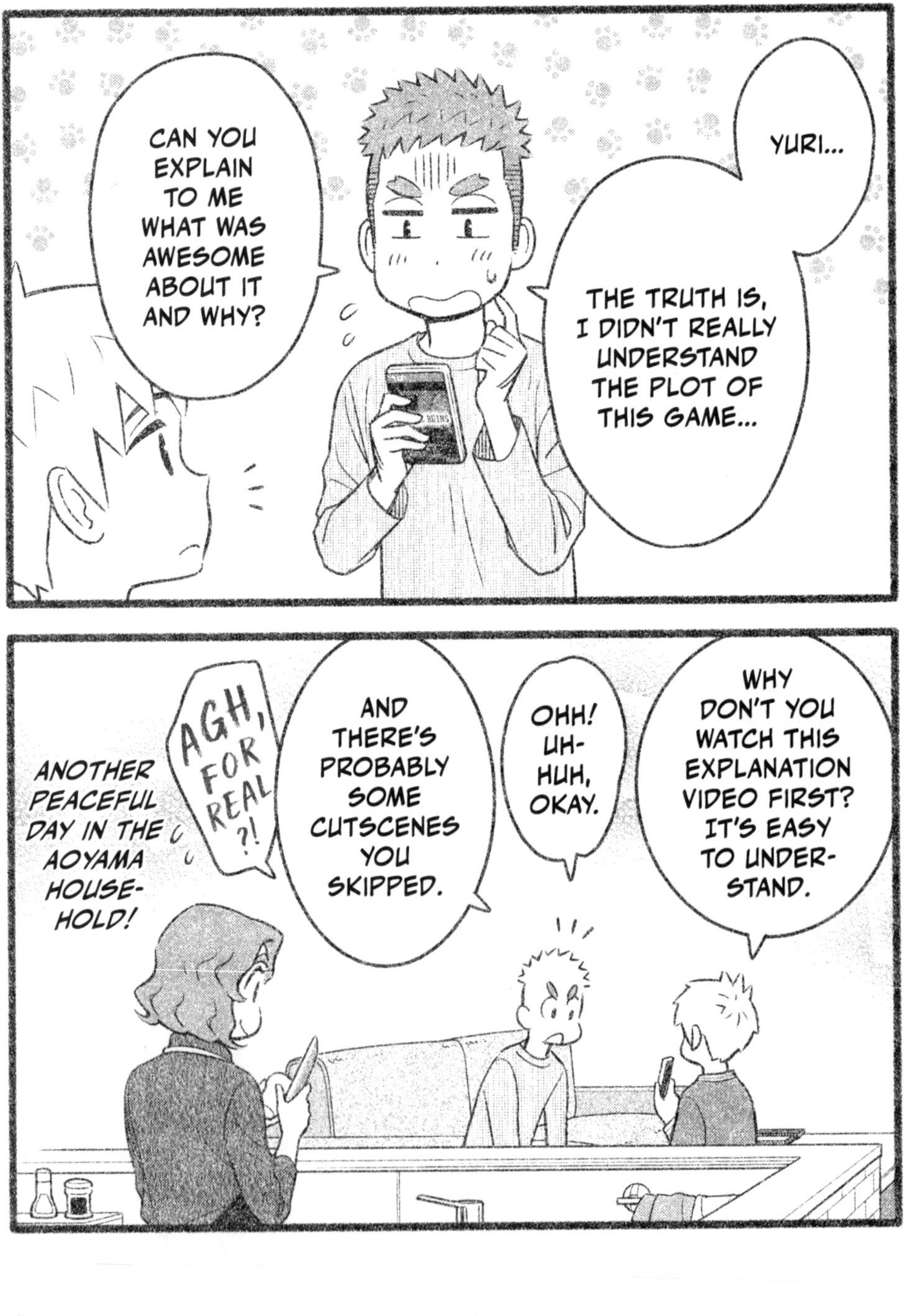
YURI...
THE TRUTH IS, I DIDN'T REALLY UNDERSTAND THE PLOT OF THIS GAME...
CAN YOU EXPLAIN TO ME WHAT WAS AWESOME ABOUT IT AND WHY?
WHY DON'T YOU WATCH THIS EXPLANATION VIDEO FIRST? IT'S EASY TO UNDER-STAND.
OHH! UH-HUH, OKAY.
AND THERE'S PROBABLY SOME CUTSCENES YOU SKIPPED.
AGH, FOR REAL?!
ANOTHER PEACEFUL DAY IN THE AOYAMA HOUSE-HOLD!

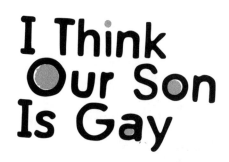

I Think
Our Son
Is Gay

# AFTERWORD

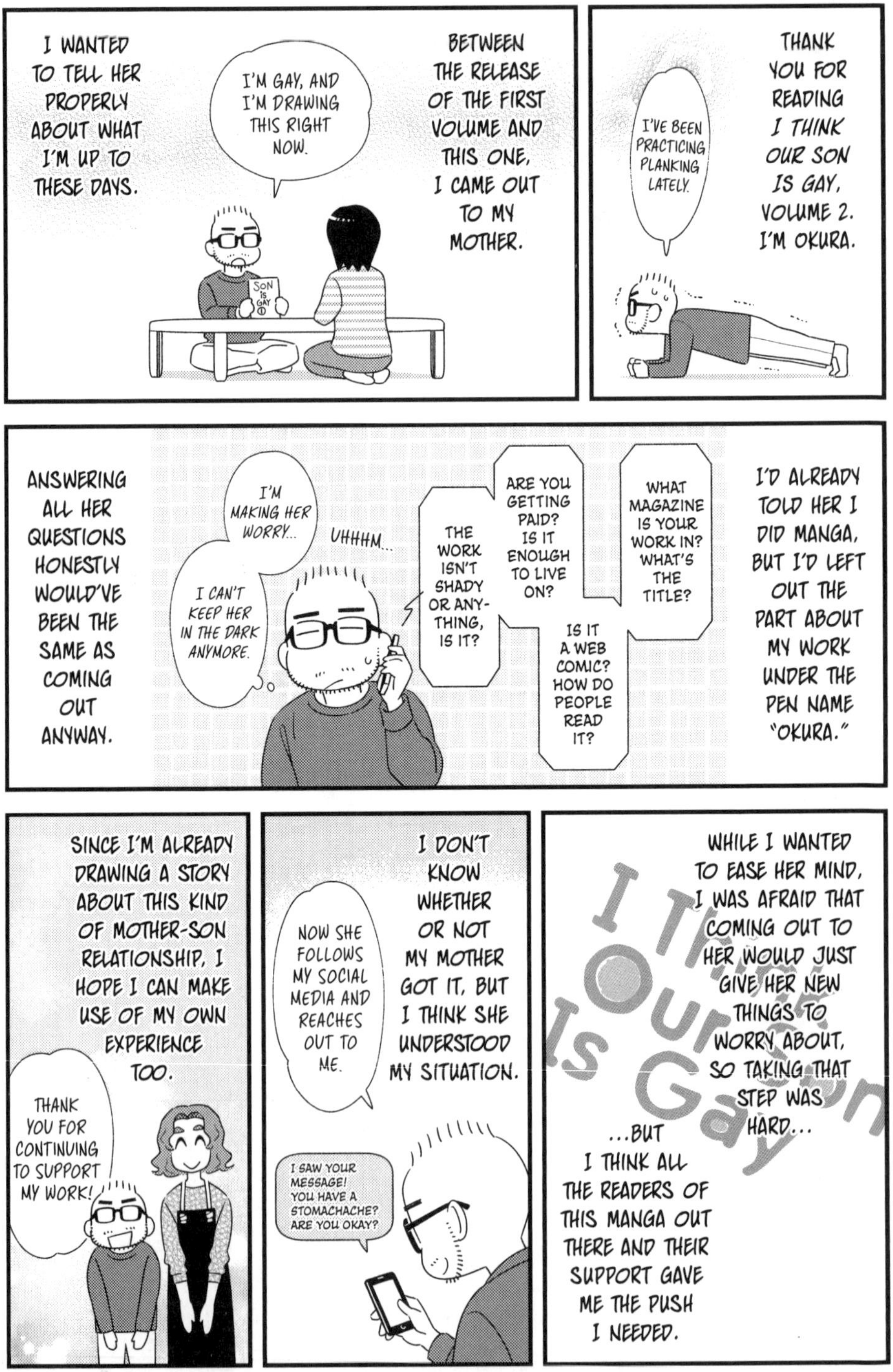
THANK YOU FOR READING *I THINK OUR SON IS GAY*, VOLUME 2. I'M OKURA.
I'VE BEEN PRACTICING PLANKING LATELY.
BETWEEN THE RELEASE OF THE FIRST VOLUME AND THIS ONE, I CAME OUT TO MY MOTHER.
I'M GAY, AND I'M DRAWING THIS RIGHT NOW.
I WANTED TO TELL HER PROPERLY ABOUT WHAT I'M UP TO THESE DAYS.
SON IS GAY ①
I'D ALREADY TOLD HER I DID MANGA, BUT I'D LEFT OUT THE PART ABOUT MY WORK UNDER THE PEN NAME "OKURA."
WHAT MAGAZINE IS YOUR WORK IN? WHAT'S THE TITLE?
ARE YOU GETTING PAID? IS IT ENOUGH TO LIVE ON?
IS IT A WEB COMIC? HOW DO PEOPLE READ IT?
THE WORK ISN'T SHADY OR ANY-THING, IS IT?
UHHHM...
I'M MAKING HER WORRY...
I CAN'T KEEP HER IN THE DARK ANYMORE.
ANSWERING ALL HER QUESTIONS HONESTLY WOULD'VE BEEN THE SAME AS COMING OUT ANYWAY.
WHILE I WANTED TO EASE HER MIND, I WAS AFRAID THAT COMING OUT TO HER WOULD JUST GIVE HER NEW THINGS TO WORRY ABOUT, SO TAKING THAT STEP WAS HARD...
...BUT I THINK ALL THE READERS OF THIS MANGA OUT THERE AND THEIR SUPPORT GAVE ME THE PUSH I NEEDED.
I DON'T KNOW WHETHER OR NOT MY MOTHER GOT IT, BUT I THINK SHE UNDERSTOOD MY SITUATION.
NOW SHE FOLLOWS MY SOCIAL MEDIA AND REACHES OUT TO ME.
I SAW YOUR MESSAGE! YOU HAVE A STOMACHACHE? ARE YOU OKAY?
SINCE I'M ALREADY DRAWING A STORY ABOUT THIS KIND OF MOTHER-SON RELATIONSHIP, I HOPE I CAN MAKE USE OF MY OWN EXPERIENCE TOO.
THANK YOU FOR CONTINUING TO SUPPORT MY WORK!

2020.2. **Okura** SPECIAL THANKS : **Watanabe**

# I Think Our Son Is Gay

## 2

### OKURA

Translation: Leo McDonagh
Lettering: Lor Prescott
Cover Design: Andrea Miller
Editor: Tania Biswas

I THINK OUR SON IS GAY Volume 2
© 2020 Okura/SQUARE ENIX CO., LTD.
First published in Japan in 2020 by SQUARE ENIX CO., LTD.
English translation rights arranged with
SQUARE ENIX CO., LTD. and SQUARE ENIX, INC.
English translation © 2021 by SQUARE ENIX CO., LTD.

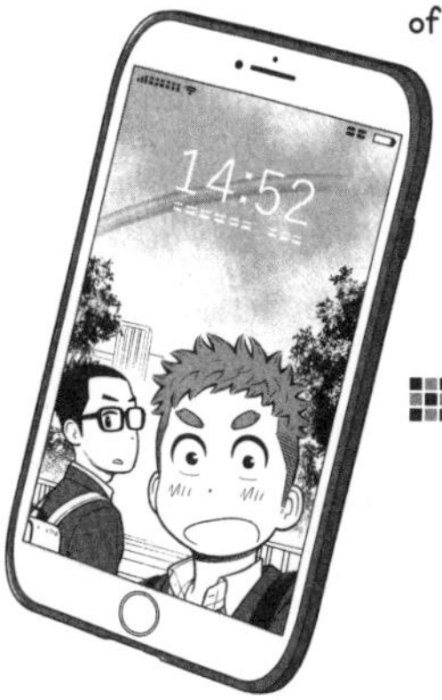

ISBN: 978-1-64609-112-6

Library of Congress Cataloging-in-Publication
Data is on file with the publisher.

Printed in the U.S.A.
First printing, October 2021
10 9 8 7 6 5 4 3 2 1

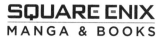

## SQUARE ENIX
### MANGA & BOOKS
www.square-enix-books.com